SPIRIT AND LETTER
IN PAUL

SPIRIT AND LETTER
IN PAUL

Arthur J. Dewey

Studies in the Bible and Early Christianity
Volume 33

The Edwin Mellen Press
Lewiston/Queenston/Lampeter

Library of Congress Cataloging-in-Publication Data

Dewey, Arthur J.
    Spirit and letter in Paul / Arthur J. Dewey.
       p.   cm. -- (Studies in the Bible and early Christianity ; v.
33)
    Includes bibliographical references and index.
    ISBN 0-7734-9703-X
    1. Letter and spirit antithesis (Pauline doctrine)   I. Tile.
II. Series.
BS2655.L47D48 1996
227'.06--dc20   95-39778
                                            CIP

This is volume 33 in the continuing series
Studies in the Bible and Early Christianity
Volume 33 ISBN 0-7734-9703-X
SBEC Series ISBN 0-88946-913-X

A CIP catalog record for this book is available from the British Library.

The Edwin Mellen Press   The Edwin Mellen Press
Box 450   Box 67
Lewiston, New York   Queenston, Ontario
USA 14092-0450   CANADA L0S 1L0

The Edwin Mellen Press, Ltd.
Lampeter, Dyfed, Wales
UNITED KINGDOM SA48 7DY

Printed in the United States of America

In gratitude to my Mother
who started it all
by giving me my first bible

and

In loving memory of my Father
who taught me the art of commentary
by his play-by-play reports

CONTENTS

Foreword ix
Introduction xi

Chapter One: Spirit and Letter in Galatians 1

I.   Introduction...1

II. A.   Galatians 3:1-5: A Rhetorical Turn....................3

II. B.   The Language of Opposition.............................6

III. A.   ἐξ ἔργων νόμου 8

III. B.   Galatians 2:15-16: 11
                The Unspoken Question

IV. A.   ἐξ ἀκοῆς πίστεως 18

IV. B.   1 Thessalonians 1:3 and
                Romans 10:16-17...................................... 19

IV. C.   Praxis and Identity................................... 21

V. A.   Galatians 3:6-14:
                Preliminary Remarks................................... 27

V. B.   The Double Magic of Tradition 28

V. C.   Some Possible Preconceptions......................... 42

V. D.   Summary 44

VI.A.   The Expansion of Interpretation:
                Tradition and Time.................................... 45

VI.B.   Tradition and Space 48

VI.C.   The Horizons of Existence 50

VII.   Conclusion.. 53

Chapter Two:	Excursus: Letter, Tradition and the Task of Interpretation	55
I.	The Dialogue within Hellenistic Judaism	56
I A.	The Figure of Abraham as an Entrance into the Discussion	56
I B.	Scripture as Conveyance of Power and Archive of Tradition	60
I C.	The Effect of the Letter: The Creation of the Autonomous Self	64
I D.	Interpretation as a Means of Unleashing the Power of the Letter	66
1.	The Letter and Allegorization	66
2.	The Letter and the Books of Wisdom	71
3.	The Letter and Jewish Apocalyptic	74
4.	Letter and the Interpretive Process at Qumran	77
II.	The Larger Cultural Dialogue	81
II A.	The Sophistic Roots	81
II B.	The Unwritten/Written Dialectic in Plato	86
II C.	Aristotle and the Classification of Tradition	91
II D.	The Cynic Counterpoint	93
II E.	Harmony, Right Reason and the the Understanding of Authentic Existence	96
II F.	Posidonius and the Scope of Interpretation	101
II G.	Roman Apocalypticism	104
	Conclusion	105

Chapter Three:	Spirit and Letter in 2 Corinthians	107
I.	Introduction	107
II.	Preliminary Questions and Strategy	108
III.	The Language Field of 2 Cor 3:6	109
III. A.	The Rhetorical Movement	109
III. B.	The Previous Correspondence	117
III. C.	The Language of Opposition: An Internal Approach	118
III. D.	The Language of Opposition Continued: 2 Cor 10-13	122
IV.	The Opponents of Paul according to D. Georgi	124
V.	The Lifeworlds of Letter and Spirit	129
V. A.	The Pauline Difference	129
V. B.	Analysis of 2 Cor 3:7-18	131
V. C.	The Task of Interpretation	139
VI.	Conclusion	142
Chapter Four:	Spirit and Letter in Romans	143
I.	Introduction	143
II.	Romans 2:29	145
II. A.	Introductory Remarks	145
II. B.	1:18-3:20: The Apocalyptic Setting	146
II. C.	Romans 2: An Analysis	149
III.	Romans 7:6	165
III. A.	Preliminary Remarks	165
III. B.	Romans 7:6 and Its Context	166
IV.	Romans 7:7-24	172

IV. A.   A Question of Strategy 172

IV. B.   "I" as Persona..174

IV. C.   Romans 7:7-24: An Analysis 177

V.   Romans 7:25a, 8:2-25: Language for a
              New World 186

              Conclusion..193

Chapter 5:   Conclusion..197

Bibliography 203

Index 215

Note: Citations from classical authors are taken from the Loeb Classical Library, unless otherwise indicated. The abbreviations used in the text and bibliography may be found in the SBL Style Sheet.

ACKNOWLEDGEMENT

The author wishes to thank Xavier University for the encouragement and support, both personal and financial, for the completion of this project. Former Dean Stanley Hedeen and Fr. Kenneth Overberg, S.J., prove the word "colleague" is no dead letter.

FOREWORD

Since Augustine gave the conceptual pair of letter and spirit a moral meaning it retained its function as a principle of interpretation but it lost its cosmic-dramatic dimension. Even the Greek and Hellenistic dialectic of the concept of the letter between the written and the unwritten was much reduced if not forgotten. This happened even more to the mythical and the magical aspects which the history of interpretation Paul presupposes had given to both concepts, letter and spirit. Only some of that was restored by the reemphasis of the mythical dimensions of eschatology by the history of religion school. Yet very soon this discovery suffered from the conflation and confusion of the eschatological with the dialectical as they evolved in dialectical theology as its apologetic tendency invaded biblical scholarship.

In that more dogmatic approach the differences between the various texts in which said pair of terms appears in Paul's letters were not taken into account. Starting from a critical observation of that state of the question, Dewey studies the historical as well as conceptual drama which takes part in the Pauline texts themselves beginning with Gal. 3. The suspense is increased by the interplay of the contextual, historical as well as theological, elements within the texts.

But I do not want to interfere too much with the reader's suspense and curiosity in following Dewey's unraveling of what he calls Paul's strategy of rhetoric which to a high degree is a movement of the subject matter itself. This does away with our customary notions of theology as a static and systematic arrangement and rearrangement of given concepts by an author who always knew best and ahead of time.

The situation of the text as a multiple interfacing of people's praxis, theory and of other historical forces Dewey brings into play. The mutual communication of the beyond and the within of the texts is shown as an essential element of production and reproduction of what we call theology. The move from Gal.3 to 2. Cor.3. becomes all the more important. In the latter text the antithetical dimension of the conceptual pair the book researches is coming out more fully than scholarship has recognized thus, my own research included.

The reasons unveiled are fascinating and they remain entrancing as the discussion moves from 2 Cor. 3 to Rom. 2 and 7. One could say that Dewey in his analysis of this movement uncovers the political momentum of Paul's dialogical thinking as it develops the radical potential of the Greek and Hellenistic concept of 'parrhesia' pointedly mentioned in 2 Cor. 3 as the citizen's right of free speech and action, now extended to all formerly disenfranchized.

Dewey has taken into account the suggestions of modern structural and literary analysis but he has not followed their often times conservative ahistorical development. Instead he has reconciled them with historical-critical approaches, not only those of history of religion and history of culture. Dewey has shown that the theology of a text cannot appear in full without the use of all such lenses. But it can and must move beyond that thus letting historical criticism do what it can do best, namely allowing the text and the past say what they have not said yet or what the in between history and use have brushed over, forgotten or silenced. The reader gets a feeling for the particularity of the texts studied that in being written became agents over and beyond the author, themselves actively creating something anew in which the careful reader, scholar as well as lay person, can participate if they use their critical imagination.

Dieter Georgi
Frankfurt/Main
September 1992

INTRODUCTION

E. Käsemann, in his provocative article on "The Spirit and the Letter," states that for some incomprehensible reason there exists no historical study of the interpretation of Spirit and Letter.[1] The meaning of this antithesis and its consequences for Paul's theology always remain "undiscussed or shadowy." He then proceeds to give his interpretation of the meaning of the antithesis of Spirit and Letter. In endeavoring to argue that underneath this usage of Spirit and Letter the apostle has a central message, which may be an approach to a theological hermeneutic, Käsemann touches on some significant historical issues.[2] Yet, since he is primarily concerned with the theological implications of this antithesis, he leaves to others the basic task of locating the question of Spirit and Letter within the movement of history.

Credit must be given to Käsemann for reopening this question of Spirit and Letter in Paul's writing. He is likewise correct when he points out that despite the slight textual basis for such an investigation there have been repeated applications of this antithesis throughout the history of

---

[1]E. Käsemann, "The Spirit and the Letter," in *Perspectives in Paul* (Philadelphia: Fortress, 1969) 138-66.

[2]Ibid. Käsemann's introduction of the question of what is the true man of the Greek tradition (p. 142) or of the question of who is truly free (p. 144) or of the relation of tradition to Letter (p. 147) should not be overlooked. Despite these historical questions, Käsemann continues to seek a theological perspective without dealing with the larger cultural dialogue out of which emerges the issue of Spirit and Letter. His consideration of the appropriate texts in Romans before that of 2 Corinthians is a decisive indication of his leaving the question of historical development to other interpreters.

interpretation.[3] The assessments have been many, ranging from calling the antithesis in question a hyperbolic straining of the truth to more elevated attempts to detect some theological principle. The major tendency, however, throughout the history of interpretation has been to see in this antithesis an expression of the issue of intent versus form or internal versus external. Perhaps the best starting point for this interpretation of Paul's antithesis is to be found among the earliest exegetes of Paul--the Gnostics. E. Pagels has shown that from the early part of the second century Gnostics used this antithesis to distinguish the pneumatics from the psychics.[4] R. M. Grant, in his treatment of the Letter and the Spirit, points to Origen as the first orthodox theologian to employ this antithesis.[5]

With Origen the commonplace distinction of form and content, inner and outer, material and spiritual, enters into the mainstream of the history of interpretation. Grant has argued that what has actually taken place is a continuation of the traditional Hellenistic methods of interpretation.[6] This may well be the case with Origen. But what is lost, both to Origen and to Grant, is the possible uniqueness of the antithesis for Paul. What might once have been an antithesis fraught with enormous eschatological and social potential has been reduced successfully in the space of a few generations to a schoolman's problem concerning the levels of interpretation.

Except for some notable variations,[7] the issue of Spirit and Letter carries on in the established tendency until the Reformation. There the

---

[3]For a fine introductory article, as well as a beginning bibliography, on Spirit and Letter, cf. G. Ebeling, "Geist und Buchstabe," *RGG*[3] 2, cols. 1290-96.

[4]E. Pagels, *The Gnostic Paul* (Philadelphia: Fortress, 1975) 19-20, 95-99.

[5]R. M. Grant, *The Letter and the Spirit* (London: SCM, 1957).

[6]Ibid., chaps. 1-3.

[7]Two notable exceptions are Augustine and Joachim of Fiore. In his *De spiritu et littera* Augustine employs the familiar destruction of inner versus outer.

distinction becomes subject to different theological perspectives. Luther grounds the antithesis upon his understanding of Law and Gospel, while Calvin sees the Spirit as the true Spirit of the Law.[8] Only the soon forgotten insights of the Anabaptists touch once more the explosive eschatological and social implications of this antithesis.[9]

The liberal-idealist tradition furthers the history of this issue. Starting from the concept of Spirit as the power of being aware of oneself and of being able to penetrate understandably the world which one encounters, this tradition then understood Letter as that which remains external, unassimilated into spiritual life.[10] Yet renewed interest into the historical meaning of both Spirit and Letter has thrown such idealistic presuppositions into serious question.

More recent interpretations have not, however, turned the tide around. One still finds investigations moving out of presupposed theological positions or attempting to arrive at them.[11] In a sense, the

---

However, in connecting the image of the "finger of God" (Exod 31:18) with the new tablets of the Spirit (chap. 28), he does reflect a sensitivity for the eschatological import of the antithesis. Throughout his *Concordia* as well as his commentaries, Joachim of Fiore shares a deep concern for the historical action and coming of the Spirit. His use of the Spirit/Letter dichotomy functions as a literary, historical and existential critique. For him the question of the coming of the Spirit meant the advent of the age of freedom.

[8]Besides the *Lecture on Romans* (chaps. 2 and 7), see the *Lectures on the Psalms*, such as Pss 9, 27, 45, 51, and 71 for Luther. The *Institutes* 2.7.2; 2.11.7 and the *Commentary on 2 Corinthians* point out Calvin's perspective.

[9]W. Klassen, "Anabaptist Hermeneutics: The Letter and the Spirit," *MQR* 40 (1966) 83-96. Also: H. Poettcker, "Meno Simon's Encounter with the Bible," *MQR* 40 (1966) 112-26.

[10]Käsemann, "Spirit and the Letter," 139. See G. W. F. Hegel, *The Phenomenology of the Spirit*.

[11]One can easily perceive this in the *TDNT* articles: E. Schweizer, "πνεῦμα κτλ," *TDNT* 6. 389-455; G. Schrenk, "γράφω κτλ," *TDNT* 1. 742-73.

history of interpretation of the antithesis of Spirit and Letter is a dramatic illustration of what happens to a text whose historical context has been either forgotten or disregarded. Indeed, there is an overriding irony in that, while the antithesis of Spirit and Letter has been used by exegetes as a fundamental principle of interpretation, the antithesis itself has usually been left with little or no historical foundation.

That the antithesis of Spirit and Letter cannot be analyzed from a purely theological viewpoint has been demonstrated clearly by D. Georgi, who has shown that in order to understand the issues within 2 Corinthians one must take seriously into consideration the opponents of Paul, along with their worldview and method.[12]   E. Brandenburger, in his work *Fleisch und Geist*, has argued quite forcefully that any further advance in the understanding of Paul must be made through an attentive analysis of the significant word-groups in light of their historical and cultural associations.[13]   Betz in his recent work on Galatians also points to similar conclusions.[14]   Further studies on the nature of Hellenistic propaganda continue to reinforce this methodological consideration.[15]

In pursuing the question of Spirit and Letter in Paul, therefore, I take it as my fundamental task to locate this famous antithesis within its historical horizon. If there is any lesson to be gained from the history of interpretation of this antithesis it is that one must be aware of the ever-present temptation to render the significance of this antithesis in some

---

[12]D. Georgi, *Die Gegner des Paulus im 2. Korintherbrief* (Neukirchen: Neukirchener, 1964).

[13]E. Brandenburger, *Fleisch und Geist. Paulus und die dualistische Weisheit* (Neukirchen-Vluyn: Neukirchener, 1968).

[14]H. D. Betz, "The Literary Composition and Function of Paul's Letter to the Galatians," *NTS* 21 (1975) 353-79.   Also, idem, *Galatians* (Philadelphia: Fortress, 1979).

[15]Cf. E. Schüssler Fiorenza, ed., *Aspects of Religious Propaganda in Judaism and Early Christianity* (Notre Dame: Notre Dame University, 1976).

atomistic fashion. Neither a reduced philological meaning nor any so-called higher theological principle does justice to the functional significance of this antithesis. In investigating this question, then, I shall listen attentively to the language of the text. This will be done by allowing various word-groups or formations to suggest the interpretive leads and clues for this investigation. The reason for this approach is the historical experience of language. For language historically expressed discloses the lifeworld of that particular conversation. Interpretation of a text is, first of all, a dialogue with the text, wherein the interpreter attempts to understand the world of meaning, the common ground recognized by those whose conversation brought about the text. Language, then, is not simply a tool for the interpreter but the space or medium in which the world of meaning comes to stand. Thus, in attempting to discover significant word-groups or equivalencies I shall try to find out how such language functions within the life-world presupposed by the text. In short, this close attention to language attempts to open up the historical horizon of the text, by determining through what is said what has been left unspoken but which forms the very basis for the historical expression of the text.[16]

This investigation is in some respects a return to the effort of Reitzenstein, who saw the need to review the term πνεῦμα within the shifting horizons of Hellenistic mystery religions.[17] He rightly perceived that Paul was involved in issues which went beyond a mere lexical understanding of spirit. He saw that Paul's use of πνεῦμα was indeed a choice among several linguistic strategies designed to speak of the fundamental drive of humanity to seek an experience of transcendence which both liberates and illuminates. Although some of the philological

---

[16]Here I am indebted to the insights of J. Barr, *The Semantics of Biblical Language* (Oxford: Oxford University, 1969); E. Brandenburger, *Fleisch und Geist*; H.-G. Gadamer, *Truth and Method* (New York: Seabury, 1975).

[17]R. Reitzenstein, *Hellenistic Mystery Religions* (trans. J. E. Steely; Pittsburgh: Pickwick, 1978).

connections remain matters of speculation, while others must be reexamined critically on historical grounds, what must not be lost is the challenge he leaves to every interpreter: to see within the very multiplicity of religious competition the hankering of humanity for divine habitation. Indeed, it will be shown that what is at stake with the issue of Spirit and Letter is the question of how the human comes to grips with powers and forces transcending existence.

Moreover, my concern for the linguistic combinations of Pauline material has been sharpened by recent investigations of Paul's use of rhetoric. Betz,[18] Church,[19] and Stowers[20] have pointed out that further exegesis of Paul must begin again to ask this literary question.[21] Indeed, this question of rhetoric has already been raised in respect to the antithesis of Spirit and Letter. Cohen,[22] in assessing Paul's understanding of Spirit and Letter, has argued that what Paul does is to play with established Greco-Roman and Jewish rhetorical canons. In his view, Paul tries to effect a mere rhetorical surprise, conditioned by his peculiar eschatological perspective. Although one can take Cohen's conclusion concerning Paul's eschatological perspective, his dismissal of Paul's rhetorical usage leaves one greatly unsatisfied. For the initial

---

[18]Betz, *Galatians*.

[19]F. F. Church, "Rhetorical Structure and Design in Paul's Letter to Philemon," *HTR* 71 (1978) 17-33.

[20]S. Stowers, "A Critical Reassessment of Paul and the Diatribe: The Dialogical Element in Paul's Letter to the Romans" (Ph.D. diss., Yale University, 1979).

[21]E.g., Betz's commentary on Galatians.

[22]B. Cohen, "Letter and Spirit in Jewish and Roman Law," *Mordocai Kaplan Jubilee Volume* (New York: Jewish Theological Seminary, 1953) 109-35.

observations of Weiss,[23] followed by Bultmann's demonstration of the rhetorical elements of diatribe in Paul,[24] along with the more recent analysis of the use of antithesis in Paul by N. Schneider,[25] have made a dismissal of the question of rhetoric rather suspect. Further, Betz, Church and Stowers have made the treatment of the rhetorical element in Paul quite necessary within any investigation which purports to deal with the historical contours of Pauline language. Thus, while my study will not undertake a thoroughgoing rhetorical analysis on all sections of Paul under consideration, I shall utilize the insights of such rhetorical canons where applicable. The reason for this is that rhetoric provides us with an opening into the possible competitive lifeworld of Paul. In dealing with attempts to persuade or dissuade, to allure and to advertise, I may find clues to the questions which underlie such strategies of competition.

Furthermore, in light of the overriding concern to locate an understanding of this antithesis within its historical context, I shall cut across significant passages from Galatians, 2 Corinthians, and Romans. By so doing I hope to discern whether there are any semantic equivalencies in Paul's language to the antithesis of Spirit and Letter. By examining such passages I shall see if there are any word combinations which may provide an important link to the thought of Paul. This line of analysis has a fourfold advantage. First, it will help limit the task, thereby rendering the investigation feasible. Second, it will help provide interpretive limits from the text itself and not from some presupposed schema. Third, the word combinations disclosed may well open up the larger linguistic field, allowing the interpreter to understand Paul's language within a broader cultural horizon. A final point is that in taking

[23]J. Weiss, *Die Aufgaben des neutestamentlichen Wissenschaft in der Gegenwart* (Göttingen: Vanderhoeck & Ruprecht, 1911) 11.

[24]R. Bultmann, *Der Stil der paulinischen Predigt und die kynisch-stoische Diatribe* (Göttingen: Vanderhoeck & Ruprecht, 1910).

[25]N. Schneider, *Die rhetorische Eigenart der paulinischen Antithese* (Tübingen: Mohr, 1970).

these letters in chronological order,[26] one may be able to see whether there is any development by Paul in regard to Spirit and Letter.

In addition to my introductory and concluding remarks, this investigation consists of four major sections. My first chapter begins, surprisingly perhaps, with an extended analysis of Gal 3:1-14. I contend that the concepts of Spirit and Letter are already implicit in the Pauline argument and that by using equivalent language Paul is placing himself within a definite intellectual tradition. In other words, as Paul meets the claims of his opposition in Galatia, he has recourse to categories and associations which not only are shared by his opposition but also are expressions of the larger cultural debate concerning meaningful lifeworlds. Paul, thus, directly in dialogue with the Galatian communities, is at the same time entering the cultural dialectic over the experience and control of transcendence in human existence. To demonstrate these points it will be necessary to consider the rhetorical twists and turns of Paul's language, the possible language of his opposition and the questions raised by their language, the interpretive strategy of Paul's antithesis, and the association of magic and curse with what is written. This will then lead to a brief consideration of the rest of chap. 3 and appropriate sections of chap. 4, where it will be seen that the lifeworlds laid bare in 3:1-14 are further drawn out and explored. In so doing, the very understanding and interpretation of tradition, viewed in its lethal and life-giving aspects, will emerge as the essential question of the extended dialogue.

The intimate relation of tradition and Letter suggested in the first chapter will be the substance of an extended excursus on Letter, tradition and the task of interpretation. For in order to grasp the significance of Paul's usage, it will be necessary to place this discussion within the larger cultural dialectic. Thus I shall explore the variety of ways in which one comes to grips with transcendent forces and powers so as to gain some

---

[26]Here I follow the most probable chronology. Cf. G. Bornkamm, *Paul* (New York: Herder & Herder, 1971).

sense of genuine identity and destiny. In the first part of this chapter I shall deal with the proximate horizon suggested by the investigation of Galatians, namely, the thought world of Hellenistic Judaism. Here one can see that, with Letter most positively understood, a definite sense of continuity of tradition and law, unwrittenness and writtenness, nature and transcendence, past and present, is dramatically achieved. Under the aspect of written Scripture, the Letter functions as a storehouse of tradition as well as the very means of unlocking the boundaries of space and time. Moreover, the person who incorporates the power and force of tradition through interpretation realizes one of the fondest hopes of the Hellenistic world: the free and autonomous individual. Indeed, it will be argued that the varied processes of interpretation become the means of unleashing the power of the Letter, thereby allowing one to come to terms with the fundamental questions of transcendence.

In the second half of the excursus I shall examine more schematically the roots and development of this dialogue. From the Sophistic debate to Roman Apocalyptic I shall attempt to illustrate the far-flung aspects of the relation of Letter and tradition to the act of interpretation. In so doing, one will be able to see how Paul is a correspondent not only to the dialogue within Hellenistic Judaism but also to the broader discussion of the Hellenistic world. within an ever-shifting dialectic, where the question is continually refined, restated, revised, and realigned, Letter and tradition emerge as fundamental interpretive concepts. The impact of Paul's language in Galatians, 2 Corinthians and Romans, then, can now be viewed within this matrix of interpretive options. In short, it can be said that before Paul can be regarded as a creative thinker, he must first of all be seen as an heir to the dialogue on Letter and tradition.

The third major division of this thesis deals with the Spirit/Letter antithesis of 2 Cor 3:6. I shall argue that Paul develops both lines of this antithesis not only out of his thinking in Galatians but also in reaction to the position of his opponents as well as to that of the Corinthian community. At stake in my interpretation is the potential overturning of what the subsequent history of interpretation has understood to be the meaning of this antithesis. I shall argue that the usual distinction of inner and outer, spiritual and material, is more in correspondence with the thought-world of Paul's opponents than with Paul. Further, I shall argue that, beginning with the shared understanding of Spirit and Letter, Paul, then reinterprets both in light of his singular eschatological perspective.

In order to demonstrate these contentions I shall again consider the language field before and after 2 Cor 3:6. An analysis of the rhetorical elements will disclose the likelihood of a competitive situation. Further, there will be concern for what can be presupposed on the part of the Corinthian community and Paul's opposition. From an inspection of previous correspondence, as well as the language of the opposition, an understanding of the need to document objectively the presence of the Spirit by both community and opposition will emerge. This positive linkage of Spirit and Letter radically determines Paul's response to the Corinthian congregation. Depending upon the contributions of D. Georgi in regard to the worldview of the opponents of Paul, I shall further deepen the cultural aspect of this question. The response by Paul, in such light, becomes not simply a surprising rhetorical flourish, but a strategic attack upon the foundations of Letter and tradition. Through the subsequent analysis of 2 Cor 3:7-18, I shall argue that 2 Cor 3:6c becomes a guiding principle of interpretation for Paul as he exposes the lethal lifeworld of the Letter while simultaneously demonstrating the lifegiving world of Spirit.

Moreover, the communal aspect of interpretation, already brought forward in the chapter on Galatians, will become quite manifest as a significant element in the entire interpretive process. For Paul's argument stands or falls upon his claim that the lifeworld of Spirit which he sets before the Corinthians is already their experience and thus the ground for sharing his interpretation with them. Furthermore, in refuting the need for some sort of objective verification of the Spirit, Paul throws open the task of interpretation onto the entire scope of history. In criticizing the notion of a controlled activity, performed only by experts and appreciated solely by initiates, Paul discloses the activity of interpretation as essentially that of re-creation by the community as it continues to advance into the future opened up by the eschatological revelation in Christ.

My final chapter considers the question whether the radical understanding of Spirit and Letter found in 2 Cor 3 is continued, or indeed furthered, by Paul in Rom 2:29 and 7:6. To determine the function of Rom 2:29 it will be necessary to place it in the context of the extended block of material from 1:18 to 3:20, where the interplay of apocalyptic and popular philosophical languages becomes manifest. Having determined the apocalyptic stage for chap. 2 I shall then pay close attention to the diatribal strategy of this chapter. The introduction of Letter and Spirit at this particular moment allows Paul not only to maintain his radical questioning of contemporary assumptions of what constitutes the human project but also to suggest that the hope of human authenticity has come true in Spirit.

However, it is not until 7:6ff. that the implications of the lifeworlds of Spirit and Letter are explored in full existential dimensions. I shall argue in this section that 7:6 both explicitly sums up the progression of thought from the previous two chapters and serves as the hermeneutical principle for chaps. 7-8. A close analysis of the problems with 7:6 will justify reaching back to previous material to understand the momentum of Paul's thought. The lifeworlds of Spirit and Letter will emerge in mythic proportions as Paul discloses the fundamental conditions of human existence. In light of this overarching antithesis of Spirit and Letter the remainder of chap. 7 and 8:2-25 will be interpreted. Once again, however, the issue of language will be raised in respect now to the "I" of 7:7-25. In order to resolve the vexing question of who is this "I" I shall consider the way in which the "I" functions as a dramatic mode of speech within the diatribal tradition. By doing so, I shall be enabled to recognize the "I" of Romans 7 as an expression of the power and force of the lifeworld of the Letter. Thereupon will follow an exegesis of 7:7ff. in light of this suggestion. What shall emerge from this investigation is that the "I", usually understood as the positive embodiment of the culture's highest aspirations, is unveiled in its utter captivity under the force of the Letter.

In contrast, 8:2ff. bring forward the liberating aspects of the lifeworld of the Spirit. Again the employment of different language signals the appearance of a lifeworld where communal solidarity, realization of the dream of human authenticity, and universal hope are characteristic of a radically new human situation. Indeed, the interpretive scope of Paul continues to widen as the chapter progresses, so much so that the cosmos itself is placed under the horizon of future possibility. The new world of Spirit includes not only the community of believers but even the entire creation.

The aim of this investigation, in response to Käsemann's call, is to situate the Pauline usage of Spirit and Letter within its historical context. However, in order to avoid the temptation to interpret this antithesis either by a theological principle alone or simply in terms of the traditional categories of inner versus outer, spiritual versus material, it is necessary to become self-conscious of the hermeneutical task that is dictated by the language of the text. Thus the entire project becomes an occasion for examining the very process of interpretation. Indeed, this is quite fitting, since the antithesis of Spirit and Letter traditionally served as an interpretive principle of Scripture. Moreover, by paying close attention to the way in which Paul's language functions, to the variety of word combinations, and to the rhetorical strategy, one discovers that Paul is an heir to a much larger cultural discussion wherein interpretation is placed at the service of fundamental human questions. *The question of the scope and promise of the interpretive act thus underlies this project.* To place Paul's concerns, intimated by his usage of Spirit and Letter, within such a context is to reactivate the basic thrust of that fundamental question, namely, how can human beings make sense of the forces and powers which transcend human existence? The interpretation of Paul's antithesis makes it necessary for Paul's interpreter to disclose that very tradition to which Paul is indebted. In that light not only Paul but also his exegete contribute to the answering of that question. The implications of such a self-conscious activity of interpretation will be discussed in the concluding section of this investigation.

CHAPTER ONE

Spirit and Letter in Galatians

I. Introduction

My investigation of Spirit and Letter in Paul begins not with the famous third chapter of 2 Corinthians but, somewhat surprisingly, with the third chapter of Galatians. My argument for this is that what will be seen as a full-blown antithesis in 2 Corinthians already is underway in this chapter of Galatians. From an extended exegesis of Gal 3:1-14, as well as noting its influence upon subsequent arguments (such as 4:21-31), I shall attempt to show how fundamental the notions of Letter and Spirit are to Paul's position within the intellectual climate of his time. My contention is that in using such concepts Paul is self-consciously placing himself in the intellectual tradition which makes interpretation subordinate to and instrumental of the fundamental understanding of god(s), world, humanity, society and history. In dealing with the situation brought about by "other" missionaries, in making clear to the Galatians what his understanding of Spirit is in relation to tradition, to Scripture and to Torah, Paul is aware of and is using common conceptual categories and associations. The distinctiveness of Paul will then be seen not in his being some sort of aberrant intellectual phenomenon but in his creative ordering and employment of contemporary intellectual categories. Furthermore, it is precisely by the way in which Paul uses these conceptual associations that the relation of Spirit and Letter becomes clarified.

This investigation will begin with an examination of Gal 3:1-14 for the following reasons. First and foremost, since this research is concerned with the question of Spirit and Letter, it will be essential to consider Gal 3:1-14, since here we find, in anticipation of 2 Cor 3:6, more than a simple intimation of the issue of Spirit and Letter. For in these verses we find a very interesting usage of πνεῦμα and γραφή (3:2, 5, 8). Indeed, Gal 3:2 is the first time in Galatians that πνεῦμα has been mentioned by Paul. Moreover, of the eighteen times the term is used in Galatians, it occurs four times within these fourteen verses.[1] In regard to the equivalent of Letter, ἡ γραφή , there is the striking fact that the first thorough going use of Scripture is located within this usage of πνεῦμα . Lührmann has even pointed out the possible use of *inclusio* regarding the issue of Spirit around the employment of Scripture.[2] The task ahead is not only to find out what is the relationship of πνεῦμα to γραφή within this context, but also to ask what is the hermeneutical value of bringing in these terms at this point within the epistle. Is there any significance to the fact that the issue of πνεῦμα is brought up within a series of rhetorical questions to the Galatians?   What underlying categories or associations have assisted or forced Paul to express himself in the way he does? Is Paul in dialogue with his opponents, with the Galatian communities, or even with a wider intellectual audience in respect to these categories of thought? Why is it, in short, that Paul chooses this moment in his letter to speak of πνεῦμα and exhibit his exegetical finesse?   My contention, in this chapter, is that Paul strategically uses πνεῦμα and γραφή at this moment in order to bring the Galatians to an understanding that the matters with which they are concerned, such as tradition and praxis, have more far-reaching implications than seems to be the case. The epistle is less an apology[3] than it is a teaching vehicle exploring the conditions of authentic

---

[1] In fact, three times in vss 2-5.

[2] Vss 5, 14; cf. D. Lührmann, *Der Brief an die Galater* (Zürich: Theologischer Verlag, 1980) 53.

[3] Especially a legal defense; cf. Betz, *Galatians*, 14-25.

existence. By employing πνεῦμα and γραφή , as well as other significant conceptual associations, Paul brings out the possibilities and powers of tradition before the Christian communities.

II. A. Galatians 3:1-5: A Rhetorical Turn

It is impossible even for the modern ear, less sophisticated to the ancient elements of rhetoric, to miss the rhetorical force of Gal 3:1-5. Recent studies, going beyond the work of Bultmann, have shown that Paul was quite capable as a rhetorician.[4a] Relying upon the work of Betz (while not subscribing to his overall formal analysis),[4b] and even more so on the research of Stowers,[5] I present a breakdown of the rhetorical elements within these five verses.   Upon inspecting these verses, a number of questions will emerge. How do these rhetorical twists and turns function? Why does Paul use them at this point? Does the rhetoric provide any clues to the lifeworld presupposed by the language?

First, let us consider the verses:

3:1a ῏Ω ἀνόητοι Γαλάται,

Insulting address, a dramatic turn from 2:21, expresses lack of perception.

3:1b τίς ὑμᾶς ἐβάσκανεν,

Rhetorical question; common rhetorical allusion to spellbinding effect.

3:1c οἷς κατ᾽ ὀφθαλμοὺς
᾽Ιησοῦς Χριστὸς προ-
εγράφη ἐσταυρωμένος;

Rhetorical use of vividness; recalls initial message; cites the audience as eyewitnesses.

[4a]Cf. Introduction, pp. xvi-xvii above.

[4b]Betz, *Galatians*.

[5]Stowers, *Paul and the Diatribe*.

3:2a	τοῦτο μόνον θέλω μαθεῖν ἀφ' ὑμῶν,	Inquiry; possible play on μαθεῖν-παθεῖν (vs 4). Inductive method.
3:2b	ἐξ ἔργων νόμου τὸ πνεῦμα ἐλάβετε ἢ ἐξ ἀκοῆς πίστεως;	Indicting rhetorical question; use of induction; antithesis.
3:3a	οὕτως ἀνόητοί ἐστε;	Expression of lack of perception.
3:3b	ἐναρξάμενοι πνεύματι νῦν σαρκὶ ἐπιτελεῖσθε;	Continuance of rhetorical question; chiastic antitheton, indicating inconsistency.
3:4a	τοσαῦτα ἐπάθετε εἰκῇ;	Rhetorical question; cf. vs 2; *dubitatio*.
3:4b	εἴ γε καὶ εἰκῇ.	Common diatribal element; exclamation.
3:5a	ὁ οὖν ἐπιχορηγῶν ὑμῖν τὸ πνεῦμα καὶ ἐνεργῶν δυνάμεις ἐν ὑμῖν	Rhetorical question, calling for a conclusion, based on the experience of those addressed.
3:5b	ἐξ ἔργων νόμου ἢ ἐξ ἀκοῆς πίστεως;	End of rhetorical question; antithesis.[6]

These verses very clearly bear the marks of diatribe: a series of rhetorical questions, indicting the addressees; an inductive method, causing the listeners to consider their experience; vivid address, placing the initial message and the community's experience before their eyes. Now the observation of such diatribal elements cannot rest there. As Stowers has shown, the elements of diatribe must be seen within the larger dialogical context, wherein a teacher-student relationship is presupposed.[7] The various methods, as evidenced in Gal 3:1-5, are used

---

[6]Ibid., 133ff.

[7]Ibid., 240-48.

by the speaker to lead the listener to a deeper realization of the issues under consideration. Thus, it is not a simple matter of noting the various elements of style but of discovering the basic strategy of communication. Such a series of questions is designed to induce the listener to a deeper basis of thought and self-reflection. The rhetorical effect of these verses, then, is not only to move away from what appears to be a personal defense of and explanation by Paul, but also to bring the Galatians directly into the argument of the letter.[8] Thus, the Galatians in these verses are directly confronted by Paul through direct address and a series of rhetorical questions. They are called ἀνόητοι twice in this rapid-fire attempt to learn what they really think. The amazement which Paul registered early in the letter (1:6ff) is replaced by a direct attack on their present understanding, which Paul can only consider a result of some bewitchment (3:1b). Immediately Paul graphically portrays the initial message within the context of their own experience, and, in antithetical fashion, asks them to decide how they came by the πνεῦμα (3:3, 5). The basis for their decision is to be found within the very confines of their communal life (3:5).[9] Throughout this questioning Paul appears quite at a loss and at the point of exasperation.[10] Now it is in this emotionally charged context that the first use of πνεῦμα is made. It is then appropriate to continue this investigation by considering the language in which this usage of πνεῦμα appears. This must be done in order to see with what other terms Paul associates πνεῦμα and thus to determine

---

[8]After Paul's apparent apologetic remarks (1:10-2:21), we tend to forget that the letter is addressed to the Galatians in regard to their abandonment of what Paul considers to be the Gospel: 1:2, 6-9, 11, 13, 20.

[9] ἐναρξάμενοι , ἐπιτελεῖσθε (3:3) and δυνάμεις (3.5) carry associations of cultic experience. Cf. ἐνάρχομαι *BAG*, p. 262.1; G. Delling, τελέω , κτλ, *TDNT* 8. 61-62; δύναμις *BAG*, p. 208.6.

[10]Cf. 3:1, an insulting direct address; 3:2, an attempt to learn but one thing; 3:3, a repeated insult; 3:4, an expression of doubt.

σ what is the issue which Paul is attempting to enlarge for the Galatians'
self-understanding.

II. B. The Language of Opposition

The first instance of πνεῦμα in Galatians occurs within the inquiry Paul
makes as to whether the Galatians have received the Spirit ἐξ ἔργων
νόμου or ἐξ ἀκοῆς πίστεως (3:2). These antithetical phrases are held
out as interpretative alternatives for the Galatians' understanding of their
reception of πνεῦμα. The words τὸ πνεῦμα ἐλάβετε strongly
suggest that the issue of tradition is involved.[11] We can see that Paul is
arguing inductively, leaving the Galatians to decide which interpretation
fits their experience. It is a given that the Spirit is present to them; what
is at stake is how the Spirit has been conveyed.[12] This antithesis is picked
up again in vs 5, but, in this case, it pertains to the question of how the
divine source provides the πνεῦμα and the powerful manifestations within
the community. In both verses the question refers to the manner or way
in which transcendent experience is acquired. Moreover, the importance
of this antithesis becomes evident by the fact that in vs 2 Paul declares
that this is what he particularly wants to find out from the Galatians and
that in vs 5 the antithesis functions as the climactic element in the final
rhetorical question. The question for this investigation is why does Paul
select these alternatives? Indeed, why does he set them in antithesis?
How is this issue over the way in which transcendent experience is
acquired related to the rest of the epistle? Does Paul pick up the language
of this antithesis from the missionaries he considers to be his opposition?
Do these phrases indicate any language field or intellectual categories with
which Paul is in dialogue? Before touching on these questions, I return to
the remaining verses of this section.

---

[11]Cf. 2 Cor 11:4: πνεῦμα ἕτερον λαμβάνετε ὃ οὐκ ἐλάβετε ,
ἢ εὐαγγέλιον ἕτερον ὃ οὐκ ἐδέξασθε . Also Gal 1:6-9.

[12]Thus, we can see the force of the surrounding antithesis.

Already in 3:1 can be found some indication of opposition, albeit indirect (τίς ὑμᾶς ἐβάσκανεν). The unnamed opposition has had a marked effect upon the communities (ἐβάσκανεν), evidently in regard to the kerygma.[13] Not only does Paul bring the Galatians directly into the discussion by turning so abrasively to them, but in doing so he graphically renders his preaching before their eyes.[14]

This vivid effect is maintained throughout vss 1-5 by the relentless series of rhetorical questions, the emotional tone,[15] and the constant emphasis upon the present situation of the community. This last point is quite evident in vs 3, where Paul, in pointing out their inconsistency, asks how their proposed present position squares with their original. Vs 5 continues to emphasize the present manifestation of the πνεῦμα and δυνάμεις within the communities. Indeed, the thrust of all the

---

[13] οἷς κατ᾽ ὀφθαλμοὺς ... ἐσταυρωμένος ; cf. Gal 1:6-7.

[14]The word προεγράφη may well be more than just a rhetorical flourish by Paul. The more common understanding of the word is "publically proclaimed". This translation seems to fit in with the proclamation of the message. Schrenk (p.xiii n. 11 above) dismisses what Betz suggests, namely, the meaning "vividly portrayed" (*Galatians*, 131). Betz argues that such a rhetorical sense would be in line with the overall rhetoric of the context. However, there may be even a further nuance to this metaphorical expression. While not immediately apparent to the reader, is there not the possible play on the word προ-γράφω ? For in vss 6 and 8 we see that ἡ γραφή becomes quite prominent, enough to be personified. Further, Paul, in speaking about ἡ γραφή , plays on the future vision of Scripture (προϊδοῦσα δὲ ἡ γραφή . . . προ- ευηγγελίσατο). Could Paul already in vs 1 be intimating with προγράφω what will later be explicitly brought out? Moreover, the demonstration in vs 13 of the literal fulfillment of Scripture by the crucified Christ calls to mind the only other Pauline usage of προγράφω (Rom 15:4) where we see that Scripture having been written beforehand is fulfilled by Christ and is now used for the encouragement of the community. Therefore, while not denying the rhetorical effect suggested by commentators, my suggestion is that the term προγράφω delivers, perhaps subliminally, an imaginative hint to the coming exegesis. See p. 43 n. 106 below.

[15]Cf. especially vs 4b.

rhetorical questions is intended to furnish a challenge to the Galatians' present deliberations.

The effect, then, of these verses is to open up the Galatians' present situation for examination. Through the series of rhetorical questions Paul shifts the focus to their communal experience. From Paul's perspective the Galatians are on the verge of succumbing to a misinterpretation of their original reception of the Gospel as well as their present experience of the Spirit. In order to make them aware of this problem, he provides an antithetical interpretation of their experience of πνεῦμα. The task now is to determine whether this antithesis is solely Paul's or if Paul is using language from his opposition. Would the Galatians have already been aware of this antithesis? Or is Paul adding a significant nuance to the understanding of the Galatians' transcendent experience?

III. A. ἐξ ἔργων νόμου

It is significant that, while the phrase ἐξ ἔργων νόμου assumes apparently hermeneutical importance for Paul in 3:2-5, its overall usage in Galatians is markedly little. The four other occurrences of ἐξ ἔργων νόμου are found in 2:16 and 3:10. The latter instance will be considered in the analysis of 3:6-14.[16] 2:16 is quite intriguing, since the phrase is employed three times. I have remarked above that in 3:1-5 there was the suggestion that the issue of the interpretation of πνεῦμα might well be tied in with the question of tradition (3:2), and that this had some relationship with the kerygma proclaimed by Paul (3:1). The connection with tradition and the kerygma might well be made also with the phrase ἐξ ἔργων νόμου . Indeed, if the defensive narrative of Paul[17] is taken

---

[16]V.A.-V.B. below.

[17]Cf. Betz (*Galatians*, 14-18, 58-62), who argues that 1:12-2:14 is the *narratio* of an overall *apologia* by Paul. I do not agree with Betz's formal analysis of the epistle. However, there is no question that this section does perform a defensive function with the epistle. The question outstanding is whether Paul is consciously writing an *apologia* or using the rhetorical techniques of defense for

into account we can see that the issue of tradition is dramatically in evidence. This relationship is increased if the opening remarks and the address to the Galatians are also investigated. Thus, Paul from the beginning of the epistle makes the point that his authority[18] does not come through any form of tradition.[19] The Gospel which he announces has come neither through human agency nor teaching.[20] Rather, his apostleship and his Gospel come through (διά) Jesus Christ. Indeed, both the purpose and his message have come through divine revelation.[21]

Yet, the problem within the Galatian communities in Paul's eyes is that the Gospel which they have received from him is being overturned by another understanding[22] which is a perversion.[23] Now, although Paul is at pains to declare his position beyond anything traditional, he, nevertheless, from 1:12 to 2:14 is engaged in the question of tradition.

---

a different purpose and therefore writing something quite other than an *apologia*.

[18]Cf. J. Schütz, *Paul and the Anatomy of Apostolic Authority* (Cambridge: Cambridge University, 1975).

[19]1:1: οὐκ ἀπ' ἀνθρώπων οὐδὲ δι' ἀνθρώπου.

[20]1:12: οὐδὲ γὰρ ἐγὼ παρὰ ἀνθρώπου παρέλαβον αὐτό οὔτε ἐδιδάχθην.

[21]1:12: ἀλλὰ δι' ἀποκαλύψεως Ἰησοῦ Χριστοῦ ; 1:15-16: ὅτε δὲ εὐδόκησεν . . . ἀποκαλύψαι . . . ἵνα εὐαγγελίζωμαι.

[22]1:6: μετατίθεσθε . . . εἰς ἕτερον εὐαγγέλιον . Other examples of μετατίθημι meaning "changing one's allegiance and adopting a new opinion" can be found in Josephus *Ant.* 20.38; 2 Macc 7:24; DL 7.37.166.

[23] μεταστρέφω (1:7) carries with it the rhetorical sense that a position has been twisted or misrepresented. Cf. Liddel-Scott 1117; also Plato *Rep.* 367A; Aristotle *Rhet.* 1376B21.

After clarifying the source of his Gospel (1:12), he notes that he formerly, before the revelation by God, had been zealous for the traditions of the fathers.[24] This latter phrase is quite general[25] and most probably pertains to the practical customs of religious lifestyle[26] advocated by the Pharisees.[27]

Thereupon in three separate scenes Paul demonstrates that his gospel is not derived from any authority, even from Cephas (1:18-24); that his gospel, not out of harmony with the Jerusalem church, frees the Gentiles from the requirement of circumcision (2:1-10); that the Jewish rules of tablefellowship are also not required by the Gospel (2:11-14). Throughout his defensive narrative Paul maintains that the necessity of taking one the particular traditions of Judaism[28] no longer exists due to the freedom enjoyed through the Gospel.[29] It is then at this point where the threefold usage of ἐξ ἔργων νόμου appears.

---

[24]1:14: ζηλωτὴς ὑπάρχων τῶν πατρικῶν μου παραδόσεων.

[25]Cf. Betz, *Galatians*, 68 n. 118.

[26]Vs 13: ἀναστροφή .

[27]Cf. Josephus *Ant.* 13.297, 290. However, this does not mean that Paul is referring here to any written tradition, which would appear later in Rabbinic Judaism. Indeed, Paul's use of written tradition in 3:6ff. might well be a forerunner of what will later emerge as Rabbinic Judaism after 70 C.E. cf. J. Neusner, *Early Rabbinic Judaism* (Leiden: Brill, 1975) 63ff. Neusner argues that before 70 C.E. the Pharisees were concerned with matters of praxis, such as rite and tablefellowship. Only in the Yavnean period do we find a fusion of the scribal and Pharisaic traditions, issuing in a union of scribal activity and rabbinic piety.

[28]Cf. 2:14, the final rhetorical question to Cephas: πῶς τὰ ἔθνη ἀναγκάζεις ᾿Ιουδαΐζειν.

[29]Cf. 2:4, 14.

III. B. Galatians 2:15-16: The Unspoken Question

In order to come to some understanding of ἐξ ἔργων νόμου a prior question must be dealt with. What is the function of vss 15-16 within the context of 2:10-21? Is this compound sentence a continuation of the speech before Cephas and others at Antioch?[30] Or does it form a separate part of the letter, making a transition and a summary of the defensive narrative that preceded it?[31]

An analysis of the sentence itself reveals that there may be contradictions within it.

Vss 15-16:

a) ʽΗμεῖς φύσει ʼΙουδαῖοι

b) καὶ οὐκ ἐξ ἐθνῶν ἁμαρτωλοί,

c) εἰδότες (δὲ) ὅτι οὐ δικαιοῦται ἄνθρωπος ἐξ ἔργων νόμου

d) ἐὰν μὴ διὰ πίστεως ʼΙησοῦ Χριστοῦ,

e) καὶ ἡμεῖς εἰς Χριστὸν ʼΙησοῦν ἐπιστεύσαμεν,

f) ἵνα δικαιωθῶμεν ἐκ πίστεως Χριστοῦ

g) καὶ οὐκ ἐξ ἔργων νόμου,

h) ὅτι ἐξ ἔργων νόμου οὐ δικαιωθήσεται πᾶσα σάρξ.

---

[30]Cf. Betz, *Galatians*, 113 n. 6.

[31]Betz has argued that this section forms the *prepositio* of Paul's apologetic letter, thereby summing up the legal content of the *narratio* and providing a transition to the *probatio*. The summary is made to appear as "the logical conclusion one would draw from the *narratio* as a whole" (p. 114). However, there are difficulties with this suggestion. First, it is not clear that vss 15-21 only summarize what has been narrated and that they state what is agreed upon and what is still at issue. Indeed, for the first time does the notion of justification appear (vss 16-17, 21) as well as ἐξ ἔργων νόμου. One could just as well argue that Paul is presenting new material to the entire argument. Second, while there is obvious forensic intention in the language in regard to the eschatological judgment of God, is it simply a matter of a legal issue (cf. vss 19-20)? Third, although this appears to be a defensive summary of Paul, the very figure of Paul (qua "I") begins to disappear from the focus of the argument (vss 19-20).

First, a-d appear as contradictory to h, since the distinction between Jew and Gentile no longer obtains in h where everyone is included in πᾶσα σάρξ . Second, c-d may not be exactly equivalent to f-h, for d does not necessarily function disjunctively to c as does g to f. Indeed, e-h seem to function as a definite interpretation of a-d, clarifying the ambiguous meaning of c-d with the disjunction ἐκ πίστεως / ἐξ ἔργων νόμου in f-g. We can also see this interpretative work in h, which probably features a scriptural quotation.[32] This need for an interpretation, indeed, a revision of a-d, is puzzling since Paul himself appears to be uttering these words. This puzzlement is increased when one asks why he continues in vss 15-16 when vs 14b represents a perfect rhetorical finish to his confrontation with Cephas. Moreover, this addition features vocabulary unknown in the letter until now.[33] These verses go far beyond a mere summary of the question of tradition which Paul has been concerned with since 1:12.

    A probable solution to this predicament is that a-d represent the self-understanding of a Jewish Christian position, most likely that of the very opposition of Paul in Galatia. Of course, this solution can only be indirectly derived; however, a reasonable case can be made. First of all, it would be especially appropriate for Paul to bring in his opposition at this point, since his entire letter to this point has been directed to the situation by the introduction of their "other gospel" (1:6).

---

[32]Cf. Rom 3:20: διότι ἐξ ἔργων νόμου οὐ δικαιωθήσεται πᾶσα σάρξ ἐνώπιον αὐτοῦ ; cf. LXX Ps 142(3):2: ὅτι οὐ δικαιωθήσεται ἐνώπιον σου πᾶς ζῶν. Rom 3:9ff. indicates that Paul is aware of a scribal tradition of proof texts from which the conclusion can be drawn that no one is righteous. However, the inclusion of ἐξ ἔργων νόμου cannot be supported by either the proof text or the later letter to the Romans as indicating that such a phrase existed in the early tradition. Obviously one cannot argue from a later letter, Romans, to an earlier one, Galatians, in an attempt to find the source of this phrase. Rather, the argument must be the other way around.

[33] φύσει, ἁμαρτωλοί, δικαιοῦται ἐξ ἔργων νόμου, διὰ πίστεωςἐκ πίστεως πᾶσα σάρξ.

His lengthy defense concerning the question of his pleasing people with his message (1:10), his former zealous observance of the traditions of the fathers (1:13-14), the introduction of the issues of circumcision (2:3ff.) and tablefellowship (2:11-14), would make eminent sense if his opposition presented another version of the Gospel which associated the proclamation of Christ with the observance of Jewish traditions (1:6-7, 8; 3:2, 5, 21b; 4:9-10, 21; 5:2, 4; 6:12), hearkening back to the font at Sinai (3:17-21; 4:21-31; 6:12-13).

Second, the verses immediately following vss 15-16 yield not only the probable accusation by the opposition against Paul but also terminology linked to that which first appears in vss 15-16. Paul counters the accusation of nullifying the grace of God (vs 21a) by overturning the traditions of the law (vs 18a) through which comes justification (vs 21b). By not providing the Galatians with the resources of this tradition, Paul becomes a transgressor of the law (vs 18b) and leaves the Galatians still in sin (vs 17a).[34] The terminology is markedly similar to that found in vss

---

[34]Vss 17-21 can be analyzed rhetorically, showing both the possible objections of the opposition but also the interpretative explanation of Paul.

vs 17a,b	εἰ δὲ ζητοῦντες δικαιωθῆναι ἐν Χριστῷ εὑρέθημεν καὶ αὐτοὶ ἁμαρτωλοί,	Objection: question introduced by εἰ δέ;
	ἆρα Χριστὸς ἁμαρτίας διάκονος;	false conclusion.
vs 17c	μὴ γένοιτο.	Rejection of conclusion.
vs 18	εἰ γὰρ ἃ κατέλυσα ταῦτα πάλιν οἰκοδομῶ, παραβάτην ἐμαυτὸν συνιστάνω.	Reason for rejection; inversion of charge vs 21a.
vs 19	ἐγὼ γὰρ διὰ νόμου νόμῳ ἀπέθανον ἵνα θεῷ ζήσω. Χριστῷ συνεσταύρωμαι·	Reason: further explanation of vs 18; argument from experience, kerygmatic terms put in existential forms.
vs 20a	ζῶ δὲ οὐκέτι ἐγώ, ζῇ δὲ ἐν ἐμοὶ Χριστός·	Reason: explanation in negative terms of how ἐγώ exists.

15-16.   If vss 17-21 do then reflect the possible objections by the opposition, then vss 15-16 may well be part of that same language field.

The third reason for arguing that vss 15-16d (that is, parts a-d) carry the self-understanding of a Jewish Christian position is external,

vs 20b ὃ δὲ νῦν ζῶ ἐν σαρκί, ἐν πίστει ζῶ τῇ τοῦ υἱοῦ τοῦ θεοῦ τοῦ ἀγαπήσαντός με καὶ παραδόντος ἑαυτὸν ὑπὲρ ἐμοῦ.	Reason: positive explanation quoting christological formula (also rendered existentially).
vs 21a οὐκ ἀθετῶ τὴν χάριν τοῦ θεοῦ·	Rejection of charge, the basis for vs 17, the inversion of vs 18.
vs 21b εἰ γὰρ διὰ νόμου δικαιοσύνη,	Objection: introduced by εἰ γὰρ.
vs 21c ἄρα Χριστὸς δωρεὰν ἀπέθανεν.	Conclusion: from vss 19-20; such would deny the experience used as evidence.

The argument brought out by Paul once again demonstrates diatribal elements within a dialogical context (cf. analysis of 3:1-5 above). The objections of the opposition (that Paul is setting aside the Law, through which comes justification and thus renders the gentiles still in a sinful condition vss 21a, b, 17a, b) are countered through argument based on Paul's own experience (cf. Betz, *Galatians*, 30, the argument called the *genus inartificiale*).   The terms δικαιόω , ἁμαρτωλοι (vs 17), διὰ νόμου, δικαιοσύνη (vs 21) and perhaps κατα λύω , παραβάτης (vs 18) would appear to be probable terms of the opposition.

The interesting use of "I" should be noted here.   Indeed, the entire argument of Paul up to this point could well have been mustered to support the common cultural view that through the internalization of tradition the "I" comes into its own. Even a rejection of traditions, as argued by Paul, could still allow for the constitution of the "I", e.g., the formation of a gnostic self. This does not happen here. On the contrary, we find that the "I" loses ground due to the experience of Paul. For him the "I" does not function as the agent through which meaning is founded (cf vs 20a). The unusual use of ὃ in vs 20b may well suggest that Paul is attempting to express something which escapes the typical language of his time. It is the relationship ἐν πίστει which becomes the ground for his argument and critique. See chap. on Romans, section IV below.

namely, that except for Paul the issue of works and faith was not considered in disjunction.[35] This argument has been advanced many times, so there is no need to rehearse it in this investigation.[36] What is capital for this investigation is to recall that the figure of Abraham, for both Jewish Christians and Hellenistic Jews epitomizes this conjunction of works and faith.[37]

The figure of Abraham plays a fundamental part in the intellectual environment of Galatians. This is due not only to the explicit connection in 3:6ff. but also to its association with the issues raised before 3:6. In a letter so self-conscious of the question of tradition and its interpretation, in the section under discussion where works, faith and δικαιοσύνη first appear, the figure of Abraham hovers in the background of the conversation. For in these very issues the figure of Abraham formed a paradigmatic link between the tradition of the past and the missionary outreach to the Gentiles. Abraham summed up the movement away from what was culturally and theologically limited to that which was universal and transcendent. In no way opposed to his ἔργα, the faith of Abraham provided the keystone to this transcultural arch. In this varied and long-standing tradition, faith was the greatest of Abraham's works, the greatest virtue of which humanity was capable. Through faith, the ἔργον διανοίας and δικαιοσύνης , the cultural ideal of the sage becomes a reality, not only as a past example but as a possibility for all

---

[35]Cf. Betz, *Galatians*, 117-18.

[36]One of the latest supporters of the thesis that the Gospel of the opponents is a Jewish Christian missionary Gospel which sees the Law as a positive means of Righteousness is D. Lührmann (*Galater*, 104-8); also Betz, *Galatians*, 116-17 nn. 33-36.

[37]Cf. Ep. Jas. 2:20-26; Sir 44:19-21; Jub 14:6, 20; 23:10; 24:11; 1 Macc 2:52; 2 Bar. 57:2; Jos. *Ant.* 1.154-55, 183; Philo *Mig.Abr.* 129-31; *Quis heres* 90-95; *De Abr.* 262-74; *De virt.* 216-19; *De praem.* 27.

those who in the present find in Abraham who does the law a figure of true worth.[38]

---

[38]Thus, in Sir 44:19-21a, during the praise of the Fathers, the role of Abraham is clearly portrayed:

Αβρααμ μέγας πατὴρ πλήθους ἐθνῶν, καὶ οὐκ εὑρέθη
ὅμοιος ἐν τῇ δόξῃ· ὃς συνετήρησεν νόμον ὑψίστου
καὶ ἐγένετο ἐν διαθήκῃ μετ' αὐτοῦ· ἐν σαρκὶ αὐτοῦ
ἐστήσεν διαθήκην καὶ ἐν πειρασμῷ εὑρέθη πιστός·
διὰ τοῦτο ἐν ὅρκῳ ἔστασεν αὐτῷ ἐνενλογηθῆναι ἔθνη
ἐν σπέρματι αὐτοῦ.

Here the faithfulness of Abraham is due to proven deeds, for which God's promise is his reward. This is also the case with 1 Macc 2:51-52:

καὶ μνήσθητε τὰ ἔργα τῶν πατέρων, ἃ ἐποίησαν ἐν ταῖς
γενεαῖς αὐτῶν, καὶ δέξασθε δόξαν μεγάλην καὶ ὄνομα
αἰώνιον. Αβρααμ οὐχὶ ἐν πειρασμῷ εὑρέθη πιστός, καὶ
ἐλογίσθη αὐτῷ εἰς δικαιοσύνην;

The faithfulness of Abraham can be expanded to include his entire life and in particular the keeping of all the ordinances (such as circumcision and the feasts. Cf. Jubilees 23:10; 24:11; 14:6, 20; 15:9ff.). The connection of the figure of Abraham and "works of the commandments" can be found in 2 Baruch 57, where it is mentioned that during the time of Abraham the "unwritten law was named amongst them" (trans. Charles). In Josephus we see that the figure of Abraham is linked to the path of virtue (ἀρετή) (*Ant.* 1.155), which God commends, declaring that a reward will not be lost on these good deeds (ἐπὶ τοιαύταις εὐπραγίαις ; Ant. 1.183). But it is in Philo that we can see the fullest cultural development of the figure of Abraham as a figure of transcendent possibilities. Thus, in *Mig. Abr.* 127ff. we find an exegetical argument supporting the claim that the ἔργα τοῦ σοφοῦ are nothing else than the words of God (λόγοι θεῖοι ; 129). Abraham is brought forward as having done all the Law which is nothing else than the divine words (φησιν ὅτι ἐποίσεν ᾿Αβραὰμ "πάντα τὸν νόμον μου." νόμος δὲ οὐδὲν ἄρα ἢ λόγος θεῖος προστάττων ἃ δεῖ καὶ ἀπαγορεύων ἃ μὴ χρῆι ὡς μαρτυρεῖ φάσκων ὅτι " ἐδέξατο ἀπὸ τῶν λόγων αὐτοῦ νόμον" εἰ τοίνυν λόγος μέν ἐστι θεῖος ὁ νόμος, ποιεῖ δ' ὁ ἀστεῖος τὸν νόμον, ποιεῖ πάντως καὶ τὸν λόγον . ὥσθ, ὕπερ ἔφην τοὺς τοῦ θεοῦ λόγους πράξεις εἶναι τοῦ σοφοῦ ; 130). It should be noted that Philo has used ἐποίησεν instead of the LXX ἐφυλαξε in his

In light of the interpretative possibilities of the Abraham tradition which considered the issue of works and faith as conjunct and not antithetical, if the Jewish Christian opponents of Paul shared this assumption (more strongly brought out by the presence of 3:6ff.), then vss 15-16d would represent part of that tradition which saw a continuity between faith and works. One could even stress the necessity of πίστις (ἐὰν μὴ διὰ πίστεως) since even for Abraham this was the essential virtue, enabling all the others virtues to become present. The appeal of "another" Gospel would be the inviting prospect of becoming like the "father of faith" who demonstrates by his example the way in which

---

quotation of Gen 26:5. The emphasis is upon the attainment of the philosophic ideal of the sage, who lives according to nature (τὸ ἀκολούθως τῇ φύσει ζῆν; **128**). The true sage is one who follows the injunctions of God in both deeds (ἔργοις) and speech (λόγοις). All this Abraham has accomplished. The specific nature of Abraham's works is seen in *Quis heres* 90-95 where ἐπίστευσεν Αβραάμ τῷ θεῷ τὸν σοφόν (Gen 15:6) is commented on. Here Abraham is called τὸν σοφόν whose trust was considered an ἔργον διανοίας . Indeed, his faith was counted to him for justice (λογισθῆναι τὴν πίστιν εἰς δικαιοσύνην αὐτῷ; Gen 15:6) because it was an ἔργον δικαιοσύνη (95). Moreover, this example is a reproof furnished by the ἱερὸς λόγος to those in the present day, who marvel at this wonder of trust. In *De Abr.* 262ff. we find a final protreptic based on ἐπίστευσε τῷ θεῷ . What is of importance is to see how this sentence is measured not in words but made good by ἔργῳ (262). Faith is then extolled (268ff.) as that one sure and enduring good, the queen of virtues (τὴν βασίλιδα τῶν ἀρετῶν ; 270). This theme is picked up in *De virt.* 216ff. where Abraham in gaining faith, gains all the other virtues, as he moves away from the knowledge of the many, the secondary, the created to the One, the Primal, the Uncreated and Maker of all (213). In so doing Abraham becomes the standard of nobility for all proselytes (οὗτος ἅπασιν ἐπηλύταις εὐγενείας ἐστὶ κανών) who abandon strange laws, customs and idolatrous worship of sticks and stones to settle in the commonwealth full of true life and vitality (πρὸς ἔμψυχον τῷ ὄντι καὶ ζῶσαν πολιτείαν ; 219). In attaining the virtue of faith, Abraham stands for the person who is truly autonomous (which is the brunt of his fulfillment of the unwritten laws; cf. *De Abr.* 5-6, 275-76; Excursus, I. A.) αὐτήκοος , αὐτομαθής , αὐτοδίδακτος (*De praem. et peon.* 27).

transcendence can be attained by both Jew and Gentile. To submit to the
Law (οἱ ὑπὸ νόμον θέλοντες εἶναι ; 4:21) through
circumcision (5:3) and the keeping of the feasts (4:9-10) would become
then an occasion of entering a tradition which assured through its praxis
the continuance of their present experience (3:3, 5).[39] The prior question
of how vss 15-16 function within their context has helped in yielding
some of the hermeneutical possibilities surrounding this section, if not the
entire letter. The introduction of works, faith and justification does not
represent a completely unknown turn to the discussion of tradition.
Rather, such terms help us to see that the matter is actually more than an
internal dispute. For what seems to be at stake, for both Paul and his
unnamed opposition, is the unspoken question of what constitutes the
praxis of genuine human transcendence. In the eyes of the opposition,
Paul could well have stood not simply as a violator of customs and taboos
but as a hindrance to the very possibility of achieving what was offered by
the transcendent witness of Jewish tradition. The "other" missionaries
could easily have seen Paul as the one who is stifling the growth of the
πνεῦμα . I now turn to the other side of the antithesis (3:2, 5) ἐξ
ἀκοῆς πίστεως in order to discover why Paul has chosen to suggest
such an alternative for the interpretation of the Galatians' experience of
the   πνεῦμα .

IV. A. ʼΕξ ἀκοῆς πίστεως
In attempting to assess the hermeneutical value of the phrase ἐξ ἀκοῆς
πίστεως the exegete may at first wonder whether this phrase is merely
a *spiel* which Paul uses in opposition to what well may be a leading
phrase of the proponents of the "other" Gospel. Is this not why he only
uses it twice (3:2, 5) and never again in his correspondence? Indeed, this

---

[39]For a provocative analysis of why the Galatians found themselves in need of
such a tradition when they began to experience the difficulties of freedom in the
spirit, cf. H. D. Betz, "Spirit, Freedom and Law: Paul's Message to the
Galatian Churches," *SEA* 39 (1974) 145-60; also D. Lull, *The Spirit in Galatia*
(Chico, CA: Scholars, 1980) 7-11.

phrase is unique in antiquity. If the phrase were of some importance, why was it not used earlier in 2:16? Since it has been argued that Paul is employing a number of diatribal elements, could this not simply represent a further example of such vivid speech? To dismiss ἐξ ἀκοῆς πίστεως in this fashion would, however, fail to touch upon the hermeneutical possibilities within this phrase. For, in adopting this phrase, Paul presents an alternative way of understanding the praxis fo the life of the Spirit. In order to see why this is so, one must not only consider the context surrounding this phrase but also take into account some possible equivalencies found in other letters.[40]

IV. B. 1 Thessalonians 1:3 and Romans 10:16-17

The question of ἐξ ἀκοῆς πίστεως becomes more complicated due to the fact that in 1 Thessalonians Paul actually uses the phrase τὸ ἔργον τῆς πίστεως (1:3)! From the context of the letter, a *captatio benevolentiae* within the introductory prayer of thanksgiving, "faith" is indeed a "work", aligned with the labor of love and the steadfastness of hope. Is this once more a mere rhetorical play by Paul? Such a position is not altogether tenable since it is precisely through this rhetorical device that Paul turns the Thessalonians' attention to the very life which they are at present practicing. He continues to praise their faith which proves exemplary for all who believe in Macedonia and Achaia (1:7). Their life of faith functions as a revelation, bearing the λόγος τοῦ κυρίου

---

[40]By itself ἀκοή can refer to either the act of hearing or to that which is heard, such as rumor or report. For the former cf. Plato Thaeat. 142D; Antig. Car. 129; Ep. Arist. 142; Josephus Ant. 8.171, 172. The latter meaning usually refers to a report which may or may not be reliable (cf. Thuc. 1:20). As report, ἀκοή can be contrasted with what is seen; hearsay versus actual sight (cf. Josephus Ant. 8.171-72). Moreover, ἀκοή can have the connotation of a report which has been passed down, sometimes through many generations (cf. Josephus C. Ap. 2.14). The positive value of the term, referring to an important report carried down through time can be found in Plato Tim. 20E-25D, where Critias speaks of a tale (λόγος) coming through Solon from the records of the Egyptian priests.

(1:8). If Paul has no problem in using τὸ ἔργον τῆς πίστεως in 1
Thessalonians, why does he have such an aversion to it in Gal 2:16; 3:2,
5? Why does he set ἔργον over against ἀκοὴ πίστεως ?[41]

Before these outstanding issues can be answered, one other text
must be investigated in regard to the connection of ἀκοή to revelation.
Rom 10:16-17 deals with the issue that not all listen to the Gospel. The
words of Isa 53:1,[42] originally referring to the revelation which Yahweh
delivered to the prophet, bear directly upon the present mission situation.
Vs 17 adds that faith comes ἐξ ἀκοῆς and ἀκοή comes διὰ
ῥήματος Χριστοῦ . From vs 18 (and from vs 14) one can discern
that ἀκοή in this context most probably refers to the act of hearing,
specifically the hearing of the proclamation of the Gospel. Now one
learned earlier that it is this hearing of the word (ῥῆμα) which brings
about a different view of righteousness. The Jews, who have not
submitted to God's righteousness, remain ignorant of the righteousness
from God (10:3). Over against the righteousness from the Law about
which Moses writes (10:5) stands the personified Righteousness of faith
(ἐκ πίστεως) both quoting Scripture and, perhaps, providing its
interpretation (10:6-7). This diatribal element[43] has the effect of breaking

---

[41]While 2 Thess 2:13 uses the term ἀκοή in connection with an oral tradition
παραλαβόντες λόγον ἀκοῆς ... ἐδέξασθε , I would argue that
the section of 1 Thess 2:13-16 is a non-Pauline interpolation into the text. Not
only does it interrupt the rhetorically moving address, but it carries an anti-
Jewish polemic quite unusual for Paul. The references to the final expression of
God's wrath, and to the persecutions of communities in Judea, may look back
upon the destruction of the Temple and its implications for the Jesus believers.
Cf. B. Pearson, "1 Thessalonians 2:13-16: A Deutero-Pauline Interpolation,"
HTR 64 (1971) 79-94.

[42] κύριε , τίς ἐπίστευσεν τῇ ἀκοῇ ἡμῶν .

[43]Cf. Teles, Περὶ αὐταρκείας ., 6H, 8H, where affairs
(πράγματα) acquire a voice, and Poverty addresses the interlocutors. Cf.
Chapter 4, p. 176.

into the present situation of those addressed.[44]   The words from Deut
30:14 given in vs 8 seem to disregard space and time in an almost gnostic
fashion as the very word (ῥῆμα) is declared the very ῥῆμα of faith
which Paul preaches. Vss 9-10 argue that the praxis of faith, located in
the personal response of the believer, is truly what the personification of
Righteousness is pointing out. Those who hear the Gospel are the ones
who can listen to Righteousness ἐκ πίστεως who speaks to their
present experience of faith.

Now in both 1 Thessalonians and Romans the issue can be
appreciated under the aspect of the praxis of faith. In the former there
was the sense that the work of faith is an effective and revealing
continuance of the message the Thessalonians received. In the latter
example ἀκοή is associated with the practical aspect of hearing the word
of Christ on which is based the contention that the righteousness of God is
a present and effective reality. It is this practical nuance by which the life
of faith is interpreted that gives us a clue to the usage ἐξ ἀκοῆς πίστεως
in Gal 3:2, 5.

IV. C. Praxis and Identity

The relationship of praxis to the phrase ἐξ ἀκοῆς πίστεως   has, in
fact, already been anticipated in this investigation. Now it is time to spell
out where this relationship has been intimated. It has been pointed out
that the entire rhetorical force of 3:1-5 forces the Galatians to reexamine
their present situation.   The antithesis of ἐξ ἔργων νόμου/ ἐξ
ἀκοῆς πίστεως was shown to be Paul's suggested way of interpreting
the transcendent experience which they enjoyed.   It has also been
remarked that 3:1 most likely refers to the original kerygma proclaimed
by Paul and now is graphically represented before the eyes of the
churches. This kerygma which the Galatians also received (ἐλάβετε ;
3:2) has become part of their experience. Yet, why does Paul use ἀκοή
πίστεως? If Paul is concerned with the actual praxis of the Galatians,

---

[44]Cf. Stowers, *Paul and the Diatribe*, 154.

why does he not use ἐξ ἔργου πίστεως, drawing on his language in 1
Thess 1:3? Would this not confront the opposition more directly?[45]

An answer to these questions can in part be made from a
consideration of the strategy of the letter up to 3:1-5. Paul has seen quite
clearly that the issue from the beginning was that of tradition and Gospel
and their practical implications. Paul does not see that the Gospel needs
any further requirement of entering into the specific traditions of the Law
in order to insure the continuance of the experience of the πνεῦμα. His
defensive narrative from 1:10-2:14 argues specifically for the freedom of
the Gospel from those traditions in which he himself was reared. He then
introduces in 2:15-16 language which we have argued to be probably in
use by the opposition. His antithetical usage of ἐξ ἔργων νόμου/ἐκ
πίστεως adds a definite interpretative direction to the debate. This
direction is sharply opposed to the understanding usually associated with
the figure of Abraham within Hellenistic Judaism. Here would be a true
figure who would fulfill the words   ἐξ ἔργου πίστεως. We have
seen that in relation to the figure of Abraham faith is interpreted as the
greatest virtue, enabling this transcultural hero to live the true life of the
wise individual. Thus, to use the phrase ἐξ ἔργου πίστεως, although it
would be perfectly acceptable in 1 Thessalonians, would represent in
Galatians a dubious strategy. To speak of ἔργα πίστεως or ἔργον
πίστεως would give the impression that Paul is simply carving out a
section of the ἔργα νόμου for the practice of faith. Moreover, it
would still leave open the interpretation that the life of faith is an
individual work of virtue. But this runs counter to Paul's contention that
justification is ἐκ πίστεως (2:16).

---

[45]This is not so far-fetched, for in Rom 3:27, within the diatribal context we
have a question, διὰ ποίου νόμου ; followed by a false conclusion:
τῶν ἔργων ; then a correction: οὐχί, ἀλλὰ διὰ νόμου πίστεως.
Paul is quite capable of using the possible objections and language of his real or
imagined opposition. Thus, the question why he does not do so in Gal 3:2, 5
becomes more perplexing.

There is a further answer to the questions raised above and it has to do with the very understanding of experience. The positive appeal of the figure of Abraham within Hellenistic Judaism lay in its possibilities for realization by Jew and Gentile alike. As we have seen above, the figure of Abraham played to the hope that the ideal was realizable in the life of the individual believer. To put it another way, the figure of Abraham, as the model of the virtue of faith, became an interpretative means of understanding the experience of Spirit. Through this given model the believer could enter into the traditions of Judaism thereby continuing to construct a self out of the materials of this religion. In this light, another way of describing the defensive narrative of Paul in Galatians is that we have before us a conscious negation of what was once the positive material for the construction of a religious identity (1:13-14). This argument against the very elements which formerly composed his identity is not a mere negation but a defense based on what has become the formative factors of a reinterpreted "identity". For the revelation διὰ Ἰησοῦ Χριστοῦ (1:1) breaks up the κανών of the experience of transcendence.[46] Both the standard for spiritual excellence as well as the means of maintaining this have been, in Paul's view, rendered ineffective.[47] Superseding them is the revelation of Christ proclaimed through the Gospel (1:11-12, 16).

The reevaluation of identity is seen most forcefully in 2:19-20. Here, where the entire defensive narrative would most logically end in a climactic self-definition of his position,[48] the language employed by Paul

---

[46]Note the juxtaposition of 1:15-16, presenting the revelatory event, which halts the progress of his life in Ιουδαϊσμος (1:13-14).

[47]This will be seen more so in the following analysis of 3:6-14 and the comments on 3:22.

[48]Cf. Betz, *Galatians*, 121; Betz considers this the *expositio* of the *propositio* where Paul presents four theses in his theological position. Although Betz is intrigued with the use of the first person singular here, suggesting that Paul uses himself as a prototypical example, applicable to all Pauline Christians (p. 121), this interpretation seems to be somewhat too static for the way in which the

suggests a revision of what constitutes the true agent of identity. The "I", so prominent in vs 19a, loses its emphasis in the subordinate clause as well as in the following exclamation. This devaluation of the "I" continues in vs 20, where the "I" is not only replaced by Χριστός as the active agent, but the very manner of present existence[49] becomes quite ambiguous, deriving its meaning from the relationship ἐν πίστει to the υἱὸς τοῦ θεοῦ. It should also be noted that the revaluation of the "I" is done through the use of what appears to be common christological terminology.[50] Not only is the identity of Paul revised but it is done in terms which would be understandable to the Galatians, thereby allowing a quick association and identification.[51]

This revision of the understanding of one's transcendent identity in 2:19-20 has great bearing upon what follows in 3:1-5. As I have argued above, the rhetorical effect of these verses is to cause the Galatians to reflect upon their present transcendent experience, that is, their life in the

---

language of these verses is moving. As suggested above (n.34; see chap. 4, pp. 172-185 below), we seem to have the vivid style of diatribe, which calls into question the very self-definition of the "I". If there is any paradigm, it is certainly not clear cut, for Paul appears to be working with the tension of the emergence of a new situation brought about through the encounter with the divine. For a similar use of language, cf. *The Mithras Liturgy*, ed. and trans. M. Meyer (Missoula: Scholars, 1976) 20, 719ff.:

> κύριε, παλινγενόμενος ἀπογίγνομαι,
> αὐξόμενος καὶ αὐξηθεὶς τελευτῶ,
> ἀπὸ γενέσεως ζωογόνου γενόμενος
> εἰς ἀπογενεσίαν ἀναλυθεὶς πορεύομαι

[49]ὃ δὲ νῦν ζῶ . . .

[50]Cf. vs 19 (with the exception of διὰ νόμου νόμῳ) and vs 20d.

[51]Here Betz (*Galatians*, 122) would be correct to speak of a "paradigmatic ego." But this should not be taken as some kind of external self similar to that of the figure of Abraham. I do not think we have the substitution of one figure by another; this would, in fact, defeat the "relatedness" inherent in Paul's graphic language.

Spirit. The language used not only suggests their present life but also the very origin of that life, the proclamation of the Gospel (3:1). The identity which has already begun to be established through their encounter with kerygma has actually been touched on in 2:19-20. The identity which Paul now sees as vital is shared in by the Galatians through their adherence to the Gospel.[52] It is the revelation through the proclamation which has brought about this new basis for identity. Here, then, we can come to understand the selection of ἐξ ἀκοῆς πίστεως . In setting ἐξ ἔργων νόμου over against ἐξ ἀκοῆς πίστεως , Paul is asking the Galatians to come to an interpretation of their experience in the Spirit. Since his opposition has probably given the Galatians hermeneutical standards for determining how the life in the Spirit is to be led, Paul provides his interpretive category, which, however, is not imposed from without, but comes from the Galatians' experience of the Gospel message. This message itself is revelatory and powerful. The presence of πνεῦμα is evidence of its revelatory effect. Further, to match the opposition's means for insuring the life of the spirit, Paul argues that the πνεῦμα is received as it has from the beginning ἐξ ἀκοῆς πίστεως , that is, through spontaneous openness to the revelation in Christ. Nothing need be imposed to insure the πνεῦμα ; indeed this would hinder the freedom of the Gospel.[53]

Moreover, it is precisely because of the presence of the πνεῦμα that the situation becomes an interpretive occasion for Paul and his opposition. The series of rhetorical questions demonstrates that for Paul, however, the ground for the act of interpretation rests within the activity of the community. The questions function, then, to continue this activity

---

[52]Thus, Paul earlier can see their change of mind as a radical rejection from the "one who called you in Christ" (1:6).

[53]Cf. 2:4. Here Romans 10 becomes significant, for there Paul spells out explicitly that the act of hearing the Gospel and confessing the Christ more than compares with the prescriptions of Moses. For Righteousness itself speaks across space and time to the reality within the believer.

by stimulating the community towards a fuller self-understanding of the meaning of living in the Spirit. It is precisely in the interaction of the questions and the forthcoming answers that the issue of identity is to be resolved. Thus, the activity of interpretation becomes essential not merely for the discerning of texts or even models (where the answers of ideals are already known) but for the practical self-understanding of the communities.[54]

This last point becomes significant when the relationship of 3:6ff. is investigated. Usually Gal 4:21ff. is seen as the first hermeneutical section in Galatians. However, it is my contention that 3:1-5 provides a hermeneutical key to the following nine verses (as well as to the subsequent argument). For as we shall see, the exegesis of the text by Paul relies upon the precondition of the Galatians' present experience and interpretation of the πνεῦμα. Not only are the hermeneutical options dealt with,[55] but also Scripture itself becomes clarified in so far as it *interacts* with those whom Paul is questioning. The meaning of Scripture cannot be ascertained in isolation from the communities' present transformation. In so far as they interpret the Spirit as coming ἐξ ἀκοῆς πίστεως will they understand how the tradition in the form of Scripture speaks across time and space to them (3:8). The text will be seen as coming to life again (through personification), because those empowered by the πνεῦμα can enter the lifeworld where Scripture speaks directly to them. Just as the Gospel was announced and proved effective in their lives, so now the Scripture will be seen in all its revelatory power as beneficial and lethal. Thus, ἐξ ἀκοῆς πίστεως is most fitting, since it not only indicates the experiential basis that Paul adopts but also provides an explicit clue to the way in which the following scriptural citations are to be interpreted.

---

[54]Cf. Excursus, where interpretation is essential for self-understanding of the communities of the Therapeutae and Essenes, chap. 2, pp. 64-70; 77-81.

[55] ἐξ ἔργων νόμου (vss 10-13)/ ἐξ ἀκοῆς πίστεως (vss 6-9).

V. A. Galatians 3:6-14: Preliminary Remarks

Following immediately what I have argued to be a series of rhetorical questions, stimulating the self-interpretation of the communities, vss 6-14 present Paul's first extended use of Scripture in the epistle. As such these two sections present an interesting juxtaposition of the terms πνεῦμα and γραφή. Indeed, this first thoroughgoing use of Scripture is found within a possible *inclusio*, where πνεῦμα is employed (vss 5,, 14). Moreover, the very terms of the antithesis by which the experience of πνεῦμα is to be interpreted become essential for the distinction of the argument in vss 6-12.[56]

I have suggested above that the phrase ἐξ ἀκοῆς πίστεως not only indicates the experiential focus adopted by Paul but also provides an explicit clue to the way in which the Scripture is employed in vss 6ff. How is this possible, since the word ἀκοή has apparently been dropped for the shorter phrase ἐκ πίστεως? And, if it can be shown that the term is significant, what does this mean for the reading of vss 6-14? Indeed, we can generalize this concern by asking what is the relation of vss 1-5 with 6-14? Why does Paul start here to cite Scripture? Does it have any connection with the issue of works, the hearing of faith, the Spirit? If Paul has located the basis of the problem within the experience of the communities, why, then, does he rely on scriptural support? Is the act of interpretation begun through the series of rhetorical questions related to the act of interpreting the Scripture? Is there anything surprising from Paul's exegesis, that is, does the process of interpretation begun in vss 1-5 continue to advance the self-understanding of the Galatians, or does the section simply confirm established knowledge?

The standard approach for investigating vss 6-14 has been to regard Paul's introduction of Scripture as common exegetical procedure. Even in Betz's analysis,[57] this section still is seen as an argument from Scripture. While there is admittedly a usage of Scripture, what has been

---

[56]Thus, ἐκ πίστεως (vss 6-9); ἐξ ἔργων νόμου (vss 10-12).

[57]Betz, *Galatians, 140-53.*

overlooked is the manner in which Scripture has been introduced and is
related to what has just preceded it, especially the final words of vs 5, ἐξ
ἀκοῆς πίστεως . If the clues given by the language of these verses
are closely attended to, then what one scholar has described as "une
fantasie ingenieuse"[58] may be discovered as a powerful display of Spirit
and Letter.[59]

V. B. The Double Magic of Tradition

In order to uncover this powerful display of Spirit and Letter, let me
begin by asking a question of strategy.   Why does Paul begin his
"scriptural proof" with Gen 15:6, if he is, in fact, trying to argue that the
πνεῦμα comes ἐξ ἀκοῆς πίστεως ? Why go to the trouble of
bringing in 'Αβραάμ, υἱοί 'Αβρααμ , and εὐλογία? Would it
have not been easier to cite Hab 2:4 (which he does in vs 11b), if a proof
text is what he wants? Moreover, only here do we find the exact phrase
ἐκ πίστεως , which he uses in vss 7-9. Could he not have stated that
this verse had been foreseen and pre-announced?[60] However, it is not so
much a matter of proof texts, as it is one of application of tradition to the
present situation which concerns Paul.   And in the very act of this
application the power of Scripture as the conveyor of tradition becomes
manifest. Thus, the figure of Abraham is brought up because, as has
been suggested above,[61] this figure has already been part of the

---

[58]A. Loisy, *L'Epitre aux Galates* (Paris: Nourry, 1916) 151.

[59]The usual analysis of this section regards this as basically the result of
working with proof texts, where the answers are already known and no further
revelation is possible. My contention is exactly the opposite, namely, that Paul
is not merely summoning well-known answers but is actually seeking Wisdom
from Scripture in light of the Christ event and thus is quite open to the
revelation which his "fantastic" speculation might unearth.

[60]Cf. Rom 1:17, where Paul does use this verse to support the contention that
the δικαιοσύνη of God is revealed ἐκ πίστεως . Only later in 4:1ff.
is Abraham brought up.

[61]See pp. 15-16, 21-23 above.

theological background of the discussion. The investigation of ἐξ ἔργων νόμου has led to the possibility that the opposition has employed the figure of Abraham as a model of life in the Spirit. By entering into the traditions of the Covenant, the Galatians can be assured of righteous standing before God. Paul explicitly mentions Abraham at this point in order to clarify his own contention that the praxis of the Spirit does not entail all the religious associations tied to this figure. On the contrary, he uses the figure of Abraham in such a way as to remove what stands out strongly in the tradition, namely, his works.

This surgical removal is performed in a most interesting way. While the figure of Abraham is brought into the argument, the emphasis in vss 6-9 rests upon those who are οἱ ἐκ πίστεως .[62] Moreover, this is done within an interpretive application of the verses cited.[63] But most intriguing is the way in which the scriptural verses are brought forward into the discussion. Directly after ἐξ ἀκοῆς πίστεως (vs 5), Paul cites Gen 15:6[64] and immediately coordinates this with the application (vs 7). Vs 8 presents Scripture speaking for itself, as Paul personifies[65] it as both foreseeing what God is presently doing as well as pre-announcing to Abraham that all the gentiles will be blessed in him. Vs 9 continues the train of thought from vs 8, noting that οἱ ἐκ πίστεως as a result (ὥστε) are now being blessed with Abraham. The coordination noted in vss 6-7[66] is actually maintained in vss 8-9. What Scripture has foreseen and preached beforehand is now taking place. What coordinates these verses is the supposition that those making the application are presently

---

[62]Vss 7, 8, 9.

[63] γινώσετε ἄρα (vs 7).

[64]Adding ʼΑβραάμ

[65]Cf. n. 44 above.

[66] καθὼς . . . γινώσετε ἄρα . . .

listening to γραφή . This seems to be a minor point until one realizes that γραφή, as the spokeswoman for tradition, has taken on what one might call magical power, transcending both space and time, linking Abraham and the gentiles, that is, the Galatians, solely through her words.[67] This magical effect occurs only for those ἐκ πίστεως who hear what is being said. Understanding (γινώσκετε) is tied directly to the praxis of faith.[68]

Thus, the way in which Scripture is presented continues the thrust of Paul's rhetorical questions in vss 1-5. The activity of life in the Spirit ἐξ ἀκοῆς πίστεως allows the Galatians to understand what many would consider to be a forced exegesis of the text. Indeed, what this hearing ἐκ πίστεως allows is to let tradition as Scripture confront them as a personified, magical force, thereby aiding them in interpreting their lifeworld in relation to the figure of Abraham. Through the words of Scripture, the Galatians are placed on equal footing with the one Hellenistic Judaism regarded as the prime example of faith. Now both Abraham and the Galatians hear what is said by γραφή. They become co-inhabitants of the lifeworld of promise and blessing (cf. 4:22ff.). The very words of tradition confirming the identity of the Galatians become through their effective power another demonstration of the πνεῦμα and δυνάμεις in their midst (3:5).

---

[67]The notion that Scripture is alive and able to know beforehand is not uncommon in Hellenistic Judaism. We can see, e.g., in Philo (*Leg. all.* 3.118) where Scripture is described as knowing (εἰδώς) the strength of the passions. Thereupon Philo quotes Ex 28:30 to present an allegorical application. In his description of the Therapeutae (*Vit. cont.* 78) Philo recounts how in the process of interpreting the sacred writings (τῶν ἱερῶν γραμμάτων) resemble a living being whose literal ordinances are like the body and the invisible mind (νοῦς) like a soul. Of course, as previously mentioned, Rom 10:6 gives us another instance of personification of Righteousness, where Scripture comes to life in the mouth of δικαιοσύνη .

[68]This would explain the use of Gen 15:6, where the activity of faith is explicitly mentioned.

That which Paul has separated from the figure of Abraham appears directly in vs 10 — the ἔργα νόμου . As this investigation will show, Paul associates the works of the Law with a cursed condition, and that this cursed condition has something to do with what is written. Whereas in vss 6-9 Paul presents a lively personification of γραφή, associating it with the promised blessing, so in vss 10-12 there is a second aspect to Scripture. The Scripture reveals its lethal aspect through its written curse.[69]

Vs 10 begins with an explanation of ἐξ ἔργων νόμου . What has been removed from the figure of Abraham surfaces now under a curse. Again, it should be noted that this explanation is tied to those who would identify themselves with such a lifeworld.[70] But the following scriptural quotation gives more than just a reason why those who are ἐξ ἔργων νόμου are under a curse; it is the curse itself. While magical possibilities are inherent in the personification of γραφή, which both foretells the future and effects people at a distance, the term κατάρα brings the reader directly into the realm of magic. One might point out that perhaps this use of κατάρα is merely rhetorical; indeed, did not rhetoricians declare (as Paul does in 3:1) that the opposition has bewitched the audience? However, an ironclad distinction does not hold up either in this instance or in the ancient world. The association of magic and rhetoric was longstanding, based on the conviction that words

---

[69]The association of works of the Law with curse certainly has part of its background in the notion of covenantal blessings and curses. Since the ἐκ πίστεως part of the interpretative antithesis is joined with blessing, the connection of curse and ἔργα νόμου is not hard to make. Certainly the use of blessing and curse was not an uncommon homilitic device in the Jewish mission (cf. Philo, *De poen, et praem.*). What is distinct is the relegation of the ἔργα νόμου to a cursed situation.

[70] ὅσοι . . . ἐξ ἔργων νόμου . The distinction made in regard to the reception of the Spirit in 3:2 or the source of transcendence in 3:5 is applied to those ὑπὸ νόμον θέλοντες εἶναι (4:21) just as ἐκ πίστεως was applied to those who identified with the faith of Abraham and heard Scripture speak (vss 6-9).

do effect affairs.[71]   Indeed, what is someone's rhetor is another's wizard.[72] Moreover, we see already in 1:8-9 that Paul is not adverse to using such magical language. Nor does the oath taken in 1:20 reduce the impression that Paul thought he could bring something about through words.

The magical nuance to the scriptural citation is further supported by the term ἐπικατάρατος . It is significant that, while it is found rarely outside of the LXX, the term has been found on funeral inscriptions.[73] Such inscriptions work on the ancient presumption that they functioned as magical letters from the dead threatening with a curse any potential violator. The combination of the written inscription plus the incantation was seen as effective speech, able to inflict a curse even at a later time. Moreover, when the curses became effective, the spell would last until it could be broken by some greater power or antidote. The association of magic and law is further seen when one recalls that the publication of law itself, when dealing with severe matters, was

---

[71]Cf. J. de Romilly, *Magic and Rhetoric in Ancient Greece* (Cambridge: Harvard University, 1964).

[72]Cf. Philostratus *Vita Apollonii* 8.7.2.

[73]Two examples first connected to Galatians by A. Deismann, *Light from the Ancient East* (trans. L. Strachan; Grand Rapids: Baker Book House, 1978) 96-97:

> ἐπικατάρατος ὅστις μὴ φείδοιτο κατὰ
> τόνδε τὸν χῶρον τοῦδε τοῦ ἔργου

and

> εἴ τις δὲ ἐπιχειρήσι λίθον
> ἆραι ἢ λῦσαι αὐτό,
> ἤτω ἐπικατάρατος ταῖς προγεγραμμέναις ἀραῖς.

accompanied with curses and imprecations to insure the binding force of law.[74]

The possibility that ἐπικατάρατος has magical currency, along with the association of written law with curse, has bearing upon the way the quotation in vs 10 is to be read. The text as we have it in Galatians does not match exactly either the LXX or the MT. The discrepancies have been explained in a variety of ways.[75] However, since a variant LXX version is unknown to us, it would be best to proceed with known texts to see if the comparison might yield any significant results.

Deut. 27:26 (LXX) and Gal 3:10 read:

---

[74]Cf. Dio Chrysostom *Thirty-first Discourse* 70; Dio speaks of practices which are guarded against ἐν τοῖς νόμοις and deserving of curse (ἀρᾶς). In his *Eightieth Discourse* we hear of the Athenians establishing a curse in connection with Solon's laws in order to prevent those who would destroy them. Dio Cassius relates that upon Caesar's death a law was published and curses invoked along with a death penalty for anyone attempting to offer victims to a dead man as to a god. He further notes that this was done looking ahead to the future (*Hist.* 44.51.2). Diodorus (*Hist.* 13.69.2-3) mentions that the law of sentence when revoked by the Athenians caused the assembly to throw the written stelae into the sea, while the sacerdotal family revoked the curse against Alcibiades. Demosthenes (*Ag. Lept.* 107) says that any form of government but democracy is forbidden by curses, laws. Herodotus (*Hist.* 1.82) notes that the Argives made a law with a curse added thereto to wear their hair short. Plato (*Critias* 119C-120D) speaks of the sacrifice of a bull which is slain over a column on which are written laws and an oath calling down curses on the disobedient.

[75]Thus Paul, quoting from memory (admittedly poor), was actually conflating different texts, had another manuscript in mind, or has intentionally changed the text. This argument is also made for 3:13, which is sometimes seen as coming from a possible Jewish-Christian midrash taken over by Paul. Cf. N. Dahl, *Testamentica et Semitica* (eds. E. Ellis and M. Wilcox; Edinburgh: Clark, 1969) 15-29. M. Wilcox, "'Upon the Tree'—Deut 21:22-23 in the New Testament," *JBL* 96 (1977) 85-99. The point which seems to be overlooked is that Paul is not concerned with our modern notions of correctness, but with how an interpreted text can effectively communicate with his audience.

ἐπικατάρατος πᾶς ἄνθρωπος   ἐπικατάρατος πᾶς
ὃς οὐκ ἐμμενεῖ   ὃς οὐκ ἐμμένει
ἐν πᾶσιν τοῖς λόγοις   πᾶσιν τοῖς γεγραμμένοις
                                ἐν τῷ βιβλίῳ
τοῦ νόμου τούτου   τοῦ νόμου
τοῦ ποιῆσαι αὐτούς.   τοῦ ποιῆσαι αὐτά.

We find: (1) the elimination of ἄνθρωπος , ἐν and τούτου in Gal
3:10; (2) the addition of γεγραμμένοις , ἐν τῷ βιβλίῳ to Gal
3:10.[76] The removal of ἄνθρωπος may well be due to Paul's intended
use of Deut 21:23 in vs 13.   It may also reflect the usage of curse
inscriptions.[77] The elimination of τούτου is rather curious. For, even
if Paul is conflating various texts, one finds that similar texts in the
vicinity of Deut 27:26 favor the retention of τούτου.[78] Why, then,
does not Paul include τούτου ? Would it not favor his argument in
1:13-2:21 and later in 3:17ff., that the Law represents particularity over
against what he represents as a more universal solution to the Galatians'
need for transcendence?[79]   However, while Paul does argue for the

---

[76]Gal 3:10 is even farther from the MT (דברי את לא-יקים אשר ארור
אותם לעשות הואת- הזואת- הזורה ; "Cursed is he who does not keep the
words of this law, in order to do them").

[77]Cf. *Defixionum Tabellae quotquot innoteurunt*, ed. A. Audollent (Paris,
1904) 75.8.

[78]So: Deut 28:61:   καὶ πᾶσαν μαλακίαν καὶ πᾶσαν πληγὴν
τὴν μὴ γεγραμμένην ἐν τῷ βιβλίῳ τοῦ νόμου τούτου
ἐπάξει κύριος ἐπὶ σέ; Deut 28:58: ποιεῖν πάντα τὰ
ῥήματα τοῦ νόμου τούτου τὰ γεγραμμένα ἐν τῷ βιβλίῳ
τούτῳ; Deut 29:20: κατὰ πάσας τὰς ἀρὰς τῆς διαθήκης
τὰς γεγραμμένας ἐν τῷ βιβλίῳ τοῦ νόμου τούτου ; Deut
29:26: κατὰ πάσας τὰς κατάρας τὰς γεγραμμένας ἐν τῷ
βιβλίῳ τοῦ νόμου τούτου .

[79]Cf. 4:21? On the other hand, the particularity of the Law could be seen as a
positive point. Philo sees that this particular Law in fact leads one onto the road
to transcendence. Cf. *De somn.* 2.175.

particular character of the Law in time and space (cf. 3:17ff; 4:24ff.), he seems here to be declaring that the curse is a general condition of the Law. Here it is a matter of lifeworld, of meaning in which those ἐξ ἔργων νόμου can find their identity. Moreover, we find that the Law is characterized, but under the rubric of writtenness. This point can be illustrated by the fact that Paul changes τοῖς λόγοις for τοῖς γεγραμμένοις ἐν τῷ βιβλίῳ . If Paul is in fact conflating texts, we can see that he goes beyond merely joining Deut 28:58[80] with Deut 27:26. Any possibility of an oral understanding of Law has been avoided by the removal of λόγοις (or ῥήματα). The elimination of τοῖς λόγοις must be seen in light of the previous discussion of ἀκοῆ πίστεως .[81] Here in vs 10 Paul is yoking the cursed condition of works of law with what has been written. This curious amalgamation is a further instance of Paul's presumption of the power of γραφή (vs 8). First we have seen that γραφή through personification foresees and transcends the boundaries of time and space to speak with Abraham and the Galatians. Now a second aspect of Scripture is brought out, that is, the power of its writtenness by which the power of tradition is demonstrated.[82] But this second power of the written text is, unlike the common presumption of Hellenistic Judaism, solely of negative effect.[83]

---

[80] τὰ ῥήματα τοῦ νόμου τούτου γεγραμμένα ἐν τῷ βιβλίῳ τούτῳ.

[81] Pp. 21-26 above.

[82] Indeed, why does Paul use τοῖς γεγραμμένοις ἐν τῷ βιβλίῳ τοῦ νόμου when τοῖς γεγραμμένοις ἐν τῷ νόμῳ could have sufficed? Is it a strategic choice?

[83] Cf. Chap. 2 Excursus below. An example of the power of Scripture is found easily in the propagandistic Letter of Aristeas. Not only are the circumstances surrounding the translation into the LXX miraculous but the text itself is filled with power and spirit. Unlike Paul's dichotomy of works of law and hearing of faith, only those who live virtuously from the Law can engage in a translation of it. True righteousness permits the interpreter, moreover, to transcend the

Finally, the question of the elimination of ἐν has led some
scholars to suggest that an official legal formula consisting of
ἐμμένειν plus dative of a participle (with or without ἐν) has caused
the change from Deut 27:26 to Gal 3:10.[84] This observation ties in with
what has been suggested earlier in regard to the connection of law and
curse.   The quotation of vs 10 could then be in Paul's perspective not
simply a quotation from Scripture but a legal formula bearing by its very
words the curse which would normally accompany such a written law.   It
should be noted, moreover, that such an association does not mean that
Paul considers the law to be at present powerless.   Rather, just the
opposite is the case.   The Law is not dead, but lethal for those who are
(εἰσίν) ἐξ ἔργων νόμου .

This view of the citation from Deut 27:26 as more than a simple
proof text is important, since from 3:1ff. there has been a decided
emphasis upon the interpretation of the present praxis of the Galatians.
The citation in vs 10 continues the task of forwarding the question of
interpretation begun in 3:2, 5.   I have argued already that in vss 6-9
Scripture is speaking directly to those who interpret their situation ἐκ
πίστεως .   Now the second part of the antithesis as it regards those who
would live such is made clear.   The vivid pattern of speech begun through

---

literal level without violation (170-71).   Indeed, the written parchment sent to
the king is considered to be the oracles of God (τὰ λόγια ; 178).   Upon
hearing of the new translation, the Jewish community pronounced a curse upon
any who would alter a word (310-11).   When the translation is read in the
presence of the king, two aspects of Scripture come through.   First, the very
spirit of the Lawgiver carries on through the words of the writings.   Second, the
king is informed of the fatal power connected with Scripture.   Those who dared
produce an unreliable translation receive misfortune (312-16).   But those who
read and rely on an accurate translation reach the divine (313).   Finally, the
letter itself is written to continue to benefit the reader who can discover for
himself the claim for such a powerful and spirit-ridden text (322).

[84]Cf. A. Deissmann, *Bible Studies* (trans. A. Grieve; Edinburgh: Clark, 1931)
248ff; W. Arndt and F. W. Gingrich, *A Greek-English Lexicon* (2d ed.;
Chicago: Chicago University, 1979) 255; Betz, *Galatians*, 144 n. 60.

the series of rhetorical questions, continued through the personification of γραφή in vss 6-9, is now actualized further by the startling association of ἐξ ἔργων νόμου with a curse which remains powerfully in effect. The alternatives which Paul brings forward in 3:2, 5 continue to work as a challenge to the audience's interpretation; for they must bear the task of deciding in which lifeworld of meaning and power they would live. This challenge of living under law or faith comes through quite strongly in vss 11-12. It is not a matter simply of the recitation of scriptural proofs. Nor is it merely the exegetical technique of citing two conflicting verses in order to produce a third for some resolution.[85] Rather,, the interpretation of these verses must take its clues from the movement of the language within the context of the historical situation. By relying on the text as written, Paul draws out the stark dilemma for those who would choose the lifeworld of works of the Law. First of all, the implicit possibility is rendered impossible by Paul's interpretation. The fact that[86] no one is justified[87] is supported by the quotation from Hab 2:4.[88] This in turn is interpreted by Lev 18:5,[89] which proves that the law is not ἐκ πίστεως , since ἐκ πίστεως is missing. The catch word ζήσεται which forms the basis for this comparison is of capital

---

[85]Cf. H. Schoeps, *Paul* (trans. H. Knight; Philadelphia: Westminster, 1961) 177-78.

[86]ὅτι (vs 11a); cf. Smyth 2586.

[87]This hearkens back to the reality given ἐκ πίστεως (vss 7-8).

[88]Paul's version differs from both the LXX (ὁ δὲ δίκαιος ἐκ πίστεως μου ζήσεται) and the MT (וצדיק באמונתו יחיה ; "The righteous shall live because of his faithfulness"); cf. 1QpHab 7.17-8.3. Here the text is unfortunately lost. However, the pesher reads that because of "the faith of the Teacher of Righteousness" God will deliver them. See Excursus, p. 78 n. 132.

[89]Also not exactly following the LXX: ἄνθρωπος is missing. Cf. p. 34 above regarding the elimination of ἄνθρωπος from Deut 27:26 in Gal 3:10.

importance. For it not only provides the link word but also hints at the destiny of both the δίκαιος and the one who does the law (αὐτά), that is, what is written. The tenses of the verbs are also important in this regard. In vs 8 it has been suggested that the effect of justification is taking place now through faith. In vs 11 we see that the written Scripture is speaking to the present situation (δικαιοῦται). Moreover, the verses from Scripture act in oracular fashion, prophesying what will be the outcome of either life choice. For those ἐξ ἔργων νόμου (vs 10) to do what is written (ποιῆσαι αὐτά) will result not in justification but in living ἐν αὐτοῖς . And, since it is already argued that this is not justification, it can only mean living under the curse (vs 10). Paul is continuing that which he has begun in vs 6, namely, letting γραφή speak for itself. Now tradition becomes clear before the eyes of the community: blessing ἐκ πίστεως or curse ἐξ ἔργων νόμου . Through his interpretation of these two possible lifeworlds of praxis, Paul has drawn upon the presumption of the power of the Scripture. The demonstration of the magical power of Scripture is made to throw light literally upon the self-understanding of the Galatians.

The spell of two lifeworlds which Paul has been creating through the drawing out of these alternatives is broken by vs 13. He does this not by reducing the magical nuance of his words but by increasing it, syntactically, rhetorically, and conceptually. Vss 13-14 contain a number of questions which bear directly upon the magical effect of these verses. First, if this is a further interpretation as on could argue, why does it not continue with the use of connective particles?[90]   Second, why does Χριστός make its appearance here and why in such language?[91]   Third,

---

[90]E.g., vs 7 ἄρα; vs 8 δέ; vs 10 γάρ; vs 11 δέ; vs 12 δέ, ἀλλά.

[91] ἐξαγοράζω is found only here and in 4:5 in the authentic Pauline corpus. ἡ κατάρα τοῦ νόμου is found only here in Paul. The function of the participial phrase γενόμενος ὑπὲρ ἡμῶν κατάρα   is quite unclear. Is there some reliance upon the cultic language of 4:4-5 (γενόμενον ὑπὸ νόμου) or is the latter dependent upon 3:13 and, thus, a Pauline interpolation into 4:4-5?

what is the reason for adding the apparent quotation from Deuteronomy? How does it function in the argument? Moreover, why does Paul say ὅτι γέγραπται and not γέγραπται ὅτι ? Does this imply scriptural fulfillment? Fourth, why is there a repetition of ἵνα in vs 14? How is this double purpose clause related to both the movement of vs 13 and the argument from 3:1ff.?

The lack of a connective particle in vs 13 is symptomatic of the function of the entire verse. Vs 13 actually serves as a break from what has just preceded. The introduction of Χριστός at this point jars the memory of the audience back to what has been mentioned in 3:1. There we had the reference to the original message of the Gospel as well as the claim that the opponents had put the Galatians under a spell. The effect of vs 13 is to bring the Galatians up short in their contemplation of the fate awaiting those who would enter the Law.

If the fate of a people is dictated by their language, then this short-circuiting of fate can be seen in asking a hypothetical question regarding vs 13a. What would the text be like without vs 13a? If one were to maintain the logic of vss 10-12 through vs 13b (minus vs 13a), one would find that the momentum and effect of the curse continues. Despite the oddity of the scriptural citation, one would be forced to conclude that the association of writtenness and curse is maintained. This can be seen in the following way. If we compare vs 13b with Deut 21:23, we find that, as with vs 10,[92] Paul does not quote the LXX verbatim (nor the MT). Assuming that Paul is using the LXX,[93] some interesting points appear. Deut 21:23 reads: κεκατηραμένος ὑπὸ θεοῦ πᾶς κρεμάνενος ἐπὶ ξύλου. Paul does four things to this verse: First, he substitutes ἐπικατάρατος for κεκατηραμένος . He removes θεός. He thus links πᾶς with ἐπικατάρατος . He adds

---

[92]Cf. n. 75 above.

[93]The argument that he is using another version is attractive but not altogether convincing. Again, it should be noted that Paul might well be more interested in effect than in exactitude.

ὁ to κρεμάμενος . One can see this work as an alignment with vs
10b. This would give us a clue that we are to read this verse within the
association he tries to establish in vss 10-12. The removal of ὑπὸ θεοῦ
goes very well with his negative association of curse and writtenness, with
his emphasis on the deadly power of that association. Also intriguing is
his emphasis of ἐπικατάρατος πᾶς and the addition of ὁ. Already
πᾶς is present in vs 10b. If Paul has removed ἄνθρωπος from his use
of Deuteronomy in 3:10, was this done with an eye to vs 13b? If so,
what is the functional significance of the phrase ἐπικατάρατος πᾶς ?

     If one considers the argument closely from vss 10ff., one sees that
Paul is claiming that the force of the curse falls upon everyone who does
not remain in the Law. His additional explanation and argument further
generalizes the situation.[94] If we then omit vs 13a, ἐπικατάρατος
πᾶς would not refer to Χριστός necessarily but, following the logic of
this association, would be another embodiment of "everyone" who falls
under the curse.

     What happens then when vs 13a is reintroduced? This question is
tied to the earlier question of the function of ὅτι linking vs 13a with vs
13b. The answer may well lie in that Paul is introducing a recollection of
the oral message (3:1) as effectively present in stark opposition to what
has just preceded (vss 10-12). But, if he is introducing such a
recollection, why does he add the participial phrase instead of stopping at
τοῦ νόμου ? He could have simply declared an end to the curse
through the redemption of Christ. But he does not. It would appear that
γενόμενος ὑπὲρ ἡμῶν adds an additional insight into the reading
which follows. The recollected oral message throws light upon what is
written. But that is not all. The use of ὅτι is not simply a quotation
formula but a causal connective, providing a reason for γενόμενος .
This reading is not to be found as a fulfillment of Scripture (which
assumes the answer is already provided), for such an interpretation
overlooked the construction of Paul's argument. Rather, the situation is

---

[94]In vs 11 οὐδείς, vs 12 ὁ δίκαιος , ὁ ποιήσας

more along the lines of the application of confessional language.[95] If we bracket out Christ's identification with vs 13b, we can see that the "everyone" who are cursed are ἡμεῖς for whom Christ has become the curse. Paul has reinterpreted the oral message that Christ has given himself for "us" by declaring that he has become a curse. Christ does so *because* it is written ἐπικατάρατος πᾶς . And because Christ has done so, Paul can reread Deut 21:23. In this light the verse from Deuteronomy literally changes before our eyes. This metamorphosis of the very letters of the text is due to an insight derived from an understanding which comes ἐξ ἀκοῆς πίστεως of the original message Paul preached.[96] Paul effects an entirely new reading from Deut 21:23 by having the oral message of the death of Jesus meet the written curse. The significance of the death of Christ, when placed up against the power and fate of tradition engenders further interpretation. This argument of Paul is made within the rapt attention of the Galatian communities. In doing so Paul tries to be even a greater magician than his opponents. For the message itself is powerful, already having produced (ἐξηγόρασεν) what it says.

This point leads us into the double purpose of vs 14. For vs 14 reveals what is the purpose of Christ's taking on the curse. Through this event the oral promise, which has been already brought to life in vss 6-9, has been given, both the blessing of Abraham as well as the promise which is interpreted as the Spirit which the Galatians and Paul already possess. Paul thus breaks the spell by showing that what the opponents promise through works of the Law are delivered already by Christ and that the cursed lifeworld the Galatians would take on themselves has been broken by Christ.

---

[95]E.g., 1:4; 2:20.

[96]Comparable revisions of a text through the act of interpretation can be found, for example, in the Wisdom of Solomon; cf. p. 73-74 n. 113.

V. C. Some Possible Preconceptions

A consideration of the language of vs 13 within its cultural context leads to some suggestive possibilities. Now, I have maintained through this analysis that Paul uses magical nuances to his speech. Perhaps more than any other so far, vs 13 suggests the common magical understanding about the voluntary death of an individual in behalf of others. I have noted already the unusual usage of ἐξαγοράζω , ἡ κατάρα τοῦ νόμου . The phrase γενόμενος ὑπὲρ ἡμῶν κατάρα is as perplexing as its counterpart in 2 Cor 5:21. And, just now, the surprising usage of Deut 21:23 has been brought forward. Yet, this language may not be so perplexing if one considers the magical notion of φαρμακός .[97] This custom, necessary either to avert harm or to repair a cursed condition, not only was recalled through traditional figures who gave their lives for their people,[98] but even is forcefully illustrated through Greek tragedy, especially the plays of Euripides. The language used to describe these actions are quite suggestive in light of NT usage.[99] Moreover, this voluntary sacrifice did not rest on the individual's decision but followed a divine demand of atoning sacrifice.[100] This demand came about through either seer or oracle.[101] Further, this sacrifice usually occurred in a

---

[97]Cf. W. Burkert, "Greek Tragedy and Sacrificial Ritual," *Greek Roman and Byzantine Studies* 7 (1966) 87ff. *Homo Necans. Interpretationem altgriechischer opferriten und Mythen* (RVV 32; Berlin/New York, 1972).

[98]Cf. Cicero, *Tus. dis.* 1.48.116-17; *De div.* 1.224.50-51; 1 Clement 50.1-5.

[99]E.g., the two daughters of Orion in Aeonia in Boetia propitiate the underworld by accepting death for their fellow citizens (ὑπὲρ ἀτῶν θάνατον ἐδέξαντο). They freely offer themselves as sacrifices to the gods (αὐτοῖς ἑκοῦσαι θύματα γίνονται). Metioche and Menippe, Antonius Liberalis 25, ed. M. Papathomopulos (1968) 43ff., and commentary 125ff. Ovid *Metamorphosis* 4.1.389ff.

[100]M. Hengel, *The Atonement* (Philadelphia: Fortress, 1981) 23.

[101]Cf. Libanius, *Declamatio* 42.24 (7.415): οὐκ ἀκούετε Πύθιον . . . καί οἱ μὲν παῖδες ἐτέθυντο. The phrase οὐκ ἀκούετε touches not only Gal 3:2, 5 but also 4:21.

situation of crisis brought about by guilt and destiny.[102] In this light the desperate measures performed by Roman generals through *devotio* can be understood.[103] However, the most common "scapegoat" in antiquity was someone either poor, crippled, maimed or a condemned criminal.[104] These worthless people were usually cursed[105] and then sacrificed for the common good.

Returning, then, to vs 13, I would simply offer this suggestion that the language Paul is using may very well find associations of this sort among the preconceptions of the Galatian communities. Vs 13 echoes the notion of a voluntary victim who buys back or off the cursed destiny, written in the book of the Law. Moreover, the quotation from Deut 21:23, functioning in an oracular fashion, gives the means whereby the curse can be taken away. Only when this action is performed is the curse broken by the Χριστός who hangs ἐπὶ ξύλου as a common criminal.[106] From the Galatians' possible perspective, the "black magic" of vss 10-12 is dissolved by the more powerful magic of vs 13. Finally, it is only after the cursed condition has been removed through this apotropaic action that Paul continues to interpret the meaning of this act. The blessing of Abraham, magically foretold by ἡ γραφή , is effected through this action. Moreover, the promise of the πνεῦμα is received διὰ τῆς πίστεως . Could this parallel the other side of the sacrificial

---

[102]Hengel, *Atonement*, 23.

[103]Cicero *De div.* 1.24.50-51; Lucan *Pharsalia* 2.304-9. Here the younger Cato prays that his blood will redeem all his people.

[104]Hengel, *Atonement*, 24-25.

[105]Ibid., p. 88 n. 94.

[106]The term προγράφω in 3:1 can also mean "proscribed", which was the fate of those "doomed for others" (Hengel, *Atonement*, 26).

act, namely, dying for the good of the people? To deny this purpose
would render the death in vain (2:21b).[107]

　　Whether what has just been suggested has any merit, what must not
be lost sight of is the basic direction of Paul's thought. It is not just a
matter of overcoming a curse but a question of understanding the role and
force of tradition as it bears upon the experience of the Galatians. Paul
may or may not be playing upon the notion of the   φαρμακός . He is,
through this magical interpretation of tradition as oral and written, placing
before the Galatians' eyes the powers of tradition in their midst. The
fated lifeworld "under the Law" is revealed and criticized by what they
have already heard. And this message continues to have effect, as it
declares that the lifeworld of blessing is the experience which they now
enjoy (πνεῦμα).

V. D. Summary

The issue of spirit and Letter, then, in Gal 3:1-14 is hardly simple. In
order for Paul to assist the Galatians in understanding what living in the
spirit entails, he had to enter into a dialogue with them, exploring the
possibilities of the way one could so live. Tradition through Scripture is
summoned to bear on this act of interpretation. Behind the summoning of
tradition was the presupposition that the Scripture was magical, that it had
power and effect beyond the limits of time and space. However, this
power was seen as limited in the sense that Scripture, precisely as written,
could only provide the condition of curse. On the other hand, the oral
message of the Christ, through which the Spirit comes, meets the curse
and breaks through the magic. The tradition of Letter must give way to
the more powerful, historical event which, in its encounter with the text,
opens up unforeseen possibilities of this tradition. Moreover, these

---

[107]An example of the use of a magical text to discover what is the meaning of
someone's death is found in *Tus. dis.* 1.48.115, where a certain Elysius asking
the reason for his son's death is given three verses *in tabellis* at the place where
the spirits of the dead are summoned.

possibilities are actually part and parcel of the praxis of the Galatians' experience.

VI. A. The Expansion of Interpretation: Tradition and Time

With the double aspect of Scripture demonstrated in 3:6-14, Paul continues in subsequent sections of Galatians to revise the understanding of Tradition. Essential to this revision are the eschatological event in Christ and the experiential basis of the Galatians' life in the Spirit. The two separate "lifeworlds" of blessing and of curse now will be viewed in light of time and space. What we shall find before us is a fusion of horizons, where the horizon of tradition is in dialogue with the new understanding achieved in 3:6-14. Some elements of the traditional horizon (as we have seen already) will be affirmed, while others are negated or subordinated. The result is that through this epistle a new disclosure occurs. A new world stands before the communities of Galatia through the medium of understanding (ἐξ ἀκοῆς πίστεως).

In vss 15-18 we find an immediate instance of this fusion of horizons and revision of tradition. In drawing an example from common legal practice[108] Paul argues that the promises given to Abraham and to his "seed"[109] are not canceled or added to by the Law which came 430 years later. In doing so, Paul greatly revises the traditional picture. First of all, the heir has been interpreted as Χριστός (vs 16). This would go against the traditional grain which includes as heirs of the promise both Jews and proselytes.[110] This revision is done with an eye to demonstrate that those ἐκ πίστεως who are blessed together with Abraham are identical with believers in Christ (3:6-14). Secondly, in temporally

---

[108]Cf. Betz, *Galatians*, 154-55.

[109]It should be emphasized that, while Paul separates the "seed" from the age of the Law, his usage of legal terminology argues for the prior legal validity and value of the promise to Abraham and thus of the oral tradition.

[110]Cf. Ps Sol 12:6; T. Jos. 20; Wis sol 12:21; cf. also Str-B 3.207-9 and Quell and Schulz, " σπέρμα κτλ ," *TDNT* 7. 536-47.

separating the covenant of promise from the law, Paul "polemically separates what Judaism tries to hold together."[111]   Instead of showing Abraham as one who knows the Law by nature,[112] by secret writings,[113] or through special revelation,[114] he argues that Abraham is not connected with the Law.   The "lifeworld" of blessing provides the inheritance (κληρονομία) apart from the νόμος.

This temporalizing of the Law immediately raises further speculation as to the function and purpose of the Law. Paul cannot avoid this issue, since it is presumably not only a key factor in his opposition's connection of the Gospel with the traditions of Judaism, but also by its very historical presence demands interpretation. To the possible objection τί οὖν νόμος ,[115] Paul continues the Law's association with a negative and temporally limited condition, declaring that it was added on account of transgressions, until the promised "seed" arrived. Furthermore, this Law is doubly mediated, delivered by angels by the hand of a mediator. A second possible objection that the Law then is opposed to the promises[116] is countered by the argument that the Law was unable to effect a life-giving condition, to bestow righteousness, since Scripture confined everything under sin in order that the promise ἐκ πίστεως might be given to those who believe (vss 21b-22). This response as well as the introduction of ἡ γραφή into the argument is not altogether clear until we recall the function of γραφή .   So far in Galatians Betz has rightly described the working of Scripture here as "almost like Fate."[117]

---

[112]Cf. Philo *Abr.* 275ff.

[113]E.g., Jub 21:10.

[114]Mek Exod 20.18.

[115]Cf. Stowers, *Paul and the Diatribe*, 181ff., where the rhetorical objection, raised by opposition, function to continue the dialogical process.

[116]See n. 115 above.

[117]Betz, *Galatians*, 175.

Paul not only shares in the pessimism of some Jewish traditions[118] but is employing the understanding of Scripture presupposed in 3:6-14. There it was argued that Scripture represents tradition in all of its power, both life-giving and death-dealing. Here in vs 22 we once more have a personification of γραφή which confines all things. But the purpose (ἴνα) of this act of confinement is to make sure that the promise comes about through the condition of faith. Thus, the Law, which disappears in vs 22 only to resurface in vs 23, becomes an instrument under the control of Scripture. This becomes quite evident in vss 23-24, where the mythic language of vs 22 is now reinterpreted existentially in regard to ἡμεῖς. Once again Paul is bringing forward the effective power of Tradition within the double aspect of blessing and curse. In viewing the function of the Law within time, Paul continues the notion that the Law bears a curse. This is evident from the fact that it was added due to transgression, that it was mediated, that it could not effect justification or give life. Yet, despite its severe limitations it functioned within the larger sphere of γραφή, which in the understanding of faith carries the promise of blessing. Moreover, the temporal location of νόμος is even indicated by the rhetorical chiasmus of vs 24, where, situated between πρὸ τοῦ δὲ ἐλθεῖν τὴν πίστιν and εἰς τὴν μέλλουσαν πίστιν ἀποκαλυφθῆναι, the "we[119] are imprisoned" and "confined" ὑπὸ νόμον. The result of this reinterpretation of νόμος is that (ὥστε) the νόμος is seen pejoratively as a pedagogue who must give way to the lifeworld of faith, wherein justification and maturity belong (vs 25; 4:1ff.). Indeed, this "lifeworld" of faith is already part and parcel of the

---

[118]Such as in 2 Esd 7:46.

[119]Whether the "we" refers to Paul and only to Jewish Jesus believers or whether it includes the Galatians may be a moot point. As we have noted earlier, the use of "I" is used quite curiously. No firm individual identity may be focused. Rather, Paul may well be implicitly equating the time under the law with being under the "elements" (4:3, 8-10).

Galatians' experience as Paul insinuates by using a probable liturgical hymn.[120]

Thus, the "lifeworld" of the promise which existed prior to the giving of the Law is found to be a reality in the present liturgical praxis of the community (vs 29).   Tradition has not been lost but critically reevaluated.   Paul does not reduce the mythic power of tradition to a simple rationalization but effectively brings out the potential and greater "legal validity" of this tradition.   At each step this is done through bringing the horizon of this tradition into dialogue with the eschatological event in Christ experienced in faith by the Galatians.

VI. B. Tradition and Space

This critical fusion of horizons occurs also in reference to the στοιχεῖα τοῦ κόσμου (4:3, 8-10). While Betz is correct in noting that a number of studies have concluded that these "elements of the word" represent "demonic forces" which constitute and control "this evil aeon,"[121] and that "the common understanding was that one was hopelessly and helplessly engulfed by these forces,"[122] nevertheless there existed also the belief that such forces were controllable or at least manipulable.[123]   The point at stake here is that Paul is deepening the interpretive quest to include the very understanding of how the cosmos is constituted and how the Galatians are to stand in relation to this constitution.   This issue of interpretation once again turns on the issue of praxis, since we find in vss 9-10 that the Galatians are tempted to return

---

[120]Cf. D. MacDonald, "There is no Male and Female: Galatians 3:26-28 and Gnostic Baptismal Tradition" (Ph.D. diss., Harvard University, 1978).

[121]Cf. Betz, *Galatians*, 204-5 n. 30.

[122]Cf. ibid., 205.

[123]Cf. Excursus below, pp. 56-57, where Abraham is regarded as an astrologer; where the interpretation of texts at Qumran was an entrance into the very elements of the Universe.

to the "elements of the world" by their observance of appointed feasts and festivals. Having explored what tradition conveys from primordial time, Paul now confronts the traditional preconceptions of the cosmos. In responding to the preunderstanding that to have some control over one's life there is a need to enter into rites which would effect this control, Paul attacks on two fronts, both of which turn upon the experience of the Galatians. First, he places the issue of the "elements of the cosmos" within a temporal frame, by using an example from the common practice of attaining one's majority.[124] The enslaved or cursed condition which we saw as associated with νόμος is now connected with the "elements of the cosmos" (4:1-3, 3:23-24). This condition is brought to a definitive end through the purposeful action of God (4:4). Once again this understanding is suggested by Paul as already part of the Galatians' experience through the probable liturgical formulae (4:4-5; 6-7). Secondly, in using the argument against superstition, common in both Jewish and Hellenistic circles,[125] Paul characterizes what would be seen as powerful as "weak and impotent" (vs 9). Again, this argument is not simply a theoretical discursus but relies upon the experience of transcendence[126] enjoyed in the present by the Galatians. The effect of this section is to enlarge the issues of the debate. The universe as well as time has come under the purview of interpretation. The momentum of the act of interpretation now encompasses within the separate lifeworlds of blessing and curse the entire universe.[127]

---

[124]Cf. Betz, *Galatians*, 203-4.

[125]Cf. ibid., 214-15.

[126] νῦν δὲ γνόντες θεόν,   μᾶλλον δὲ γνωσθέντες ὑπὸ θεοῦ. For the "gnostic flavor" of this verse, cf. Betz, *Galatians*, 215-16 nn. 24-27.

[127]That this movement of interpretation is not unusual at this time can be seen from a number of examples. One notable discussion which works upon these presuppositions is the dialogue in Cicero *De deorum nat.* Cf. chap. 4, pp. 186-193.

VI. C. The Horizons of Existence

A final indication of this interpretive act of revision through a critical
dialogue with tradition comes in 4:21-31. Again in diatribal fashion Paul
directly questions those who would wish to be ὑπὸ νόμον (vs 21).[128]
Once more, as we have seen in regard to 3:1-5, the act of interpretation
occurs within a dialogical situation. Paul assumes the perspective of those
wanting to submit to the requirements of Torah, or, as I have described it,
who wish to enter the lifeworld of the Jewish traditions. He then
proceeds to allegorize the traditional story of Sarah and Hagar and their
sons. It is significant that although Paul uses a quotation formula
(γέγραπται γὰρ ὅτι) he is not very much interested in quoting the
text of Scripture. This is another indication that Paul is in fact concerned
with the tradition and its effect and not with a correct text. At the same
time, his interpretation is given under the rubric that he is letting the Law
itself speak through his allegorical interpretation (τὸν νόμον οὐκ
ἀκούετε ;) to those who would interpret its meaning. First, he
distinguishes through his summary of the Abraham tradition the two sons.
That one born of the slave woman is κατὰ σάρκα ; the one of the free
woman is δι᾽ ἐπαγγελίας (vs 23). He then proceeds to allegorize
the "women" of the tradition. Now, if this were the usual form of
allegory, we would find Paul moving from the material level to the more
spiritual. The common understanding of "Letter and Spirit" as outer and
inner meaning[129] would be a basic assumption in this interpretive
movement. However, just as the distinction of the two sons reaches back
to the two different lifeworlds found in 3:6ff., so now the two women are
linked with two covenants which are immediately differentiated between
that which is both spatially and temporally limited (from Mount Sinai,
corresponding to the present Jerusalem) and that which transcends such
limitations. Moreover, the first covenant delivers her sons into slavery

---

[128]Cf. Stowers, *Paul and the Diatribe*, 240-47.

[129]Cf. Excursus, pp. 65-70.

with herself, while the second is free and is the mother of those presently in dialogue (vss 24b-26). Here, then, is a further instance of bringing the effect of tradition directly into the present. While it may be true to say that Paul is relying upon Apocalyptic traditions of a heavenly world,[130] it is not entirely correct to say that this lifeworld remains "above" waiting for the sons of the free woman to ascend to it.[131]

This last remark can be clarified by considering the succeeding verse. It is only here that Paul gives a scriptural citation (Isa 54:1). It should not be lost on the interpreter that this verse in the tradition was an oracle,[132] playing a great role in Jewish eschatological expectation. The effect of this verse is not simply as a proof text for vs 26; rather its very appearance at this point functions as a surprise, speaking directly to the eschatological miracle in the midst of the Galatians. Here the oracular power of Scripture has been invoked to yoke the dream of a universal metropolis to the experience of the Galatian communities. Paul has continued to let the tradition speak for itself and in doing so throw light on the new situation of the present. Thus, the application in vs 28 makes eminent sense. The direct address to the Galatians (ὑμεῖς, δὲ, ἀδελφοί . . . ἐστέ) once more links the primordial promise with the Galatians. Moreover, the past tradition throws light on the division between those who would live in the different lifeworlds. Just as it happened in the past so now it is the case (ὥσπερ τότε . . . οὕτως καὶ νῦν). Finally, the negative power of tradition is brought forward in vs 30, where Paul lets γραφή speak for herself a curse that the slavewoman and her offspring will not share the inheritance of the son of the free woman.

In looking over this section, we can easily see the topography of understanding writ large. Paul summons the past once more to illumine

---

[130]Cf. 2 Bar 4:1-6.

[131]Contra Betz, *Galatians*, 246.

[132]Cf. ibid., 248 n. 102.

not only the present lifeworlds of those who would enter the Law and those through the promise, but also the destiny of those involved. Scripture itself casts light and dark shadows of unexpected blessing and fateful curse. Thus, the interpretive movement is not simply a use of allegory and then typology,[133] but rather an engagement with the meaning of tradition as certain elements are brought forward into the act of understanding. Certainly Betz is correct in noting that this section depends upon the use of induction, allowing the Galatians to come to their own conclusion.[134] Yet, an analysis of method alone does not adequately convey the power of these verses. This final scriptural experiment in Galatians continues to build on the insights brought about in 3:1-14. Paul is engaging the Galatians in a reconsideration of the very horizons of their existence. Tradition, with its topography of past, present and future, is brought directly to bear by the interpretation of γραφή. Paul is not presenting apologetic arguments for his position but is inviting, even enticing, the Galatians to enter more boldly in the lifeworld of faith. At the same time, he is sharpening the dualism which has been uncovered in 3:6-14. The two epochs which Scripture has thrown light on can be found throughout the course of time, encompassing the elements of the cosmos. The choice, which has been there since 3:2, 5, is now clearly drawn by this interpretation of the offspring of the slave woman and free woman. Throughout all this, the fundamental position of Paul has been to use the activity of interpretation to seek a basic understanding of those ἐκ πίστεως in regard to issues which certainly transcend the text. The basis of all of this activity of interpretation is the πνεῦμα given through their belief in Christ. The ability to interpret the life of transcendence (τὸ πνεῦμα) is given to those who understand ἐξ ἀκοῆς πίστεως .

133Ibid., 239.

134Ibid., 240.

From this fundamental openness comes the power to confront the enormity of tradition in both its blessing and curse.[135]

VII. Conclusion

Through this close analysis of the language of Galatians, it has become evident that what is at stake is nothing less than the fundamental understanding of the Spirit. Both the "other" missionaries and Paul base their interpretive positions upon the experience of Spirit already at work within the Galatian communities. However, through the investigation of the rhetoric and significant word groups, it has become clear that the issue of tradition figures greatly into the opposition's interpretation of the experience of Spirit. For them, the presence of the Spirit can be maintained and furthered through the practice of the works of the law. Such a lifeworld, whose κανών of spiritual experience is Abraham, promises not only a continuance of their present spiritual life, but an entrance into what was regarded as the Hellenistic world's oldest culture and tradition. In completing their original belief with the practice of the Law, the Galatians were offered an identity and destiny which transcended the limitations of space and time.

From Paul's perspective there existed no continuity between the lifeworld given ἐξ ἀκοῆς πίστεως and that ἐξ ἔργων νόμου . While adopting the language of his opposition, Paul throws the understanding of tradition into radical questioning. For him the eschatological event in Christ has cast both tradition and identity derived from its internalization into a double light. Indeed, the experience of the Spirit, which he shares with the Galatian communities, allows Paul to look upon tradition in a discontinuous fashion. Tradition as the

---

135This dualism of lifeworlds continues in the hortatory sections of Galatians. The two spheres of life, κατὰ πνεῦμα and κατὰ σάρκα become further instances of this vision. For Paul is concerned not with simply providing an ethic but in showing that this is the way one lives in the new creation (καινὴ κτίσις ; 6:15). This is the only κανών (6:16), transcending the exemplary one of Abraham's works.

personified oral promise, reaching back to primordial time, can be understood by those ἐξ ἀκοῆς πίστεως to help interpret their present experience. On the other hand, tradition, as written, associated with the Law, is unveiled as cursed and, at best, a temporary confinement. It is the power of the Spirit, given through belief in the Christ, that permits Paul to discover the life-giving and lethal powers which tradition holds for those who seek to employ it. Paul's letter to the Galatians thus paints in broad, mythic strokes the lifeworlds of those who would live either ἐξ ἔργων νόμου or ἐξ ἀκοῆς πίστεως . His subsequent argument continues to reinforce this double vision of tradition. Not only in temporal terms but even in spatial images does he seek to show the implications of each lifeworld for the Galatian communities. What appears, then, at first to be a matter of cultic or religious concern becomes very quickly an issue which determines how one interprets the very powers and forces of existence.

It is in light of such explosive possibilities in regard to the task of interpretation that one must ask how far-ranging were such concerns. Whether understood positively or negatively, tradition and γραφή figure significantly in this interpretive discussion. Before I turn to Paul's explicit use of Spirit and Letter, it is thus incumbent upon me to consider the understanding of tradition and Letter (γραφή) within a larger cultural context. This cultural dialogue over tradition and Letter has already been suggested by what has been disclosed in my analysis of Galatians. It is now important to find out just how far this discussion extends. How much does the experience of Spirit summon up fundamental associations with Letter and tradition? Is Paul, in other words, through his response to the Galatians, entering into a wider debate over how humanity can come to grips with transcendent forces and powers so as to gain some sense of identity and destiny?

CHAPTER TWO

Excursus: Letter, Tradition
and the Task of Interpretation

In the preceding chapter I have argued that in order to understand the basic terms of Paul's position it is necessary to see his thinking within a decided cultural dialectic. For Paul the task of interpretation is not a limited intellectual exercise but a fundamental human activity whereby one comes to grip with transcendent forces and powers so as to gain some sense of genuine identity and destiny. In this Excursus I shall attempt to demonstrate that, while Paul may greatly differ in his own answer, he is very much part of the larger cultural dialogue which asks how it is possible for a human being to come to terms with the powers and forces which transcend one's existence. To do so, I shall first deal with the more proximate horizon of this discussion. This has already been suggested in the previous chapter, namely, the thought-world of Hellenistic Judaism. Then I shall widen the scope even more to indicate how this question already was at the basis of the Sophistic debate and continued to be taken up in a variety of ways in the Hellenistic intellectual tradition.*

---

*Although the claim will be advanced in this section that Letter and Spirit are seen to a large extent as compatible, the term "spirit" may seem to disappear from the discussion. However, as was made clear from the outset, this study is interested in not merely lexical citations but equivalencies of meaning. Thus, in using such terms as "transcendent forces and powers", I seek to widen the horizon of the discussion and by so doing to locate the question of spirit and Letter within its far-ranging conceptual context.

I. The Dialogue within Hellenistic Judaism

A. The Figure of Abraham as an Entrance into the Discussion.

In bringing forward the figure of Abraham in Galatians 3 Paul
provocatively chose what was for the Hellenistic Jewish mission a model
of continuity and authenticity.[1] Indeed, for the Hellenistic Jew seeking a
means of dealing with the large theological and cultural issues, such as
custom and nature, virtue and spirit, general and particular, writtenness
and unwrittenness, the figure of Abraham readily presented itself. In
short, the forces of tradition as well as the possibility of cultural progress
met in Abraham. For Josephus the figure of Abraham is patently one of
cultural and intellectual advancement.[2] By being the first to reason that
there is one God, Abraham provides a revolutionary breakthrough for the
development of humanity.[3] Moreover, his behavior matched this
intellectual achievement.[4] Yet such remarkable capacities did not
foreclose further advances for humanity; on the contrary, the entire thrust
of Josephus' account emphasizes that with Abraham civilization has taken
a major step towards the betterment and perfection of humanity.[5]

With Philo an even fuller presentation of Abraham as model of
human progress and perfection is given. In *De Virt.* 211-19 Philo
introduces the figure of Abraham[6] into his discussion of what constitutes

---

[1] See above, pp. 15-18.

[2] Abraham is a man of understanding, with rhetorical and logical skills. *Ant.*
1.154.

[3] By reasoning beyond his astrological findings, he came to this breakthrough.
Ant. 1.155-56.

[4] *Ant.* 1.155.

[5] *Ant.* 1.21ff.

[6] The figure of Abraham is anonymous throughout this section, emphasizing, its
universal application. Cf. the figure of Solomon in *Wisdom of Solomon* 7.

true nobility.[7] As a standard (κανών) for all proselytes,[8] Abraham serves as a type of identification for those who have abandoned the particularity of strange laws and monstrous customs, which reverence wood and stone, and who come to a living commonwealth where Truth is president.[9] This universal standard, himself born of an erring Chaldean astrologer,[10] comes out of the past as the most ancient member of the Jewish race. His migration from the land of his birth becomes in Philo's understanding a search for Truth.[11] Reason and inspiration meet in this intellectual journey. Not only does he understand[12] that the knowledge of the many, secondary and created, signified by astrology, leads to ignorance of the One, the First, the Uncreated but also he becomes inspired[13] to seek clearer visions of God's existence and providence. Reason, faith and virtue coincide in this movement. He is spoken of as the first to believe in God since he grasped the conception that there is one transcendent cause.[14] Moreover, this belief is conceived of as the first of all virtues.[15] Thus, Abraham becomes the bearer of the truly

---

[7] The true nobility, while coming from a guilty lineage, by their own lives become worthy of fame and imitation. Cf. *De praem.* 152.

[8] *De virt.* 219.

[9] Ibid.

[10] While for Philo Abraham is not an astrologer, his insight into reality agrees with Josephus' presentation. See above.

[11] Cf. *De Abr.* 68-88; *Quis heres* 96-99.

[12] ἔννοιαν λαβών ; *De virt.* 214.

[13] ἐπιθειάσας ; *De virt.* 214.

[14] *De Virt.* 216.

[15] Ibid.

great and royal soul.[16] His nature is revered as one who surpasses normal human perfection.[17] Furthermore, the fundamental relationship which he seeks is the very company of God. And this is evidenced by the divine spirit lodged in his soul, transforming him both internally and externally, filling his audience with understanding.[18] Accordingly, this man was the paradigm of the truly kingly soul, a prophet, an elect friend of God.[19] Philo can sum all this up by declaring Abraham's life to be an unwritten law.[20]

Now it is in *De Abrahamo* where the continuity of tradition and law, unwrittenness and writtenness, nature and transcendence, past and present, is dramatically achieved. The express purpose of Moses, according to Philo, in setting down the life of Abraham was not merely to praise him but to let it serve as a protreptic to those in the present who are inspired by such a figure.[21] The lives of the ancients are presented before the particulars of the Jewish Law because they are, as it were, archetypes of what later may be termed copies.[22] These men are, in effect, the laws living and endowed with reason.[23] Such lives demonstrate first that the ordinances enacted later are not contrary to

---

[16] Ibid.; cf. De Abr. 261.

[17] *De virt.* 217.

[18] Ibid.; cf. *Quis heres* 265, 266. This prophetic inspiration and gift of divine presence can take the form of cosmic mysticism. Cf. Georgi's remarks about the pseudo-Orpheus fragment, wherein the mystic vision granted to Abraham becomes a basis of mediation to others. Georgi, *Die Gegner*, 74.

[19] *De virt.* 218.

[20] Ibid., 194.

[21] *De Abr.* 4.

[22] Ibid., 3.

[23] ἔμψυχοι καὶ λογικοὶ νόμοι; Ibid., 5.

nature and second that, since the ancients embodied in their lives what later was to be written out and have done so with ease, later generations can take encouragement in following such written laws.[24] These first men were autodidacts, relying not on external authority, but conforming freely with nature.[25] The written record of these lives then forms a memorial and a means of effective encouragement. Moreover, the memorial of these men extends beyond the written record, for, since they lived in conformity with nature, nature itself provides a recording of their lives' significance.[26] On the other hand, the written record itself becomes a means of transcendence, for by it the flames of virtue are kept alive, promoting further goodness in the readers' souls.[27] In specifically touching on Abraham, Philo portrays him as one who has contemplated the order of nature and can live in conformance with this order.[28] His migration is that of a man of wisdom, who removes himself from theological error.[29] Throughout Philo recounts the events of Abraham's life with an eye towards discovering insight for the present through allegorical interpretation. The result of such a study is that Abraham can be truly called the "elder", in the sense of "first" of the human race. By his wisdom and faith is he so entitled.[30] The life of Abraham echoes what Moses said of him, namely, that he did the divine law.[31] For

---

[24] Ibid., 5.

[25] Ibid., 6.

[26] Ibid., 11.

[27] Ibid., 23.

[28] Ibid., 61ff.

[29] Ibid., 68, 82.

[30] Ibid., 271-72.

[31] Ibid., 275.

Abraham, taught by unwritten nature, anticipates the meaning and force
of the written law. Indeed, as Philo concludes, he himself is a law and an
unwritten statute.[32]

In summary, one can say that the figure of Abraham represents for
Hellenistic Judaism a remarkable confluence of various cultural
conceptions. In Abraham the unwritten, living example and the later
written law become one. A particular historical personage comes to stand
as a universal figure for proselyte and Jew alike. For the former he is a
model of conversion, welcoming the convert into a citizenship of
universal proportions. For the latter he confirms what the particularities
of the Mosaic Law demand. For both he is the archetype of the true
ruler, a figure of the internalization of virtue. For those who take to heart
what Abraham signifies there is a world of meaning, a commonwealth of
the virtuous. Spirit is not divorced from tradition, nor the unwritten from
the written. On the contrary, the figure of Abraham substantiates the
written law, declaring to those listening to the Law that the very spirit
which invaded Abraham can also be theirs. Thus, the figure of Abraham
serves as a fundamental interpretive model by which proselyte and Jew
can gain a transcendent understanding of both identity and destiny.

B. Scripture as Conveyance of Power and Archive of Tradition

Having seen that the figure of Abraham represented a basic continuity
between unwritten and written law, one can now move on to consider the
understanding of tradition under its written aspect. Scripture, for
Hellenistic Judaism, presents no sharp break with such self-taught men of
old. On the contrary, one can say that it brings to fruition this unbroken
tradition. In fact, precisely as written, Scripture indicates the presence of
a living tradition. Scripture comes to be seen as a conveyance of the
power of tradition, functioning as a storehouse for tradition, as well as the
very means of breaking through the boundaries of space and time to come
upon eternity.

---

[32] νόμος αὐτὸς ὢν καὶ θεσμὸς ἄγραφος ; *De Abr.* 276.

This sense of continuity of tradition between the unwritten and written is the basis for Philo's treatise on the Decalogue.[33] Indeed, the ancient examples of transcendence are followed now by the written Law which is the major demonstration of God's power and presence. Thus, according to Philo, the Law given in the desert was not a human invention but the oracles of God.[34] Both Philo and Josephus are at pains to show that the giving of the ten commandments to the people was done in a special way through the very voice of God.[35] At the same time, this divine intervention through the Law given to Moses represented another advance for human civilization.[36] The Lawgiver, himself, becomes the type par excellence of those who embody the written and unwritten aspects of the Law,[37] for he truly conformed and understood the relationship of humanity to the law of nature.[38] This correspondence, already noted in regard to Abraham, was not something invented by Philo. As Georgi has shown, this correspondence of nature, patriarchs and the written laws was a commonplace within Hellenistic apologetic tradition.[39] Such written legislation presupposes the ordering of the individual life and both presume an understanding of nature, which leads to the imitation and following of nature.[40] Thus, the legislation of Moses symbolized explicitly this overarching understanding of continuity.

------

[33]*De Dec.* 1.

[34]Ibid., 15.

[35]Ibid., 15, 19, 32, 39, 41, 45-49. Also Josephus *Ant.* 3.89-90.

[36]*C. Ap* 2.151-63.

[37]*Vit. Mos.* 1.4; 2.69-70.

[38]Ibid., 2.48; cf. *De opif.* 3.

[39]Georgi, *Die Gegner*, 161.

[40]Ibid., 162.

Now the oracular event at Sinai is documented by the tablets which Moses left inscribed.[41]   The Decalogue in its written form becomes sacred, so much so that Josephus states that it is impossible for him to utter it πρὸς λέξιν , although he will endeavor to give his readers its δυνάμεις .[42]   Philo also regards the written laws as mysterious and attempts to bring to light their hidden meaning through allegorical interpretation.[43] Furthermore, while the oracles of God as written are thereby fixed and past, this does not mean that they have lost either power or significance.   What has been said just now about Josephus and Philo indicates this.   Moreover, as Georgi has pointed out,[44] the unchangeable nature of the written text reflects the eternal nature of God.   The written text, then, as fixed and past, becomes mysterious and its initial inaccessibility serves as an occasion for interpretation.

The sacred character of the written laws can also be seen not only from the reinforcement they give to the divine experience of Moses[45] but also in their function as a heavenly letter.[46] They are written by the hand of God.[47] The recipients and possessor of the letter from heaven were raised above the rest of humanity and possessed a form of taboo.[48] The letter from heaven bestows on this fortunate group blessing and happiness,

---

[41]Josephus *Ant.* 3.90.

[42]Ibid.

[43]Philo *De Dec.* 1.

[44]Georgi, *Die Gegner*, 169 and n. 3.

[45]Josephus *Ant.* 3.101.

[46]L. Röhrich, "Himmelsbrief," RGG[3] 3 (1959) 338-39.

[47]Josephus *Ant.* 3.101; Philo *Mig. Abr.* 85; *Quis heres* 167.

[48]Georgi, *Die Gegner*, 166.

which is precisely, according to Josephus, what is promised by such oracles.[49]

Furthermore, these written tablets, preserved in the ark,[50] become the basic archive for the Jewish people, which was saved until after the destruction of Jerusalem by Babylon.[51] This concern for preservation as possession of divine power continues in the concern for accuracy for the ˋΙουδαικὰ γράμματα . The *Letter of Aristeas*, for example, indicates how much, even in its Greek translation, the apologists felt the importance of accuracy. Not only is there a curse attached for anyone who would dare change the translation but it is soon made clear that the law "of sacred and divine origin" will be the cause of great misfortune to those who attempt any disrespect.[52] Josephus, himself, is cautious, at least at the beginning of his *Antiquities*, to set forth the precise details of the written records.[53] This concern for accuracy and the preserved document was not based simply on the need for literary or legal reliability; rather, because the texts were understood as conveyances of holy might and power such a scrupulous attention was maintained.[54]

Finally, all of Scripture, not simply the Decalogue, can be seen as τὰ ἱερὰ γράμματα .[55] The corpus of sacred writing carries within it the power and spiritual resources of the Jewish tradition.[56] Both the

[49]*Ant.* 3.75, 77, 88.

[50]Ibid., 3.138; *Vit. Mos.* 2.97.

[51]Cf. Eupolemus in Jakoby 3.723.5.5.

[52]*Ep. Aris.* 311, 313ff.

[53]*Ant.* 1.17.

[54]Georgi, *Die Gegner*, 167.

[55]Cf. G. Schrenk, " γράφω κτλ ," *TDNT* 1. 742-73, esp. 762-63.

[56]Cf. below, where the unleashing of the power of the Letter is examined through various Jewish traditions, pp. 66-81.

work of Philo and the *Letter of Aristeas* take this as a precondition. The
Letter, then, means more than the written text as such. It refers thus to
the tradition conveyed by both the divine men of old and the written laws.
Indeed, the tradition surrounding the figure of Abraham not only is
continued through the written laws but is even enhanced and given a firm
basis in divine inspiration.

C. The Effect of the Letter:
The Creation of the Autonomous Self

It is time now to consider what happens to the one who confronts this
powerful archive of tradition. What world of meaning emerges for the
reader or listener?   Further, how is this lifeworld appropriated
effectively?

It has already been pointed out that, according to Philo, the
purpose of Moses for setting down examples of the unwritten law was
fundamentally protreptic,[57] helping to bring into being the commonwealth
where virtue is the true test of citizenship.[58]   In taking to heart the
κανών of Abraham, the interpreter incorporates the figure of the kingly
soul.[59] Moreover, the figure of Moses presents the greatest instance of
this royal paradigm for those who seek true wisdom.[60]   Indeed, it is the
Lawgiver who calls the human race away from its sins and to the words
of God, written in the book of the Law.[61]   The choice echoes that of
Deuteronomy 30: it is a matter of life or death.[62]   For if one seeks an

---

[57]Cf. n. 21.

[58]*De Abr.* 25, 89; *De virt.* 198, 219; *De gig.* 61: *De opif.* 3.

[59]*De virt.* 216; *De Abr.* 261.

[60]*Vit. Mos.* 1.158-59; 162.

[61]*De som.* 2.175.

[62]Cf. Deut 30:15, 19. *Quod Deus* 50.

image of the good and free man,[63] there are not only the living examples of Jewish tradition but even the words of God given by Moses. One need not traverse lands but see that the roots of freedom are "in your mouth, in your heart and in your hand."[64] There is still opportunity for the human race to spring up anew in wisdom,[65] the true commonwealth can be begun, if the word of Scripture is heard and obeyed.[66]

A dramatic instance of how this kingly soul comes about.[67] is given by Philo in *De spec. leg.* 4.160-69. In commenting on how a ruler comes to understand the law, Philo presents what amounts to be the true παιδεία. The philosopher-king becomes a reality through the internalization of the Law, indeed, in the very process of writing. The instructions for this begin with the Book of Deuteronomy. The king is to write out in his own hand a summary of the Law.[68] Through the process of writing out the Law and of becoming more and more familiar with it each day a striking effect is reached. The activity of writing and rereading brings about what one would today call an internalization of the Law.[69] In order to express this, Philo renders the internal soliloquy of the ruler in the first person singular. The words are written in order to rewrite them in the soul and receive in the mind characters of script more divine.[70] This internalized writing becomes the basis of sovereignty, now

---

[63]*Quod prob.* 62ff.

[64]Deut 30:14 in *Quod prob.* 68.

[65]*Quod prob.* 71.

[66]*De conf. ling.* 196-98.

[67]Cf. *Quod Deus 159-61; De gig.* 64.

[68]Cf. Deut 17:18-20.

[69]Cf. Josephus *Contra Ap.* 2.178; Philo *Vit. Mos.* 2.4.

[70]*De spec. Leg.* 4.163.

formed in the image of the archetype of God's kingdom.[71] The dreams of Hellenistic kingship, wherein the true judge is the one who possesses the text within his breast, thereby becoming the preserver of the state and of himself,[72] is held out to the reader of the Jewish Scripture. The active combination of the written word with its internalization produces a further embodiment of the true law of nature, which is articulated through the Law of Moses. Not only does this demonstrate the superiority of the Jewish religious tradition, but it allows entrance into this tradition as well as the haunting dream of the hellenized world. The person who internalizes such an understanding of Scripture is, in effect, constructing a self out of this tradition. He incorporates the powers and forces promised in this figure. This construction is seen in conformity with the law of nature, as one finds one's true role in the universe before God. The Letter, therefore, functions in a most positive way, enabling the reader (and writer) to set on the true road to freedom. The autonomous individual is thus a creation of this assimilated tradition.

D. Interpretation as a Means of Unleashing the Power of the Letter.

1. The Letter and Allegorization

From what has been argued so far, it would be difficult to consider that the employment of allegory by Jewish writers rests upon the infirmity of the Letter. On the contrary, allegory becomes an effective interpretive method precisely because of an original confidence that the Letter does, in fact, convey power and meaning.

---

[71]Ibid., 4.164.

[72]Plato *Laws* 957D; for a seminal essay on this question, see E. R. Goodenough, "The Political Philosophy of Hellenistic Kingship," *Yale Classical Studies* 1 (1928) 55-102..

The fixity of the written Letter, mentioned above,[73] is directly linked to the ancient world's appreciation of stability and endurance. Time witnesses to the excellence of what has been handed down.[74] Moreover, the written laws not only attest to the worth of Moses,[75] but, as written, partake of the unchangeableness of God.[76] Further, because of this association with the image of God and nature, the Letter serves to direct attention to the immortal and incorruptible, thereby transcending the boundaries of time and space.[77]

Respect for the fixity of the Letter, furthermore, leads to what some might consider a paradoxical result, namely, the transcending of specific texts. The fixed character of the Letter leads to the view that the Letter is capable of transcending itself.[78] Georgi has already shown that, while Josephus and Philo stress their fidelity to the Letter, both go beyond their stated bounds in expanding, harmonizing and paraphrasing their

---

[73]See p. 62 above.

[74]Thus, Josephus considers time to be the surest test of worth (*Contra Ap.* 2.279) and the witness to the excellence of both lawgiver and revelation from God which has been handed down. In *Hypoth.* 6.6.9 Philo notes that for more than two thousand years Jews have not changed a single word written by Moses.

[75]The excellence of Moses is attested by the fact that his laws are "firm, unshaken, . . . stamped, as it were, with the seals of Nature herself" (*Vit. Mos.* 2.14). The laws remain secure from the day enacted and into the future, for they are "immortal" (ibid.).

[76]Cf. Georgi, *Die Gegner*, 169.

[77]Cf. *Mig. Abr.* 93; Georgi, *Die Gegner*, 170. This last remark can be illustrated by recalling my treatment of the figure of Abraham (section I.A. above). The heroic life of eternal value in its written form enjoys a means of transmission. The power of the ancient heroes is now permitted to transcend their lifetimes (cf. Jos. *Ant.* 3.317, 322; Philo *Vit. Mos.* 2.43).

[78]Cf. *De op.* 6.

written sources.[79]   The reason for this is that those who continue to interpret the sacred text understand their work as part of a larger tradition, which extends down to the present.[80] The engagement with the Letter becomes a point of contact between the divine power inherent in the text and the power which surrounds the text through tradition.[81]

Such a conception already underlies the work of Aristobulus, who enjoins those who would understand the real (φυσικῶς) meaning of the Pentateuch to be directed by the spirit of Moses.[82] Moreover, if there are problems, seeming contradictions, in regard to the literal level of the text, there is no cause for alarm, but for further, discriminating reflection. The literal level becomes a directional, a sign, pointing to a more profound meaning.[83]

It is with Philo that the Jewish tradition of allegorical interpretation comes to its most comprehensive expression. From his perspective of continuity between nature and law, custom and reason, unwrittenness and writtenness, the power of the Letter is unleashed through this interpretive method. Nevertheless the discernment of Truth is not always clear and easy. Throughout his writings Philo grants the difficulty or opaqueness of the literal level.[84] However, by distinguishing between the literal level and the inner meaning of the text, for those who are capable of understanding a solution exists. Indeed, the text itself through its own ambiguous letters furnishes the clue.[85]   Perhaps the most dramatic

---

[79]Georgi, *Die Gegner*, 171.

[80]Ibid., p. 172.

[81]Ibid.

[82]Eusebius *Prep. Evan.* 8.10.4.

[83]Ibid., 8.10.2.

[84]E.g., *Leg. all.* 3.4,236; *De post. Caini* 51; *De agr.* 27,157; *De plant.* 36.

[85]Cf. *De plant.* 36.

instance of the work of allegorization is found in Philo's treatise on the Therapeutae. As genuine representatives of the contemplative life, they are dedicated to the "knowledge and contemplation of natural events" according to the "sacred instructions of the prophet Moses."[86] In reading the sacred writings, they seek wisdom through allegory, for they consider the literal text as symbolic of something whose nature is revealed through such analysis.[87] Moreover, there seems to be an expansion of tradition[88] in that not only do the Therapeutae possess "writings of the men of old" but they see them as models of allegorical interpretation.

Philo later describes how this allegorical exposition of texts was understood by the community. Such exposition was performed within the communal liturgy:

> The exposition of the sacred scriptures treats the inner meaning conveyed in allegory. For to those people the whole law seems to resemble a living creature with the literal ordinances for its body and for its soul the invisible mind laid up in its wording. It is in this mind especially that the rational soul begins to contemplate the things akin to itself and looking through the words as through a mirror beholds the marvellous beauties of the concepts, unfolds and removes the symbolic coverings and brings forth the thoughts and sets them bare to the light of day for those who need but little reminding to enable them to discern the inward and hidden through the outward and visible.[89]

The task of the interpreter is of crucial importance. For the leader of such exegesis must grasp the ψυχή of the Letter. But, in order for this to happen, the interpreter must somehow possess the λογική ψυχή.[90] The interpreter sees the Letter not as an obstacle but as a mirror

---

[86]*De vit. con.* 64.

[87]Ibid., 28.

[88]Georgi, *Die Gegner*, 175-76.

[89]*De vit. con.* 78 (Loeb trans.).

[90]Georgi, *Die Gegner*, 177.

(κάτοπτρον)   of the νοῦς .   Furthermore, the Therapeutae, as
expositors of the sacred text, appear to follow the directions suggested by
Aristobulus, since they heed the sacred instructions of the prophet
Moses.[91] As one enters the allegorical process in studying the Law, one
discovers the same spirit which possessed Moses and inspired the men of
old.[92] Just as the translators of the Septuagint experienced the "purest of
spirits, the spirit of Moses,"[93] so now anyone who searches the writings
will come under the influence of the same spirit. This is the spirit shared
by all who are wise,[94] who in studying the Law and the customs of the
fathers reach the state of self-education.[95] When one, then, allegorically
interprets Scripture, one is no longer a hearer but a true spectator of
divine and everlasting truth.[96] The divine spirit ever at Moses's side[97]
both underlies and justifies this method of interpretation.

In sum, then, one can say that the allegorical method is founded on
the assumption that the Letter serves as a powerful conveyance of the
forces of tradition. Both the fixity and the ambiguity of the Letter provide
the occasion for the discovery of the inner meaning and spirit of the
tradition.   The act of interpretation becomes a progressive revelation,
which transcends time and space. The Letter, thus, is actually included in
that which exceeds it, i.e., that universal font, spirit, mind, which upholds
all that is. Given this understanding the Letter serves as a most positive
entrance into the mysteries of the universe.

---

[91]*De vit. con.* 64.

[92]*De gig.* 62-64.

[93]*Vit. Mos.* 2.40.

[94]*De gig.* 23ff.

[95]*De fug.* 166-69.

[96]*De sacr. Abelis et Caini* 7, 76-79.

[97]*De gig.* 55.

2. The Letter and the Books of Wisdom

A further aspect of the Wisdom Movement, where the Letter is positively employed to unleash the power within and surrounding tradition, can be found in what is commonly known as the Wisdom literature.* Despite historical and conceptual differences, one finds in this literature a constant concern for transcendence, knowledge and illumination brought about through the interplay of Letter and tradition.

Right from its outset the intention of the book of Sirach is clear: built upon past written tradition[98] it is now translated and published[99] so that the wisdom tradition might continue its advance to the benefit of those who would live ἐννόμως.[100] The pre-translation edition has already transformed unwritten tradition into written form. Now the advice of Jesus, as well as the statutes of the Lord, are fixed for meditation,[101] thereby transcending time and place.[102] Even the understanding of Covenant is transformed along the lines of the wisdom school. The writings of Moses, the wise and the prophets are combined with the sayings, the discourses and riddles of the wise, so that all may be pondered and studied.[103] The covenantal blessing now rests with the one

---

*Indeed, the subsequent sections on Apocalyptic and Qumran Literature can also be seen within the wide-ranging Wisdom Movement. What one finds are variations on the quest for transcendence, knowledge and illumination. Furthermore, this entire half of the Excursus must be seen within the larger matrix suggested in the second half. The interpretive quest for making sense of the powers and forces of existence, of seeking the way of wisdom, underlies the discussion of the entire chapter.

[98]Prol. 1-4.

[99]Prol. 31.

[100]Prol. 14, 36.

[101]6:37.

[102]Prol. 29ff.

[103]39:1-3.

who will be filled with understanding.[104]   True meditation will furnish
the right education[105] as well as a memory that will last forever.[106]
Finally, the retelling of ancient and recently past heroes, recorded and
unrecorded, in an honorable litany[107] sets the stage for the claim that for
those who listen this lineage will continue.[108]   Wisdom will advance
through the school that employs such an understanding of writing and
thought.

While there is a decided reaction against the encroachment of
Hellenism[109] in Baruch the amalgamation of wisdom and Letter is still
maintained.   Indeed, the book of the Law is the place where Wisdom
resides.[110] A sense of hiddenness now pervades the dialectic of tradition
and interpretation.   What in Sir 24:23 stood for an open and inclusive
view of Wisdom and the Law now in an inverted and exclusive sense
becomes the modus operandi for all those who understand the writing of
the pseudonomous Baruch.   Nevertheless, as the entitling of the book
indicates, tradition is still perceived as powerful, so much so that for
those who can return to Wisdom in Torah, there is understanding,
strength and peace.[111]

---

[104]39:6.

[105]39:8.

[106]39:9.   All this is for the one who boasts in the νόμος of the Lord's
Covenant, 39:8.   In contrast the curse of the Covenant rests on those who
forsake the law of God, 41:8-10.

[107]44:1-51:29.

[108]51:23ff.

[109]Cf. M. Hengel, *Judaism and Hellenism* (Philadelphia: Fortress, 1974) 1.
169-70.

[110]Bar 3:29-37.

[111]Bar 3:14.

The Wisdom of Solomon continues this momentum of reinterpretation, attempting to see a continuity of God's sovereignty and Covenant through a complete reconstruction of the sense of reality. This work is not simply a protreptic which, incorporating the values of Hellenism, synthesizes all within a vision of the biblical understanding of God.[112] To view it as such would miss the creative interrelationship of tradition and interpretation which the redactor was attempting to achieve. The numerous disruptions, expansions, contrasts and collections of material, the constant shifts in form, content and tone, suggest that communication is more an end than a means. And this communication is that through the very reading of the text, in grasping the playful use of various traditions, the reader enters into the new reality, the world governed by Wisdom herself. Reality is not something out there but is participated in as one comes to see that Wisdom radically forms the consciousness of the royal individual.[113] In this instance the written text

---

[112]J. M. Reese, *Hellenistic Influence on the Book of Wisdom and Its Consequences* (Rome: Biblical Institute, 1970) 157.

[113]The Wisdom of Solomon throughout is engaged in a rewriting and reinterpretation of tradition. For example, the Enoch reference (4:10-15) has now been read in light of the paradigmatic narrative of the fate of the just one (chaps. 2-5). The story of Enoch becomes the story of a youth, causing the reader to wonder at the change and the intended meaning. Another instance is the combination of sapiential sayings of comfort (3:1-6) with a prophetic oracle of salvation (3:7-9). The integration of the two in a wisdom poem effectively denies the reality of death and denounces it with further instances of transformation. The interest stirred up in chap. 6 as to what constitutes the royal personality shifts from speculation about the kings of the earth to an inspection in chap. 7 of the reader's own hopes as to what is an authentic king. The presentation is typical here, not specific. The dualism of existence before and after conversion to Wisdom (vss 1-6; 7-14) is determined by the way reality is perceived (cf. chaps. 2-5). The reader is challenged to go beyond commonplace distinctions in order to resolve the problem on the level of knowledge and ignorance. Those who do not possess Wisdom are the truly fated. The retelling of the entire Passover Haggadah in typified fashion becomes an occasion to perceive that reality is truly the miraculous appearance

provides the stimulus not only for entering into a universal tradition but for reenvisioning the entire nature of reality.

3. The Letter and Jewish Apocalyptic

A further variation of the use of the Letter as a means of unleashing the power of tradition can be found in Jewish Apocalyptic writings. In this tradition the Letter bears the forces of the past ahead towards a determined future. Within this literature the fate of the elect becomes inextricably linked to what has been written in a transcendent realm. Thus, the Letter not only discloses the future but does so associated with an irrevocable and collective power.

In retelling and expanding the biblical narrative, the Book of Jubilees remarkably binds together customs, writtenness, law, fate, blessing and heavenly tablets. The purported vision given to Moses occurs upon his reception of the tablets of the Law. The subsequent history is dictated to Moses by an angel from heavenly tablets.[114] The angel utters what has already been written in heaven, so that both time and custom are seen in reality to be a working out of what has been eternally ordained. Time permits Israel to discover how the eternal decrees are worked out in the living tradition and customs.[115] Furthermore, through written books the ancient fathers hand on to their posterity what they have discovered of these eternal decrees.[116] Writing

---

of Wisdom. The plague of darkness nicely illustrates the new perception. For those initiated into Wisdom, the whole world is illuminated (17:20). But for the uninstructed, a false consciousness overcomes them (17:1). To know Wisdom is to know complete righteousness and knowing God's power is the root of immortality (15:3). True knowledge becomes the cutting edge of this new consciousness of reality. For a fuller treatment of this, cf. D. Georgi, *Weisheit Salomos* (Gütersloh: Mohn, 1980).

[114]Jub 1:29.

[115]E.g., 4:5; 6:17, 22; 50:13.

[116]4:17-20.

becomes a major instrument thus in the furtherance of their culture. Moreover, these records serve as testimonies of the friends of God for future generations.[117] Simultaneously the deeds of those on earth are recorded in the heavenly books of life and death. These will furnish testimony for the Day of Judgment.[118] Thus, the sense of continuity already discerned in the work of Philo and Josephus continues here with an increased tension. As the reader adopts this understanding of fidelity to this eternal pattern, he is faced with a heightened sense of destiny. One's actions not only partake of the customs and laws eternally decreed but also are entered onto the roll of fate.

The Book of Enoch continues this connection between writtenness and fate. In this book, which exhibits an increased level of tension as the fate of the righteous and the evil ones, the recording of what has been seen in the heavens and on the heavenly tablets serves as a counsel for succeeding generations of the wise.[119] The seer, privy to the mysteries of the universe as well as to the record from Uriel,[120] finds himself present before the books of the living.[121] He is commanded to read all that is written on the heavenly tablets, including the deeds of humanity.[122] Thus, under what may well have been oppressive circumstances,[123] the Book of Enoch presents a written record of what has been heavenly ordained. As a heavenly letter, the book carries advice for subsequent generations, under the guise that it is a hidden document

---

[117]E.g., 10:17; 19:9; 30:20ff.

[118]E.g., 5:13ff.; 30:22.

[119]82:2-3; 104:12ff.

[120]33:3-4.

[121]47:3.

[122]81:2.

[123]103:2ff.

intended only for those of understanding.[124]   Moreover, this eschatological vision allows posterity to interpret present events, not merely past narratives, in light of an assured future.   Control is maintained through a written tradition which passes on these visions and is reinforced through the ancient figure of Enoch as a model of righteousness.

A final example of the momentous function of Letter in Jewish Apocalyptic can be found in sections 78-86 of 2 Baruch.   This pseudepigraphic epistle is sent to the tribes in captivity.   While it is not termed a heavenly letter, it does bear transcendent marks.   Carried by eagle across the Euphrates,[125] it is written to make known the mystery of times,[126] comforting the people in distress.[127]   In speaking of the coming consummation, the letter helps to prepare the peoples' hearts,[128] enabling them to remember the Covenant.[129]   And just as the fathers delivered the traditions of the law to present generations, so now the letter delivers the traditions of the law to future generations.[130]   Finally, the letter serves as an object of meditation within the congregations, who bear Baruch in mind as he does likewise through this letter.[131]   Thus, not only does an ancient figure serve as an agent of transmission, but, within this eschatological perspective, the letter itself functions as a transcendent

---

[124]Cf. n. 119.

[125]78:1; 87:1.

[126]81:4.

[127]82:1.

[128]83:7-8

[129]84:7.

[130]84:9.

[131]85:1-3.

vehicle, going beyond the bounds of space and time to deliver a hidden mystery and judgment. Once again the written document contains fated and fatal destinies which only those who wisely interpret will be able to understand and thereby receive comfort.

It is clear from these brief examples that for Jewish Apocalyptic, Letter conveys both power and tradition. The heavenly visions and/or tablets serve as the basis for an earthly edition. These documents carry with them not only the future of Israel but of the entire world, now viewed under the rubric of righteousness. As a vehicle for transmitting what is hidden, these texts confirm the future in the present. Further, as the issues of oppression and justice become more marked, the Letter comes to stand as a force for liberation, as it continues and revises the ancient tradition.

4. Letter and the Interpretive Process at Qumran

A final and quite distinct interpretive tradition which relies heavily upon the effective power of the Letter can be found in the writings from Qumran. Not only is there a firm conviction underpinning the act of interpretation that the Letter is effective, but there is the added dimension of belief that the Letter will be accomplished within the lifetime of the community. Such preconceptions of interpretation could be maintained because of the abiding inspiration of the Teacher of Righteousness who claimed to have received his understanding from God. Thus, while the act of interpretation depends heavily upon the Letter of the text, the oral tradition, initiated with the Teacher of Righteousness, leads to a further step in the process of reading and revising Scripture. Indeed, what comes about is the production of new words, *pesharim*, which, in turn, become part of the sacred records of the community.

One finds, then, for example, in the Commentary on Habakkuk 6.12-7.5, the vision which Habakkuk has written down on tablets so that "he made it read easily" is explained in this way. The vision is made known to the Teacher of Righteousness "to whom God has made known all the Mysteries of his servants the prophets." In typical pesher fashion of the sect, the text is applied to the community's own history and self-

understanding. Thus, the interpretive key to the Letter is given solely
through the inspiration of the Teacher of Righteousness, whose oral
tradition, received from the mouth of God, will be passed on to the
endtime.[132]

A second instance of reinterpretation of tradition through a
reworking of the Letter can be seen in the Damascus Document. After a
preliminary account of the circumstances which brought about the arrival
of the Teacher of Righteousness,[133] an invitation is given in the first
person singular[134] where the Teacher declares that he will "uncover your
ears"[135] so that you may understand the works of God[136] and choose
what God desires. Then follows[137] a revision of the history of Israel
which runs from the going astray of the earliest heroes to the present.[138]
The figure of Abraham provides one of the few bright moments in an
otherwise dim and errant history.[139]   However, the Covenant is

---

[132]Thus pHab 2.1ff. not only notes the oral tradition received from the mouth
of God, but also says that in the last generation the message will come from the
mouth of the priest to explain the words of the prophets. Moreover, the sense
of continued community tradition is so strong that the famous verse from Hab
2:4, "the righteous will live by his faith," is explained in terms of the
community who will be delivered from their affliction by the "fidelity"
(באמונתו) of the Teacher of Righteousness. Cf. pHab 7.17-8.3.

[133]CD 1.1-2.1.

[134]Not unlike W.S. 6.21-25.

[135]CD 2.2.

[136]CD 2.14.

[137]Again like the W.S.; cf. pp. 73-74 n. 113 above.

[138]CD 2.17-4.12.

[139]He is called a friend of God (cf. Jub 19:9; also pp. 56-60 above) who kept
the commandments and did not choose his own spirit. He hands down these
commandments to Isaac and Jacob. Cf 1QS 5.8-9; 1QS 3.18-4.26.

discovered again in its authenticity by the converts of Israel, the sons of Zadok.[140]   Thus, the entire history of Israel, and especially the understanding of Covenant, filtered through the inspiration of the Teacher of Righteousness, becomes constitutive for the communal self-understanding. The oath of admission to the community declares that one will follow the Covenant as it has been revealed to "the sons of Zadok."[141] Those entering the community are instructed by a "novice master" in the Mysteries.   They enter into the communal life of interpretation, the study of the Law, whereby the whole community may act according to what the prophets have revealed by the holy Spirit.[142]

In the Hodayot one finds a series of hymns which graphically illustrate the understanding of the Teacher of Righteousness as an interpreter of divine mysteries. Begun most likely as an autobiographical collection, perhaps in conscious imitation of the Psalms, the anonymous format of these hymns in the first person singular allows the community contemporaneous and subsequent to incorporate these experiences within the communal life and worship. In a true sense these hymns parallel the exegetical work of the community. For, just as the inspiration of the Teacher of Righteousness has enabled them to effectively interpret the texts in terms of fulfillment, so in singing these hymns the experience of an individual becomes enacted and lived out in a corporate tradition.[143]

---

[140]CD 6.2--7. Interpreting Num 21:18 the well becomes the Law, the princes who dig the people of the community and the rod, through a play on מחוקק, the Teacher of Righteousness.

[141]1QS 5.9.

[142]1QS 8.15-16

[143]Specifically, one can see that the Teacher of Righteousness has come to know the marvelous mysteries, that is, the established law and wisdom (1QH 1.15-20). This is made known to the one whose ear is uncovered (1QH 1.21), whose face is illumined (1QH 4.5), whose mouth is opened (1QH 10.7), who has been raised from dust to understanding (1QH 11.12), to whom a fountain has been opened (1QH 11.19; 12.13), whose heart is uncovered (1QH 12.34; 14.8; 18.24), whose tongue is graven with precepts (1QH 18.11). This intensely personal revelation is brought about solely by the presence of God.

Finally, this enterprise of interpretation must be situated with the overarching concern for the fate of humanity. With the law of generations and times set before creation,[144] and the form of the world "graven" before God, with its unending cycles and seasons,[145] the task of the true interpreter is to preach to the Elect,[146] who shall enter into the company of the Sons of Heaven,[147] because the Spirit of God has been granted to them to keep God's precepts graven on the tongue.[148] They are delivered from the fate of humanity which is caught in the net of Sheol.[149] By reading the Book,[150] by studying the Law,[151] one can enter into the everlasting Covenant, most particularly in the eternal working out of the feasts and seasons.

Thus, once again, within this unique exegetical tradition, one can observe how the act of interpretation, now stimulated and controlled by

---

God has set understanding in his heart (1QH 2.17-18), established truth in his mouth, sealed up the Law within (1QH 5.11, 25), made known the secret of Truth (1QH 11.9-10), put the Spirit within, the Knowledge, the Mystery as power (1QH 11.11, 12, 13); 16.10), engraving everlasting happenings on his heart (1QH 18.27). It is for this graced one to illuminate the face of the many (1QH 4.27), to present a Law within (1QH 5.11), to manifest the power of God before men (1QH 5.15), functioning as truly as the other servants of God (1QH 14.25; 7.10, 14), proclaiming the message before all (1QH 18.6), announcing the good tidings to the humble (1QH 18.14).

[144] 1QH 1.19.

[145] 1QH 1.24.

[146] 1QH 2.13.

[147] 1QH 3.22.

[148] 1QH 18.11.

[149] 1QH 3.9, 19, 25-29.

[150] 1QS 6.7.

[151] 1QS 8.15.

oral tradition, heavily relies upon the positive function of Letter. There is again no sense of disassociation but a working harmony which gives rise to more written material and the furtherance of the oral tradition. Insight, illumination and understanding are the very purpose of this undertaking. Futhermore, as in singing, so in engaging in the work of midrash, the community not only enters into the Spirit of the Teacher of Righteousness but discovers its place in the graven eternal decrees of the universe.

From what has been brought forward so far, one can see that the concept of Letter is very much tied in with a larger cultural dialogue. From these brief examples within Hellenistic Judaism, one can observe how the Letter functions in a most positive vein, advancing the varied traditions of Hellenistic Judaism within the process of interpretation. Through the positive appreciation and employment of Letter, the Hellenistic Jew came to grips with transcendent powers and forces, and, in so doing, gained some sense of identity and destiny. Through the Letter, in short, a positive lifeworld opened up. It is time now to widen the scope of this excursus to see how these concerns are part of an older and broader cultural dialogue, where the search for mastery over the forces and powers transcending one's existence spawned a variety of responses. I shall begin this necessarily short account with the Sophistic debate.

II. The Larger Cultural Dialogue
A. The Sophistic Roots

During the time of the Sophistic debate a new generation of thinkers and rhetoricians emerged, divorcing νόμος from φύσις, convention and artificial contrivance from what is natural.[152] While it is neither possible nor necessary to rehearse the history of this development,[153] it should be

---

[152]Cf. W.K.C. Guthrie, *The Sophists* (Cambridge: Cambridge University, 1971), 55-56; F. Heinemann, *Nomos und Physis* (Basel, 1945; reprinted, 1965).

[153]Cf. Heinemann, *Nomos und Physis*; A. Lesky, *A History of Greek Literature* (trans, J. Willis and C. de Heer; New York: Cornell, 1966) 340ff.; Koester, " φύσις κτλ ," *TDNT* 9. 251-77.

pointed out that once this distinction gained validity, a significant intellectual movement was underway.[154]

In making such a distinction between what is artificial and what is natural,[155] a number of interpretive possibilities come into play. In each instance the individual employing such categories carved out a self-understanding which enabled him to negotiate the political demands of the Greek city-state. Thus, in contrast to viewing the passage of time as a descent from a "Golden Age", those who supported the notion of νόμος over φύσις , following the understanding that life evolved from inanimate matter, possessed an unqualified optimism and belief in the advancement of civilization.[156] They rejected any notion that νόμος was innate or divinely ordained from the beginning.[157]   Indeed, Protagoras, the greatest of the Sophists, based his entire enterprise upon such civilized advancement.[158] Success in political life is made possible through the acquisition of ἀρετή by teaching and effort. The νόμοι , in turn, come to be seen as being laid down by the state to teach political ἀρετή .[159] They serve as guidelines for the educated individual.[160]

---

[154]Lesky points out the permanence of its effects: "But what they broke up was never put together again in Greek life, and the questions which they posed have never been suffered to lapse in the history of western thought down to our day" (*History of Greek Literature*, 341).

[155]As to the originator of this distinction, much heat but little light has been shed. Cf. Guthrie's discussion, p. 58 n.1.

[156]Guthrie, *The Sophists*, 62ff.

[157]Ibid.

[158]Cf. DL 9.55; *Prot.* 320ff.; Guthrie, *The Sophists*, 63-68; Lesky, *History of Greek Literature*, 345-47.

[159]*Prot.* 326D.

[160]Instances of this positive understanding of νόμος occur in numerable places. In his play *Sisyphus* Critias points out how laws and justice have

Any return to nature would thus represent a regression to savagery and destruction. A second interpretive response in terms of these categories is that of realistic self-interest. It does not directly oppose φύσις to νόμος ; rather it is based on the observation of political life. The figure of Thrasymachus is exemplary of this position.[161]   He argues that whether a state is a tyranny or a democracy, the ruling powers make laws with a view towards their own self-interest. Rights for subjects are what are truly beneficial to those in power. What is termed just or honorable is simply what has been decided on by those in control of the decision making.   Νόμος, therefore, is not entirely removed but is placed in a "realistic" perspective.[162]

---

brought humanity out of disorderly life (frag. 25).   Democritus upholds the benefits of law in frags. 47; 174; 245; 248; 264.   In the last he says that self-respect should be established as a νόμος in the soul.   In frag. 181 he indicates that Law is not all-powerful and can be only kept by those convinced of it.   In Xenophon's *Mem.* 4.4.12ff.   Socrates argues that although laws might not be "by nature" the essence of justice, it consists in keeping them.   Indeed, Socrates' refusal to escape his death sentence is based on his respect for law (*Crito*).   In the so-called Anonymous Iamblichi, where the stock arguments of the age are manifest, the author contends that ἀρετή confers benefit on the greatest number of people.   This is accomplished by the assistance of laws, since they create and preserve human life.   Even a tyrant would eventually be overcome by the people's allegiance to law.   Further examples of this pervasive idea are: Lysias *Second Oration* 18-19; Demosthenes *In Aristogeiton* no. 25, 15-20; Isocrates *Panegyricus 28ff.'* Diod. *13.26.3.*

[161]*Rep.* 1.336Bff.

[162]Historical corroboration can be found in the work of Thucydides.   The most famous example of this is the tragic Melian debate (5.85-111).   Instead of responding favorably to the Melian suit for justice, the Athenians declare such to be unrealistic and not in the nature of things (5.104).   Further examples in Thucydides are: the Athenians' address to the Spartans (1.76.2); Hermocrates' warning (4.60.1); Pericles' recognition of the tyranny of Athens (2.63.2); Cleon's claim to reconcile justice with self-interest (3.40.4).   Such a position is a witness to the troubled circumstances of the late fifth century, where historical developments concretized the distinctions between convention and nature.   If νόμος is a construct, either of the past or present, then it can be altered, and

Perhaps the most dramatic spokesperson for the position of φύσις over νόμος is that of Callicles in Plato's *Republic*.163 As the champion of φύσις, Callicles preaches that there is such a thing as natural justice, and it is simply that humans living to the utmost of their powers should give free play to their desires. Under the rubric might is right, the existing human νόμοι are utterly unnatural, representing attempts of the weak and worthless to thwart the designs of the powerful. In carrying out this third interpretive position to its logical conclusion, Callicles declares the truly just man to be neither the democrat nor the constitutional monarch but the tyrant.

The strongest historical proponent of φύσις over νόμος is Antiphon. In the fragment *On Truth*164 the dictates of law are seen as artificially imposed by human agreement, whereas those of nature are just. Law enforces what is both painful and artificial upon nature to the detriment of life, freedom and pleasure. Antiphon uses the necessity of nature to transcend various national or racial boundaries. He further argues for an egalitarian viewpoint, challenging the Greek prejudice of noble birth and race.165 In condemning the convention of law as an absurd restraint, he tries to show the force and benefit of φύσις to those who would acquire an enlightened self-interest.

Now it is in this larger debate over νόμος and φύσις that the question of the written and unwritten law comes into play. The relationship of the written and unwritten laws is symptomatic of the changing nature of this period of intellectual history. Guthrie expresses this well:

---

by whom better than those who are powerful to do so? Further examples of this can be found in Gorgias *Helen* 6 (DK 2.290); Aristophanes *Clouds* 11.1075ff.

163*Rep.* 492Aff.

164OP 1364, frag. 1 (frag. 44A DK).

165Ibid., frag. 2 (frag. 44B DK).

> For some, the phrase (i.e., unwritten laws) denoted certain eternal moral principles, universally valid and overruling the positive laws of men because their origin was from the gods. This conception is best known from the splendid lines of Sophocles in the *Antigone* (11.450ff.), where Antigone defends the burial of her dead brother contrary to the edict of Creon. . . . However, with the spread of democratic ideas the phrase took on a new and more sinister meaning. The codification of law came to be seen as a necessary protection for the people. Not only Euripides (Suppl 429ff.) saw it as a guarantee of equal rights and a bulwark against tyranny, but also in practice the restored democracy at the end of the Peloponnesian War expressly forbade a magistrate to make use of unwritten law (Andocides, *De Myst.*, 85).[166]

The reason for the turning against the unwritten laws, which formerly stood for the archaic tradition valid for everyone at all time,[167] can be found in the separation of νόμος from φύσις. While the divine aspect of the unwritten laws faded into the background, the power of the tradition of the unwritten laws came to be associated more and more with φύσις. The appreciation of φύσις as a fundamental force and power in the universe, which destroyed the barriers erected by νόμος,[168] guiding the wise citizen solely by the law of ἀρετή,[169] enabled the Greeks to continue to define themselves in a transcendent fashion. However, as the ideal of a paternal aristocracy gave way to the Greek πόλις, a grave danger occurred in espousing the unwritten laws insofar as they became more or less identified with the force of φύσις. The ἰσονομία of the written constitution was threatened:

---

[166]Guthrie, *The Sophists*, 22-23.

[167]E.g., Hesiod *Erga* 276; Heraclitus frag. 114.

[168]*Prot.* 337C.

[169]Antisthenes, D.L. 6.11.

> Just as physis could be invoked either to uphold humanitarian
> ideals or interests of aggression and the overthrow of
> constitutional government, so the idea of unwritten law, which
> originally emphasized the moral government of the universe,
> could in a more democratic society, appear simply as retrograde
> and a menace to the hard-won assurance of human rights that
> now was written into the statute-book.[170]

This, indeed, was the state of the question when Plato came upon the
scene. On one side of the spectrum stood the dream of equality of all
citizens under a written code, while on the other side stood the ideal of
the man of nature, who saw law a mere infringement upon desires and
liberty. It was for Plato to attempt a synthesis of this traumatic antithesis.

B. The Unwritten/Written Dialectic in Plato
In respect to the relationship of the unwritten to the written, the work of
Plato apparently contains two distinctive lines of thought. What one
encounters in the *Phaedrus* and the *Letters* seems to contrast sharply with
what is indicated in the *Laws*.

In attempting to ask what constitutes authentic learning and
knowledge, with the bulk of the discussion centering around the issue of
rhetoric, Plato raises a question concerning the propriety of writing in a
section near the end of the dialogue.[171] In order to investigate this, an
ancient tale is recounted about the origin of writing. Evidently the god
Theuth brought forth this invention, claiming it to be an elixir of memory
and wisdom.[172] The god-king Thamos denies this, declaring the
invention to be just the reverse, i.e., a source of forgetfulness, which
would allow reliance on external devices and not on oneself, thereby
giving but the appearance of wisdom. Socrates then goes on to criticize

---

[170]Guthrie, *The Sophists*, 126.

[171]*Phaedrus* 274B.

[172]274E.

writing. Just like painted pictures, written words stand silently before the questioner.[173] Helpless to defend itself, the written word appears to say the same thing. In contrast, there is another kind of word, written with intelligence in the soul of the learner.[174] Phaedrus calls this the "living and breathing word"[175] of which the written word is a mere image. The true husbandman of speech, then, will sow his words not in ink[176] but in noble souls, where the process of wisdom will ever continue.[177] In apparent contrast to all he has written, Plato declares that writing for the noble one will be but pleasant amusement, that even written political constitutions are of little worth.[178]

A continuance of this line of thought is found in the *Letters*.[179] In *Ep. 7* Plato indicates that it is not only impossible to put real teaching in writing[180] but that to attempt this shows that either gods or mortals have blasted the wits of the writer.[181] In *Ep. 2* one finds that what is written on a tablet is at best a riddle which only dialogue can solve.[182]

---

[173]275D.

[174]276A.

[175]λόγον . . . ζῶντα καὶ ἔμψυχον(276A).

[176]276C.

[177]277A; cf. pp. 64-66 above.

[178]278C.

[179]As to the question of authenticity, cf. Lesky, *History of Greek Literature*, 511, 539.

[180]*Ep. 7*, 341Bff.

[181]344D.

[182]*Ep. 2*, 312D.

Moreover, the only way to safeguard the purity of one's teaching is never to commit it to writing, lest the untrained unwisely use it.[183]

This apparent contradiction of both writing and in the process rendering the attempt at best an amusement may well point to the possibility of a double heritage of Plato, that of oral and written traditions.[184] But, it should also be noted that even the written work is not intended to remain on the written level. The whole tendency of the Platonic dialogues is protreptic and paraenetic, urging the reader to see himself as the one truly addressed in the discussion at hand.[185] Thus, when one considers the *Laws*, which combines both what is written and unwritten, one should not forget that this dialogue, too, succeeds when what has been written calls the reader to recognize that its reality only comes to stand in the thinker who carries this out for himself.

Written in the somber twilight of his life, Plato's *Laws* comes to grips with the dreams and the experience of the Sophistic period. In leaving to his posterity a "more modest proposal" as to the nature of a just society, Plato considers the building blocks upon which humanity can hope to construct a political life. In this vein he taps the ancient traditions of a Golden Age by beginning with the myth of an innocent, yet primitive, postdeluvian society. Once there may well have been such a group of humanity in an age when there was no need of a lawgiver, when lives were regulated by customs and tradition.[186] Later, he mentions the received tradition that an age of bliss existed, wherein humanity was ruled by divine guidance, allowing internal concord and happiness.[187] Yet,

---

[183]314A-C.

[184]Cf. H. J. Krämer, *Arete bei Platon und Aristoteles* (Amsterdam: Schippers, 1967).

[185]Cf. K. Gaiser, *Protreptik und Paränese bei Platon* (Stuttgart: Kohlhammer, 1956).

[186]*Laws* 680A.

[187]713C-E.

time and experience have brought about corruption; men are no longer ruled by God.[188] Only in some rural and remote places does a trace of that idyllic life remain.[189] The task of the lawmakers of the *Laws* is to attempt to reproduce as much as possible that life of the age of Kronos.

Plato indicates his indebtedness to the Sophistic debate by declaring that to return to justice, there must be a life according to law. Either regulate human life by law or return to the wildness of beasts. The reason for this is that there is no man so naturally endowed to know what is good for the human community and who also has the power to effect this good.[190] In contrast to Callicles' superman, who lives by nature's liberty, humanity's fragility and mortality will lead, according to Plato, to self-seeking, blindness, and ruin, both individual and communal.[191] Yet, Plato cannot dismiss theoretically and possibility that an individual could be born with a capacity for governing, thereby needing no laws whatsoever. But, here it must be observed that Plato introduces into the notion of φύσις the understanding that nature is an intelligent and moral force. Thus, when he says that neither law nor ordinance has any sovereignty over true knowledge (ἐπιστήμη), that it is unlawful for the νοῦς to be subject to anything, but should be ruler of all,[192] he is presupposing such an association. However, realism sets in with the subsequent observation that such a phenomenon is not to be found, except in faint traces. Therefore, humanity must choose the next best path — that of law and order.[193]

---

[188]713E.

[189]680D.

[190]874E-875A.

[191]875C.

[192]875C-D.

[193]875D.

Education becomes the means of bringing this commonwealth of
law into existence. Plato, then, is very much in the Sophistic tradition in
regard to the function of education. But, for Plato, education is a mixture
of tradition and convention.   While this education leads children
according to the rule which is pronounced right by the "voice of the
law,"[194] this "voice of the law" would be backed up by the experienced
elders of the people. The good citizen would be one who obeys not only
what the legislator has written but also what he has commended.[195] Both
written and unwritten law would thus figure in the formation of the
citizen. Indeed, for Plato there is no antithesis between them; rather, the
unwritten laws form the connecting links between what has already been
written and enacted, as well as with the law yet to be committed to
writing. Like the elders who preserve the spirit of the law, the unwritten
law serves as a shield for all that has been written, providing a necessary
substructure upon which all the written can be built.[196] The production,
then, of the lawbook of such a society would mark the appearance of the
best and finest literature.[197]   In fact, this recording would be both
pragmatic and utopian.   Not only would it set down the decisions
lawgivers have made but it would also indicate what the society considers
to be the better, providing in written form society's expectation of the
future.[198]

The Example of complete internalization of the law is found in the
figure of the just judge. To become such, one must keep the matters of
justice ever before the eyes.   There is then no study so potent

---

[194]659D.

[195]822E-823A.

[196]793B-C. Cf. M.Abot 1.1.

[197]859A.

[198]644D.

(κυριώτατα) than that of the law to make one a better human being. The text of the lawgiver becomes the touchstone (βάσανος σαφής) which the just judge will possess ἐν αὐτῷ. His embodiment of the law will preserve the rectitude of the community and serve as protection from those who are fatally attached to evil[199]

While Plato dismisses as unrealistic the notion of a human so naturally endowed as to perceive what is right and effect this for society, the appearance of the figure of the just judge permits the ideal of the authentic individual to resurface through the process of self-education. In Plato's understanding, both the unwritten laws of old as well as the written laws of society, if brought to fruition through the process of education, actually cooperate to sustain the utopian dream of an autonomous individual. Thus, in viewing both φύσις and νόμος as intelligent forces, Plato effects a synthesis of what the fifth century saw as fundamentally antithetical. In so doing Plato offers to his audience the possibility of interpreting the universe within this autonomous paradigm.

C. Aristotle and the Classification of Tradition

A common starting point in the investigation of Letter and Spirit is the *Rhetoric* of Aristotle.[200] In relating the antithesis of Letter/Spirit to what is found in the *Rhetoric*, one could then too quickly conclude that this antithesis is fundamentally a rhetorical ploy. However, without anticipating the following chapter, it is necessary to consider the context of the unwritten/written antithesis within the *Rhetoric* itself.

The first instance of the use of written/unwritten as categories comes up in Aristotle's distinction between law which is general and law which is particular. The general law is the unwritten laws recognized by all, while the particular is that written by the state.[201] In 1.13, however,

---

[199]957C-E. Cf. Philo's indebtedness to Plato, pp. 64-66 above.

[200]Cf. Cohen, "Letter and Spirit," Intro., p. xvi, n. 22 above.

[201]*Rhetoric* 1368B.1-13.

Aristotle uses the same terminology regarding νόμος in a different aspect. After noting that the law which is general is based κατά φύσιν and is divined by all, he then divides the particular law into written and unwritten.[202] In this section Aristotle is concerned primarily with the classification of just and unjust actions. Here he sees that there can be just and unjust actions which exceed what the written laws take notice of as well as the possibility that the written laws of the state cannot take into account every specific instance of law. What is not written becomes a supplement to what is written. At the same time, Aristotle has not lost sight of the universal implications of the general law, quoting both the *Antigone* and Empedocles as support.[203] While Aristotle may appear inconsistent in his overall presentation of written/unwritten law, he is not contradictory. In short, he can hold that there are two kinds of unwritten law: the first, the particular customs and traditions of the community; the second, the universal, natural laws long held by all.

The significance of these distinctions can be found within the forensic character of the work. As a handbook for orators engaged in the activity of the polis, such distinctions aid in interpreting the law.[204] Of course, it should not be overlooked that in presenting such distinctions, Aristotle relies heavily on the sophistic tradition. The employment of such traditional distinctions can assist one in interpreting the human act as just or unjust in regard to the entire context of the situation. One must

---

[202]1373B.1ff.

[203]1373B.10ff.

[204]In 1375A.ff (1.15) one can see how each understanding can be put to good use. If the written law runs counter to the case, then the advocate must employ the argument from the unwritten law, which would call the juror to consider the unwritten law as more in tune with the justice of the case, since the written law does not satisfy the requirements of equity. The reverse argument can be employed when the written law favors the case. The juror would be urged not to neglect what was written in a vain attempt to be wiser than what has been approved by written law.

look not simply to the law but to the lawgiver, not to the letter (λóγος) but to the intention (διάνοια), not to the action per se but to the purpose, not to the part but to the whole.[205] Thus, while one does not find in the *Rhetoric* anything on the order of the Platonic synthesis in regard to the categories of written/unwritten, one can see that these categories can figure prominently in the political questions of the day. Such distinctions provide basic categories and strategies for public argument. Letter as written and tradition as unwritten continue to play a positive role in the task of political interpretation.[206]

D. The Cynic Counterpoint

In marked contrast to both Plato and Aristotle[207] stands the Cynic tradition. While it is quite true that there can be no easy systematization of the Cynic movement due to its rich diversity and individuality, one can, within the lines of this project, detect that this tradition in its own peculiar way continues to respond to the fundamental questions of the Sophistic debate. The quest for the autonomous individual, interpreted through such antithetical categories as φύσις and νόμος, is not only maintained but radically conceived. Thus, from Antisthenes, Diongenes

---

[205]1374B.11ff.

[206]On the other hand, the inclusion of such antithetical categories can lead to an eventual reduction of the issues to simply matters of rhetoric, especially within a different political climate. This can be seen in the work of Quintillian where once again the distinction of letter and intention is spelled out. For him the issue is basically one of determining the strategy of the argument and then using either the letter (*scriptum*) or the intention (*voluntas*). Cf. 7.6.4.-8. Once more the various possibilities are paraded for the advocate's selection. However, there is a decided loss in regard to the universal implications of these categories. While the question of equity (*aequitas*) can be raised in support of the unwritten law, that is, the intent of what is written, there is no further concern for the broader implications of this position. The vision of the polis has been replaced by the practical concerns of the lawyers of the empire.

[207]As well as to the Stoics, below pp. 96-101.

down to Dio Chrysostom, through the pseudepigraphical examples of the wise,[208] one can find a constant theme that one can be self-sufficient, that one can live κατὰ φύσιν and not κατὰ νόμον, that for the virtuous the life of the gods is theirs.   In emphasizing a life of practice, unencumbered by theory, the Cynics maintained that virtue alone was of value, that vice was to be rejected, and that anything else — such as the advanced studies of the Stoics — was a waste of time.   Governed neither by chance nor by opinion, the wise man led an authentic life of active virtue.

A text which not only illustrates issues but also touches on the matter of this investigation is the Ninth Letter of Heraclitus.[209] Addressed ostensibly to the Ephesian lawgiver Hermodorus, this letter purports to give advice to the Ephesian recently banished for his legislation granting citizenship to freedmen.   Such an expulsion is symptomatic of the vice generally rampant throughout cities.[210]   Indeed, while written laws are not seen in a negative light by Pseudo-Heraclitus, they are situated within the larger issue of citizenship by chance (τύχη), i.e., by birth, and by behavior. Citizens by birth are not virtuous by that alone. The contrary is usually the case.[211] He then cites the example of Sparta, where citizenship is not a matter of certification (οὐ γράμμασιν) but of behavior (ἀγωγῇ).   The true citizen has so internalized virtue that he can go off bearing the country within himself.[212]   Returning to the Ephesians, the writer argues that if the

---

[208]E.g., Odysseus, Heracles, Socrates.

[209]H. Attridge, *First Century Cynicism in the Epistles of Heraclitus* (Missoula: Scholars, 1976).

[210]11.4-5.

[211]11.9-10.

[212]1.17: ἐν ἑατῷ φέρων τὴν πατρίδα ἔρχεται .

Ephesian is a true citizen then he is actually a citizen of the world.[213] This is because the earth is common territory of all, wherein νόμος is not some written statute but is god.[214] While the common person may fear the νόμος because of the wrath of some avenging Fury, the wise man recognizes that the gods are his fellow citizens. Here, most dramatically the Cynic self-confidence of dwelling with the gods through virtue is manifested.[215] The letter alternates, then, from paradoxical apostrophes to the Ephesians to advice to Hermodorus and thus to a final diatribal outburst against the Ephesians.[216]

In reviewing this pseudepigraphic letter, one discovers an example of how the Cynics drew on the resources of their tradition. Such diatribal speech and scholastic letter writing were a means of continuing a movement focused sharply on the life of virtue. Not attempting to argue from the fields of advanced research, the writer concentrates his purpose on turning humans away from vice and to the task of active virtue. The employment of antithetical categories, such as nature/custom, freedom/slavery, letter (as document)/ god are quite strategic. Moreover, the ancient figure of Heraclitus becomes the exemplary figure, testifying to the real possibility of virtue in the present time. The letter, then, is no simple exercise of rhetoric. Rather, its protreptic and paraenetic character entice the reader to sustain the vision that the autonomous individual, in fundamental equality with the divine, was a real possibility.

---

[213]11.21-22: εἰ ἀγαθός, κόσμου πολίτης .

[214]11.22-23: νόμος ἐστὶν οὐ γράμμα ἀλλὰ θεός ; cf. 2 Cor 3:6.

[215]Contrast the Stoic hesitancy to assert attainment of perfection, which the Cynics claim is not only possible but has been attained by various wise men in history. Cf. the figure of Abraham, pp. 56-60 above.

[216]The Ephesians, thinking themselves free, are actually slaves to passion (11.4-7). This unfreedom is contrary to nature (11.8-19). Moreover, this advice is prophetic ((11.4-5). If men but follow nature they will obey the laws written by Hermodorus. Finally, the Ephesians are really enslaved masters, ignorant of what they truly can be and of their possible fatal inheritance.

Thus, the dream of the true citizen within a true cosmopolis continues to shine through this particular tradition.   Moreover, while anything of convention, such as external documentation, is rejected, the written letter itself is used as an effective medium to present this vision to the world.

E. Harmony, Right Reason and the Understanding of Authentic Existence

To appreciate the variety of responses which were made to the continuing cultural question of how one can come to terms with forces and powers transcending one's existence, I shall now briefly indicate how two philosophic traditions, Pythagoreanism and Stoicism, advanced this question, especially in regard to their methods of relating the individual to the whole.

Despite the shrouded and mysterious origin of Pythagoreanism,[217] as well as the problematic character of its revival,[218] this philosophical tradition is important for this investigation, since through its influence[219] and its continued presence[220] it offers a fundamental response to the

---

[217]Cf. Guthrie, *History*, 1. 146-70.

[218]Cf. C. de Vogel, *Pythagoras and Early Pythagoreanism* (Assen: Van Gorcum, 1966); H. Thesliff, *An Introduction to the Pythagorean Writings of the Hellenistic Period* (Acta Academiae Aboensis, Humaniora 24/3, 1965).

[219]Cf. Plato's *Timaeus*.

[220]For its continued presence in literary sources, cf. Seneca *Ep.* 108.34; Ovid *Metam.* 15.153ff.; Cicero *Tusc.* 1.17.39; 4.1.204; *Resp.* 1.10.16; *De leg.* 1.33; *De off.* 1.56; Pliny *Nat. hist.* 34.36.   The oldest testimony of revival of Pythagoreanism as a philosophy comes from Alexander Polyhistor's account in *DL* 8.25-35.   In the first century B.C.E. a stream of Pythagorean pseudepigrapha breaks out. Cf. Cicero *Tim.* 1.1: Seneca *Nat. quaest.* 7.32.2. Of course, the first century features the career of Apollonius of Tyana, who regarded himself a true disciple.   Also from the first century C.E. we find Moderatus of Gades (cf. Plutarch *CQ* 8.7.727).   Finally, there is Nicomachus of Gerasa, who in true Pythagorean fashion considers mathematics as the condition for the attainment of wisdom (*Arith.*, Intro. 1.3.3-6).   For the

question of how the human relates to the universe. Moreover, its insight may well throw light upon the cosmic associations with Letter.[221] Now the philosophy of Pythagoras rests upon a "mathematics of nature."[222] Its originality lay in the insight that the chaotic mass of unformed matter could be organized by perceiving the true elements which were underneath appearances. All things owed their existence to the initiation of numbers.[223] The task of the philosopher, then, working from the presupposition that everything was composed of numbers,[224] was to perceive the true ἁρμονία of the κόσμος in order to reproduce this order in one's soul.[225] This harmonious relationship could be considered to partake somewhat magically[226] in that fundamental, living sympathy which permeates all things.[227] Philosophy becomes a conscious initiation into this cosmic sympathy through the recognition of limit and harmony. In perceiving the orderliness of the cosmos through the active study of number, geometry, music and astronomy, the contemplative discerns an actual change in his nature, becoming assimilated to the divine. The labor of the philosopher is then not to change the world but to become attuned to its reality. Progress comes about through this discovery of the path of

---

possible connections of Pythagorean through on the Hellenistic notion of kingship, cf. Goodenough, "Political Philosophy," 64, 68, 71, 76, 91.

[221]Cf. Gal 4:9; also Excursus, pp. 62-63 above.

[222]Guthrie, *History*, 237.

[223]Aristotle *Meta.* 987B11.

[224]Ibid., 987B28; 1090A20.

[225]Guthrie, *History*, 288.

[226]Ibid., 182ff.

[227]Cf. Sextus Empiricus *Math.* 9.127.

harmony.[228]   Such an understanding of reality, conveyed originally
through oral tradition,[229] survived mainly through the platonic scholastic
tradition of the Hellenistic period, and was rejuvenated by the revival of
platonic speculation in the first century B.C.E.[230] In respect to the issues
and categories already advanced in this investigation, such an
understanding of reality not only provided much of the basis for the
platonic synthesis but in its continued attraction presented the possibility
of interpreting the universe through a particular medium, i.e., number,
which served to open the power and harmony of the cosmos to the
sympathetic individual.[231]

The Stoic contribution to the continued cultural quest was to situate
the basis for human thought and action within a dynamic, rational
universe.   Because of the presence and providence of the λόγος
σπερματικός ,[232] nature was interpreted not merely as a physical
power but as that which brings forth and preserves with a specific aim
according to each thing.[233]   Indeed, it is termed an artistic fire going on
its way to create.[234]   From Chrysippus onward the term πνεῦμα is
employed to describe that which gives coherence, pervading the whole
cosmic sphere, functioning both throughout the universe as a whole and
within each individual body.   The πνεῦμα turns the universe into a

---

[228]*DL* 8.33.

[229]*DL* 8.15, 17.

[230]Cf. p. 96 n. 220.

[231]For an example of the influence of the Pythagorean fascination with number
and its use in interpreting the Letter, cf. Philo *De opif.* 100.

[232]*DL* 7.136.

[233]*DL* 7.148-49.

[234]*DL* 7.156.

dynamic continuum, interrelating its different parts.[235] Thus, as the individual acts in accordance with one's nature, one acts in concert with the rest of the universe, since the πνεῦμα grounds all in cosmic sympathy.

Chrysippus expresses well the traditional understanding of how one lives a live according to nature:

> For our individual natures are parts of the nature of the whole universe. And this is why the end may be defined as life in accordance with nature, or, in other words, in accordance with our own human nature as well as that of the universe, a life in which we refrain from every action forbidden by the law (ὁ νόμος ὁ κοινός) common to all things, that is to say, the right reason (ὁ ὀρθὸς λόγος) which pervades all things, and is identical with this Zeus, lord and ruler of all that is. And this very thing constitutes the virtue of the happy man and the smooth current of life, when all actions promote the harmony of the daimon dwelling in the individual man with the will of him who orders the universe.[236]

The task of the Stoic was to seek wisdom in order to find out how one can live in accordance with this right reason. As Long puts it, "the goal of the progression is life in accordance with mature human nature, i.e., a life governed by rational principles which are in complete harmony with rationality, goals and processes of universal Nature."[237] The individual becomes educated, discerns what the καθῆκον consists in, discovering that all social virtue is based upon Nature's inherent Reason. In accepting the external circumstance of his life, in coming to decide what is κατὰ τὴν φύσιν, the Stoic not only is a spectator of what God has brought forth but becomes an active interpreter of the universe.[238] Thus, the

---

[235]Cf. A. Long, *Hellenistic Philosophy*, (London: Duckworth, 1974), 152-58.

[236]*DL* 7.88 (Loeb ed.).

[237]Long, *Hellenistic Philosophy*, 188.

[238]Cf. Epictetus 1.6.20: οὐ μόνον θεατήν, ἀλλὰ καὶ ἐξηγητὴν αὐτῶν.

Stoic continues to support the traditional ideal of the wise man who is godlike,[239] who alone is free,[240] since he alone can judge and act according to the true dictates of Nature. In him law and reason exist by nature and not by convention.[241]

Moreover, it is precisely due to the conviction that the cosmos is orderly and that all within the cosmos can be apprehended in a rational manner which grounds the employment of allegory by the Stoics. Discrepancies in the texts of Homer, for example, are cleared up under this horizon of understanding. The Letter and Nature are perceived in a reciprocal relation. Because the universe is meaningful, the text must be, and when through the process of allegorization it is shown the rational nature of the cosmos is further demonstrated.[242] Nevertheless, there was a price for such a unified system. Since every event must have a cause,[243] with the all-pervading πνεῦμα or λόγος directing all things intelligently, it was impossible for anything to simply happen by chance. Such a possibility of chance is due to the fact that the cause has not yet been uncovered.[244] While arguing carefully for the existence of free will,[245] the Stoic can understand God to be both νοῦς and εἱμαρμένη.[246] With the passage of time, like the unwinding of a rope,

---

[239]*DL* 7.119.

[240]*DL* 7.121. Also, the Stoic alone is king (7.122).

[241]*DL* 7.128.

[242]Cf. R. Grant, *Letter and Spirit*, 6-9.

[243]Arnim, H., *Stoicorum veterum fragmenta* (Dubuque: W.C. Brown, 1964), 2.945.

[244]*SVF* 2.967.

[245]Cicero *De fato* 39-44.

[246]*DL* 7.135.

bringing nothing new,[247] the task of the individual becomes a matter of meeting one's destiny as part of the overall fate of the universe.

F. Posidonius and the Scope of Interpretation

While the debate over what is authentically his material still remains much a matter of debate and refinement,[248] there is no doubt over the influence of Posidonius upon the intellectual climate of his age. Indeed, the task of coming to grips with the forces and powers transcending one's existence continues with his work. Thus, through the notion of Cosmic Sympathy and its relation to history, Posidonius furthers the interpretive movement attempting to bring all matters of time and place within the understanding of universal principles. Since the divine, which is a rational πνεῦμα, pervades all being,[249] he could undertake the task of discovering this πνεῦμα in all matters through his prolific research. This universal research project, in turn, becomes for subsequent thinkers and historians, such as Diodorus, the foundation for a universal history. In Posidonius' eyes the wise man, engaged in such labor, stands firmly grounded in the movement of time, winning the benefits and insights for the advancement of civilization. The haunting ideal of the wise lawgiver which has emerged in this investigation exists as a real possibility for Posidonius in order to bring the commonwealth of humanity to formation.

Posidonius' position in regard to the wise man who shepherds the advancement of humanity can be found in *Epistle 90* of Seneca. In contrast to Seneca's view that the original Golden Age has been corrupted through avarice and artifice,[250] Posidonius' argument would hold that

---

[247]*SVF* 2.944.

[248]Cf. J. Dillon, *The Middle Platonists*, (Ithaca: Cornell, 1977), 106ff. for the summary of the debate.

[249]Edelstein, Frag. 100.

[250]*Ep. 90*.3, 8, 10, 18-19, 24, 27, 29, 31.

from the beginning all things were under the jurisdiction of the wise and that, even when vice and tyranny stole into the world,[251] laws were still framed by the wise. As time progressed the role of the wise did not diminish but aided in the various inventions which have made for humanity's advancement. Now, the reason that the rule of the wise and their inventions have come about, indeed, the reason that the work can continue through the researches and speculations in all areas of the universe, is that all things are interacting and connected. Through the use of this principle, which may well not have been original to his thought, he can attempt to take into interpretive focus the vast variety of his encyclopedic information in order to create a vision of the whole.[252]

A significant consequence of this thinking is dramatically seen in the writing of Diodorus Siculus.[253] In composing a universal history under the view that the divine πρόνοια directs nature and humanity through the laws of fate to a common relationship,[254] Diodorus sees that from the study of history humans can learn from mistakes and insights of the past, as well as making effective use of it in the present.[255] As the means whereby humanity's activities can be combined, written history constitutes itself as the guardian of these achievements, a witness to the deeds of evil doers and benefactors.[256] This recording of history becomes a way of immortality for those destined for extinction, a divine

---

[251]Ibid., 5, 6.

[252]Thus, because there is a vital, rational spirit pervading the universe, assimilating all things to itself (Edelstein, Frag. 101), one can even study divination to learn more of the ineluctable chain of causation (Cicero *De div.* 1.125).

[253]*D.S.* 1.1-5.

[254]1.1.3.

[255]1.1.4-5.

[256]1.2.1-2.

voice of remembrance.[257] Like the divine being of Posidonius, History, through its written transmission and viewed in a universal light extends through the entire inhabited world, bringing ruin on every ill and insuring a perpetual transmission to posterity.[258] The educated one, who sees the universal purpose and thrust of history, is brought out of barbarian existence into the world of civilization.[259] To study history means entering the true metropolis of philosophy which is ever prepared to ennoble human character.[260]

The quest for the autonomous individual who can somehow come to grips with the forces and powers transcending his existence has through the hands of such thinking now become welded to the historical destiny of Rome. This advancement of Rome now is the occasion for the concretization and furtherance of those earlier concerns. In the eyes of Posidonius, Diodorus et al.,[261] the Empire affords the possibility for the sage to advance in wisdom through political action. Moreover, the act of writing history becomes the task for the wise in order to educate those who would partake of this destiny. Tradition, then, will not only be seen as securing the value and immortality of the individual but also be used as a controlling perspective. All who enter the lists of this tradition do so under the rubric of benefit to the advancement of the historical destiny of Rome. A further concretization of Roman destiny and the Letter is found in the final section on Roman Apocalypticism.

---

[257] 1.2.3.

[258] 1.2.5.

[259] 1.2.6.

[260] 1.2.2.

[261] E.g., Plutarch, especially in his *Lives*.

G. Roman Apocalypticism

The fusion of history and destiny becomes a significant element in the following examples of Roman Apocalyptic writing. In each case the progress of Rome follows on the iron laws of destiny as the renewal of the world and the hope of civilization rest upon the shoulders of those destined to govern the Empire. For one to continue to ask about the possibility of the individual to come to terms with the transcendent forces and powers of existence, there is the necessity to identify this quest with the grand procession of the Empire.

In the *Fourth Eclogue*, then, one finds a self-conscious announcement that the long-sought Golden Age returns with the birth of a child.[262] Through this ever-lasting song, all the virtues of the past, as well as the presence of the gods with humanity, form part of the reconciled aspect of the new age. Nevertheless, this new age is exactly what has been spun by the Fates for Rome.[263] The fixed will of Destiny becomes manifest in time and place for the entire world to witness and enjoy. The sixth book of the *Aeneid* continues to unveil this fated renewal.[264] Through Anchises' prophecy the destiny of Aeneas and of Rome is laid bare. Caesar Augustus becomes the culminating point, the one who is promised to bring the age of Saturn back. The Roman rulers become through this prophetic utterance the instruments of destiny in effecting the Roman mission..

Perhaps the most dramatic instance of the association of the destiny of Rome with the spinning of Fate occurs in Ovid's *Metamorphoses*. Indeed, not only does one find a further vision of what Fate consists in, but also one comes upon the written and unchangeable character of such destiny. Thus, when Venus attempts to prevent the assassination of Julius Caesar, she is shown by Jupiter the records of all that happens on tablets

---

[262]*Fourth Eclogue*, 4ff.

[263]46ff.

[264]*Aeneid*, 6.755ff.

of brass and solid iron. Such massive tablets fear no destructive power, since they are eternal and secure. Venus can only read her descendent's fate engraved on everlasting adamant.[265]

Each poetic piece then attempts to open up, if only briefly, the destined lifeworld of Rome. The writings themselves serve to further this particular understanding of a future which has been eternally engraved. In some respects one has come full circle from the Sophist debate, where the fundamental categories of νόμος and φύσις, set off in antithetical opposition, enabled thinkers to move out of what had been perceived as a constraining situation. But here, in these poets, one finds an intimation of reconciliation, wherein the destiny of Rome carries with it the renewal of nature as well as of convention. Moreover, the attempts at an interpretive understanding which takes in universal issues now become concretized in the relentless unfolding of the Roman tradition. The Letter continues to function in a most positive vein, as propaganda, inviting people to find the realization of their quest for transcendence in the majestic march of the Empire.

Conclusion

Through this admittedly brief and necessarily schematic Excursus I have tried to disclose that the issues which Paul has raised and continued to deal with come from a larger cultural dialogue. Paul is correspondent not only to the dialogue within Hellenistic Judaism but also to the much broader discussion which can be traced back to the Sophistic debate. The human task of coming to grips with the powers and forces transcending human existence has set in motion an interpretive quest to which there has been a variety of responses. Further, one can see, even from this brief investigation, that a continual refining and restating of the question has been accomplished through the distinguishing, opposing, combining, realigning, and reworking of fundamental categories. It is within this ever-shifting dialectic that the concepts of Letter and Tradition emerge,

---

[265]Ovid *Metamorphoses* 15.745ff.; cf. 11.810-15.

for the most part, as positive, interpretive concepts.   Thus, the appreciation and employment of Letter as a mean of unleashing the power of Tradition within Hellenistic Judaism are derived from and continue to explore the issues which haunted the   οἰκουμένη .   This does not deny the particularity of the responses either by Hellenistic Jews or by Paul. On the contrary, the very force of their particular claims is due to the universal concerns with which they deal.   The point of this Excursus has been to indicate that when Paul entered into this intellectual dialogue there already existed a variety of associations available for Paul's particular response.   The impact of his specific choices, seen already in the chapter on Galatians as well as in the following chapters on 2 Corinthians and Romans, can now be viewed within this matrix of possible interpretive options.   Paul, therefore, not only is a creative thinker in regard to the issue of Letter and Tradition but is first of all an heir to this dialectic.

CHAPTER THREE

Spirit and Letter in 2 Corinthians

I. Introduction

Now it is time to turn in this investigation to the explicit usage of πνεῦμα and γράμμα in 2 Cor 3:6. I have argued in chapter two that the antithesis of πνεῦμα and γράμμα underlies the thinking regarding the two different lifeworlds found in Galatians. Now I shall argue that Paul continues to develop both lines of this antithesis due in a very large part to the position of his opposition as well as to that of the Corinthian community. At stake in my line of interpretation is the potential overturning of what the subsequent history of interpretation has understood to be the meaning of this antithesis.[1] The usual distinction of inner and outer, spiritual and material, meaning will be seen more in correspondence with the opponents of Paul rather than with Paul. Moreover, in contrast to the position that Paul has extended himself beyond contemporary categories to produce this simple rhetorical flourish due to his singular eschatological perspective,[2] I shall argue that Paul, at least, begins with an understanding of πνεῦμα and γράμμα shared by his contemporaries and that, working with these presuppositions, he distinguishes his position from theirs. His argument, then, is neither some sleight-of-hand nor a mere tour de force adopted for the occasion; on the contrary, in using the antithesis of πνεῦμα/γράμμα, Paul is

---

[1]See Introduction, above.

[2]See Introduction, p. xvi n. 22.

summoning some of the most potential cultural counters in his attempt to come to grips with the implications of the Christ event.

II. Preliminary Questions and Strategy

For the majority of interpreters in the history of interpretation of 2 Cor 3:6, the meaning and function of πνεῦμα and γράμμα have been remarkably straightforward. The γράμμα has come to signify the outer, material, external meaning, while the πνεῦμα represents the inner, spiritual, and internal meaning. Indeed, this verse has then been utilized in interpreting other difficult texts by using the outer/inner distinction as a principle of interpretation discovered within Scripture itself.[3]   The problem with this longstanding usage is that such an understanding of the πνεῦμα/γράμμα antithesis leaves much to be explained in regard to the relation of vs 6 with that of the surrounding context. For, the most obvious difficulty is that vs 6, if read in its entirety, is not confined to the problem of interpreting a text. The antithesis is used to modify the new covenant to which Paul is a minister. Furthermore, from the preceding Excursus on Letter and tradition, it is not altogether warranted to assume a radical distinction between πνεῦμα and γράμμα. On the contrary, a positive tie between γράμμα and πνεῦμα occurred in many instances.[4] To declare simply that this antithesis is a rhetorical flourish does little to help matters, since, as I have argued in chapter one, the employment of rhetoric only serves to open up the question of purpose of such rhetoric.[5] Finally, the intensification of the antithesis in vs 6c only adds to the dilemma. For what is the reason for the association of life and death with πνεῦμα and γράμμα? Does this hearken back to the findings disclosed in Chapter One?

---

[3]Cf. R. M. Grant, Introduction, p.xii above; also see P. Richardson, "Spirit and Letter: A Foundation for Hermeneutics," *EvangQuart* 45 (1973) 208-18.

[4]See Excursus above.

[5]See Chap. 1, pp. 3-6.

The raising of such questions concerning the meaning of vs 6 makes it rather clear that the usual interpretation of πνεῦμα/γράμμα must be deemed unsatisfactory at best. In the following sections, then, I shall try to come to terms with the meaning of πνεῦμα and γράμμα in light of its particular historical context. To do so the surrounding linguistic field in regard to its rhetorical style and antithetical force will be considered. What shall become evident is that there is a decided lack of apparent connection between the use of this antithesis and the surrounding concerns. In order to reach some line of connection, the issue of self-recommendation and its relation to πνεῦμα and γράμμα will be raised. This direction of questioning will lead to the work of D. Georgi in order to discover what Paul shares with his opponents in regard to these issues. Using some of the insights of Georgi, particularly in regard to vss 7-18, I shall, then, attempt to determine how Paul, in dialogue with both the Corinthians and his opposition, discloses a world of meaning which continues his Galatian response. 2 Cor 3:6 will then be seen not simply as an interpretive principle of texts but as a hermeneutical basis for the fundamental forces of history and culture.

III. The Language Field of 2 Cor 3:6
A. The Rhetorical Movement

To come to some understanding of the language field and line of thought leading to 3:6 requires first of all an appreciation of the rhetorical elements which open up to us the possibilities of a vigorous debate. Although the interpreter is subject to the difficulties of a fragmentary text,[6] one can still discern a variety of rhetorical forms.

---

[6]I am in agreement with the argument that 2 Corinthians is actually a redaction of a number of fragments, namely: 2:14-6:13, 7:2-4; 10-13; 1:1-2:13, 7:5-16; 8; 9; 6:14-7:1 (non-Pauline interpolation). Cf. G. Bornkamm, *Die Vorgeschichte des sogenannten Zweiten Korintherbriefs* (Heidelberg: Winter, 1961). The fragment which contains 3:6 is the earliest of the extant fragments. This fragment strikingly departs from the text at 2:13. The narrative, telling of Paul's departure from Troas to Macedonian in order to meet with Titus, breaks off sharply and is not resumed until 7:5. It has been noted by Weiss that these two parts surrounding 2:14-7:4 fit together "like fragments of a ring." As one

   The fragment containing 3:6 begins with an extended thanksgiving prayer (2:14-16).[7] In these verses there is a thanksgiving formula in its

---

reads through this fragment we see that it differs greatly from the surrounding sections in tone (more demonstrative, assertive or even defensive, rather than reconciliatory), style and argument. Although the subject matter is akin to that described in 1:1ff., one finds that in this fragment the situation appears to be earlier, hoping for reconciliation, while 1:1ff. mentions the achievement of this.

[7]To simply conclude that we are at the original beginning of the fragment because, along the lines of the other authentic Pauline letters, we have a thanksgiving may be overlooking some significant problems. For, despite the fact that we find in 2:14-16 an expression of thanksgiving (χάρις), the object of thanks (τῷ θεῷ), and the reason for thanksgiving (ὅτι . . .), as can be found in the opening thanksgivings in the Pauline corpus (Rom 1:8; 1 Cor 1:4; 2 Cor 1:3; Gal 1:6 (which plays upon the expected pattern); Phil 1:3; 1 Thess 1:2; Phlm 4), the only usage of τῷ δὲ θεῷ χάρις as well as the infrequent inversion of this, χάρις δὲ τῷ θεῷ, appears not at the beginning but *in medias res*. Cf. Rom 6:17; 7:25; 2 Cor 8:16; 9:15. In 1 Cor 15:57 we have the only other instance of τῷ δὲ θεῷ χάρις. There are no parallels in the OT (LXX). But τοῖς θεοῖς χάρις does appear elsewhere. Cf. Xenophon *Anabasis* 3.3.9-15 and *Cyropaedia* 7.5.70-74. In each case we can see that the thanksgiving is used within a rhetorical situation for a particular effect upon the audience's attention. The thanksgiving signals a change in aspect of the situation. Further, the thanksgiving attempts either by giving a basis or by providing an example or both to generate feeling and action within the audience. Lastly, some of these thanksgivings attempt to provide solutions or ways out which had not been within the horizon of the immediate discussion. The thanksgiving becomes a stroke of good fortune and benefaction. While from the examples in Paul it would be difficult then to sustain a position that 2:14-16 represents the original opening thanksgiving of the fragment, the two examples from Xenophon, however, would caution this conclusion, since in both we have a thanksgiving after either a brief address or short defense. Moreover, these thanksgivings become pivotal for the ensuing arguments. Thus, while 2:14-16 may not have been at the original opening as in the other Pauline letters, because of the length of the fragment which follows it, and because it seems to generate the tone and style of the developing argument, I would suggest that it most likely occurred soon after the beginning and functions as an interruption to a defensive situation or accusation.

fullest manifestation.[8] There is the one to whom thanks are offered (τῷ θεῷ), the expression of thanksgiving (χάρις), and the reason for thanksgiving (ὅτι . . .). Furthermore, there is an extensive description of the one thanked through participial parallelism (τῷ . . . θριαμβεύοντι . . . φανεροῦντι . . .). Moreover, two further parallelisms occur in the section indicating the reason for thanksgiving (a. ἐν τοῖς σοζομένοις καὶ ἐν τοῖς ἀπολλυμένοις ; b. οἷς μὲν ἐκ θανάτου εἰς θάνατον, οἷς δὲ ὀσμὴ ἐκ ζωῆς εἰς ζωήν).

This thanksgiving is in turn followed immediately by a rhetorical question (2:16c).[9] Vs 17 continues this rhetorical movement by indicating a defensive stance, suggested not only by the rhetorical topos of the sophist as a hawker of truth[10] but also by a marked antithesis (οὐ . . . ὡς οἱ πολλοὶ καπηλεύοντες . . . ἀλλ᾽ ὡς ἐξ εἰλικρινείας, ἀλλ᾽ ἐκ θεοῦ . . . λαλοῦμεν).

The next sentence continues the rhetorical momentum with two more rhetorical questions (3:1). Indeed, the second rhetorical question actually contains two in itself. 3:2-3 is, in effect, a purposeful *captatio benevolentiae*.[11] In 3:1 Paul rhetorically dismisses the need for letters of recommendation as well as the charge of self-recommendation. He does not stop with this declaration alone, but indicates through a series of participles not only the nature of the letter but also its effect and communal ground (ἡ ἐπιστολὴ . . . ἐγγεγραμμένη . . .

---

[8]J. Robinson, "Die Hodajot-Formel in Gebet und Hymnus des Frühchristentums," in *Festschrift für E. Haenchen*, 194-235.

[9]Cf. Joel 2:11. Here we find the closest OT (LXX) allusion. Quite striking is that this chapter's context well suits the triumphal thanksgiving of 2:14-16.

[10]Cf. Plato *Protagoras* 313Dff.

[11]Cf. Quintilian 4.1.5ff.; cf. H. Lausberg, *Handbuch der literarischen Rhetorik* (Munich: Heuber, 1973) 152-60.

γινωσκομένη   . . .   ἀναγινωσκομένη   . . .   (ὑμεῖς)
φανερούμενοι . . . ἐπιστολὴ . . . διακονηθεῖσα . . .
ἐγγεγραμμένη). Further there is the appearance once again of
antithetical language (οὐ   μέλανι ἀλλὰ πνεύματί . . . οὐκ
ἐν πλαξὶν λιθίναις ἀλλ᾿ ἐν πλαξὶν καρδίαις
σαρκίναις) Vs 4 adds an assertion of confidence (with πεποίθησιν
emphasized) which is then immediately qualified by another antithesis in
vs 5 (οὐχ ὅτι ἀφ᾿ ἑαυτῶν ἱκανοί . . . ἀλλ᾿ ἡ ἱκανότης
ἡμῶν . . .). The sixth verse actually begins as a modifier of τοῦ
θεοῦ, throwing the emphasis more actively upon θεός and further
subordinating the position of ἡμεῖς. The πνεῦμα/γράμμα antithesis
arises then as another modification, this time of the καινὴ διαθήκη.
Vs 6c,, however, shifts the emphasis from a modification of διαθήκη
to the very action of πνεῦμα and γράμμα.

   In this brief examination of the various forms which lead up to 3:6,
one finds within such short a space a remarkable fluidity. The movement
goes from an elaborate thanksgiving to a rhetorical question, a defensive
explanation, more rhetorical questions, a *captatio benevolentiae*, and an
assertion of confidence modified by the reason for this confidence.

   Within the rapid-fire movement of this rhetorical onslaught by Paul
three particular aspects begin to emerge. Paul has taken his position
within a horizon where the matter at hand is revelatory, a situation of life
or death, and is somehow associated with the question of competence. In
regard to the first aspect, one sees described in the thanksgiving (2:14-
16b) the universal triumphant scene of Christ, whose worldwide progress
resembles the advance of Dionysius.[12] This universal triumph is revealed
through ἡμεῖς through whom God manifests the fragrance of his
knowledge. Furthermore, this revelatory activity proves to be both death-
dealing (ἐκ θανάτου εἰς θάνατον) and lifegiving (ἐκ ζωῆς
εἰς ζωήν). The triumphal pageant's revelation has eschatological

---

[12]Cf. Euripides *Bacchae* 11.

markings, since this manifestation is intrinsically linked with the fate of humanity, destined now for life or death.[13]

    This dualistic aspect of life or death not only directly relates to 3:6 but it is actually continued from 2:14 up to 3:6 and even beyond it.[14] Thus, on the "death" side one can note the following:

Those who hawk the word of God	2:17
Those who use letters of recommendation	3:1
the letter written in ink	3:3
the letter written on stone	3:3
regarding oneself as self-sufficient	3:5
covenant of the letter	3:6
the letter kills	3:6

On the other side of the ledger, a positive series within this remarkable line of antithesis can be discerned:

"We" who speak sincerely	2:17
"We" who speak ἐκ θεοῦ, κατέναντι θεοῦ, ἐν Χριστῷ	2:17
"We" need no self-recommendation	3:1
"We" make no use of letters of recommendation	3:1
letter written πνεύματι on fleshly tablets of heart	3:3
competence is from God	3:5
new covenant of spirit	3:6
the spirit gives life	3:6

One notices not only the sustained antithetical tension throughout this section, but also that the life-death issue introduced in 2:15-16 is intertwined with the further aspect of competence. The first indication of this is in 2:16c (καὶ πρὸς ταῦτα τίς ἱκανός). While this might

---

[13]Cf. Excursus, pp. 74-77.

[14]3:7ff; see pp. 131-132 below.

be an allusion to Joel 2:11,[15] the tie-in with vs 17, featuring the antithesis between the genuine speaker and the sophist must be considered. Moreover, this question, bearing such rhetorical background, is linked to the issue of who is "able" to utter such things in the presence of God and from God as a source (κατέναντι θεοῦ, ἐκ θεοῦ). Furthermore, this issue of competency is apparently connected with how one is perceived as competent. The use of ὡς by Paul,[16] distinguishing those hawking the word from those who speak sincerely, comes sharply into play. Indeed, when the issue of competency resurfaces in 3:5, where Paul distinguishes the source of his competency (ἐκ τοῦ θεοῦ) from self-sufficiency (ἀφ' ἑαυτῶν ἱκανοί), he again reiterates the perceptual question (ὡς ἐξ ἑαυτῶν).

It is within the concern for competency that the issue of letters of recommendation arises (3:1-3). Both the rhetorical questions and the following *captatio benevolentiae* play upon the word ἐπιστολή. Having first denied the need to produce any letter of recommendation, Paul then dramatically shifts the reference of ἐπιστολή to the community with whom he is in dialogue (ἡ ἐπιστολὴ ἡμῶν ὑμεῖς ἐστε). Not only does this new "letter" play to his audience but the community is made part of the progress of the revelatory triumph. This is quite vividly expressed by φανερούμενοι, referring distinctly to the community. Moreover, while this "letter" is ministered to by Paul, continuing his agent function (2:14, δι' ἡμῶν; 2:15, εὐοδία ἐσμέν), the letter itself is an ἐπιστολή Χριστοῦ. It would appear that the community functions as a heavenly letter,[17] which continues the process of the revelatory procession in 2:14-15. Moreover, the eschatological situation indicated in 2:15-16 continues in the community. This "letter" of Christ is written not in ink but in the Spirit of the living

---

[15]See p. 111 n. 9 above.

[16]Cf. ὡς, BAG, 898.3.2; BDF, 425.3.

[17]Cf. L. Röhrich, "Himmelsbrief", RGG[3], 338-39.

God. While Paul may to some extent be playing upon the Hellenistic distinction of what is written in ink and what is written on the soul or heart,[18] the distinction is not merely one of external versus internal or artificial versus natural. Rather, the language appears to come from the eschatological visions of Ezekial and Jeremiah:

καὶ δώσω αὐτοῖς καρδίαν ἑτέραν καὶ πνεῦμα

καινὸν δώσω ἐν αὐτοῖς καὶ ἐκσπάσω τὴν καρδίαν

τὴν λιθίνην ἐκ τῆς σαρκὸς αὐτῶν καὶ δώσω αὐτοῖς

καρδίαν σαρκίνην.   Ezek 11:19 (LXX)

καὶ δώσω ὑμῖν καρδίαν καινὴν καὶ πνεῦμα καινὸν

δώσω ἐν ὑμῖν καὶ ἀφελῶ τὴν καρδίαν τὴν λιθίνην

ἐκ τῆς σαρκὸς ὑμῶν καὶ δώσω ὑμῖν καρδίαν σαρκίνην

Ezek 36:26 (LXX)

ὅτι αὕτη ἡ διαθήκη, ἣν διαθήσομαι τῷ οἴκῳ Ἰσραὴλ

μετὰ τὰς ἡμέρας ἐκείνας, φησὶν κύριος Διδοὺς δώσω

νόμους μοῦ εἰς τὴν διάνοιαν αὐτῶν καὶ ἐπὶ καρδίας

αὐτῶν γράψω αὐτούς· καὶ ἔσομαι αὐτοῖς εἰς θεόν

καὶ αὐτοὶ ἔσονταί μοι εἰς λαόν.   Jer 38:33 (LXX)

What is significant for our investigation is that while the passages from Ezekial and Jeremiah may have served as a horizon for 3:3c, Paul is not quoting verbatim.[19] This has already been noticed in Chapter One.[20] Moreover, there is a decided nuance in Paul's antithesis. Instead of the antithesis between the stoney heart and the fleshly one, Paul distinguishes

---

[18]See Excursus, pp. 58-60, 86-87, 93-96.

[19]One can easily see how these texts could function as missionary documents in the first century.

[20]Cf. Chap. One, pp. 34-36, 36-38, 50-51.

between the stoney tablets and fleshly tablets of the heart. This antithesis is in line with the preceding distinction between the letter written in ink and one written in Spirit. Thus, while the prophetic texts provide us with an eschatological aspect, they do not explain Paul's curious distinction between stoney and fleshy tablets.[21]

What we have thus found so far is that within 2:14-3:6, replete with rhetorical twists and turns, a number of issues emerge. But with this emergence comes the question: what is the line of thought connecting the issues of revelation, life and death, self-recommendation, letters of recommendation, new covenant, competency and ministry? What world or worlds of meaning are at play here? What historical situation is the basis of such a curious line of development? Moreover, if one were to move beyond 3:6 into 3:7-18, the problem becomes even more complicated. The comparison of the ministry of Moses with the ministry of the Spirit, the surprising interpretation of Exodus 34, the amount of energy spent with the written "letter", are but a few of the questions which seem to have no immediate connection with the line of thought already advanced. In order to make some sense of this predicament, I turn to the previous correspondence with Corinth to see if there are any intimations of the issues that have been just now disclosed. Then, taking a clue from the rhetorical elements in the text, I shall investigate the language of opposition to determine the reason for the issues which have emerged. In other words, what world of meaning does Paul share with either the community or his opposition? 2 Corinthians 10-13 will then be brought in to see whether there is anything there to help fill out this many-faceted dialogue.

---

[21]Cf. Excursus, pp. 86-87, 93-95.

B. The Previous Correspondence[22]

From 1 Corinthians one can find that, while there is no apparent need for Paul to recommend either himself or provide some means of recommendation, his dialogue with the community does presuppose intimations of the issues which have been disclosed in the fragment under consideration. Although Paul is at great pains to redirect the focus of interpretation of the community away from an individualistic spiritual position to one which seeks the upbuilding of the community, he does share with the community certain understandings of the life in the Spirit. First, the presence of the Spirit both enables revelation (1 Cor 2:10) and makes those in the Spirit competent to judge spiritual affairs (1 Cor 2:12, 15-16).

Secondly, the presence of the Spirit was manifested through demonstration (1 Cor 2:4b; 12:8ff.; 14:23-25) of power and the various gifts. Thirdly, the presence of the Spirit was indicative of the final age (1 Cor 1:8; 7:29, 31; 10:11), wherein the scriptural account of the wilderness experience becomes an instructive warning to those in the community (1 Cor 10:6ff.). This last point, however, should be tempered by the fact that it is Paul in 1 Corinthians who repeatedly introduces a distinction between the present and the future (e.g., 1 Cor 1:7-8; 3:13; 4:5; 13:12-13; 15:20ff.) in order to prevent misconstruing the presence of various spiritual demonstrations for the presence of the endtime. The Corinthians may well have interpreted the message and their pneumatic experiences along the lines of a detachment of the spiritual from the world and, hence, from communal responsibility.[23] Despite these intimations within 1 Corinthians, there are a number of unresolved questions. First,

---

[22]1 Cor 5:9 would indicate that there had been an earlier letter to Corinth which has been lost. Speculation that 2 Cor 6:14-7:1 is that letter fails to consider how unpauline this fragment is, both linguistically and theologically. Cf. H.D. Betz, "2 Cor 6:14-7:1: An Anti-Pauline Fragment?" JBL 92 (1973) 88-108; H. Conzelmann, 1 Corinthians (Philadelphia: Fortress, 1975) 2-5.

[23]Cf. Conzelmann, *1 Corinthians*, 14-16.

why does Paul emphasize so dramatically the eschatological presence in 2
Cor 2:14ff.; 3:3; 3:6, when he had recently advised for a more patient
vision? Secondly, why is there a need for recommendation from one who
has been consulted by the Corinthians on such practical matters? Why
must Paul adopt such a polemical tone from the outset in this fragment?
What situation could have resulted in what seems to be a decided shift in
relations?

C. The Language of Opposition: An Internal Approach

The first suggestion of opposition within this fragment is found in the
negative comparison of 2:17.   Indeed, this explanation (γάρ) at first
seems unexpected after 2:14-16. A possible clue to a connection can be
found in the rhetorical question πρὸς ταῦτα τις ἱκανός . Not only
does it convey the dramatic sense of the universal and eschatological
scene of vss 14-16, but it also touches on the issue of competency within
the following verses. By his comparison in vs 17, Paul immediately
distinguishes between the genuine and non-genuine messenger. Indeed, it
is not simply a matter of a hawker of God's word versus a sincere
messenger, but rather the additional antithetical phrase (ἀλλ' ὡς ἐκ
θεοῦ) relates the question of competency to the very basis or ground of
one's speech.24

This relation of competency and the source of one's action recurs
in 3:5. Again Paul is at pains to distinguish that he does not consider his
competency to come from himself (ἐξ ἑαυτῶν) but from God (ἐκ
τοῦ θεοῦ). However, this reiteration of his own understanding of the
question of competency must be seen within the dialogue with the
Corinthian community. The rhetorical questions raised in 3:1, which,
along with the *captatio benevolentiae* of 3:2, attempt to dismiss both the
charge   of   self-recommendation   and   the   need   for   letters   of
recommendation, allow the reader an entrance into the possible self-

---

24Thus,   κατέναντι θεοῦ ἐν Χριστῷ   (2:17) becomes even more
significant for it defines for Paul a possibly forensic sphere and position of his
preaching.

understanding of the community. In employing such rhetorical tactics Paul has anticipated what may well be the Corinthians' perspective, namely, that without some sort of letter of recommendation Paul is left vulnerable to the charge that he is merely recommending himself.[25] Moreover, this new perception of Paul by the community would seem to be brought about by others who preach and employ such letters of recommendation.

The definite note of confidence in 3:4[26] takes on, then, added significance in light of the dialogue with the Corinthian community. This declaration is made only after deflecting the charge of self-recommendation and with further clarification (διὰ τοῦ Χριστοῦ πρὸς τὸν θεόν). Indeed, Paul is careful to assert his competency as minister of the New Covenant only after noting that God is the source and active granter of such competence (vss 5-6a).[27] Now it is precisely in the context of the question of competency that the distinction between γράμμα and πνεῦμά appears. The New Covenant is "of Spirit" not "of Letter." A question which immediately arises is: if Paul through his previous antithetical distinctions has anticipated the Corinthians' possible association of competency and letters of recommendation, could not this antithesis of γράμμα and πνεῦμα be an anticipation of a similar association? Moreover, from vs 6 and what follows (vss 7-18)[28] one can see that Paul is separating the New Covenant of lifegiving Spirit from the fatal Letter, associated with the ministry of Moses (3:7ff.). Could Paul not also here be anticipating the Corinthians' possible connection between the New Covenant and the ministry of Moses? In other words, the

---

[25]Cf. 4:5, ἑαυτοὺς κηρύσσομεν ; 5:12, ἑαυτοὺς συνιστάνομεν.

[26]Note the emphatic position of πεποίθησιν.

[27]Paul has already intimated his ministry in 3:3, διακονηθεῖσα ὑφ' ἡμῶν, but there the emphasis is upon the Corinthians' role as the revealing ἐπιστολὴ Χριστοῦ.

[28]See pp. 131-132 below.

positive association of γράμμα and πνεῦμα, of New Covenant and the ministry of Moses, might very well be the presupposition of Paul's antithetical response. Furthermore, the overarching question of competency, out of which Paul's distinctions are made, must play a fundamental role in this line of possible association.

Finally, despite the recurring declarations of confidence (3:12; 4:1; 4:16), based upon the conviction that his ministry is of the πνεῦμα, of δικαιοσύνη (3:8, 9), that it has an enduring glory (3:11), in contrast to that of Moses, the competency of Paul's ministry has been placed in question by the probable charge[29] that his gospel is veiled (4:3). This veiled condition of his gospel may be due to the fact that Paul bears the message not through any extraordinary means but by his fragile humanity (4:7-12). By proclaiming his gospel in such a fashion, Paul could well have left himself open to the typical rhetorical charge that he is really indulging in deceit and deception (4:2) by not demonstrating the full power of his message.[30] While he declares that the Corinthians should

---

[29]Note that Paul grants the condition εἰ δὲ καὶ ἔστιν . . . , which he then turns to his advantage by putting it into the eschatological framework established in 2:14-16. Also, the introduction of this possible charge is quite abrupt, yet it is strategically placed after he has "unveiled" the ministry of Moses and only after he prepares the listeners by anticipating the charges of deceit (4:2).

[30]Such language is typical in attempting to expose the limitations and deceit of a false religious group. E.g., in *Spec. leg.* 1.314-23, Philo opposes the followers of mystic rites who reserve the benefits for a few and avoid the public. Moses forbids such a path and opts for a public way of life, where virtue is for the common good and a spectacle of vision for all. Just as nature does not conceal its works, so neither should the virtuous one. Cf. *Phaedrus* 243, 247, 249; Soc. 1.2; Dem. 6.31 in *The Cynic Epistles*, ed., A. Malherbe (Missoula: Scholars, 1977). Paul is quite aware of this rhetorical strategy and takes his position right from the start of this fragment in a public context (2:14). Indeed, the entire world is the forum for the issue. Moreover, he points out his sincerity (2:17) of speech which is done in God's sight. Further, this public proclamation has been confirmed and augmented by the Corinthian community (3:2).

take their advantage from his writing against those who are proud of their public appearance (ἐν προσώπῳ , 5:12), it is precisely because Paul has not publicly demonstrated the power of his gospel that renders him susceptible of such charges.[31] Thus, in inspecting the possible traces of opposition within the rhetorical twists and turns of this fragment, one can discern that the issue of competency is very much a determining question. Through noting the possible anticipations by Paul of the community's presuppositions, one can detect that the issue of competency is directly related to the confirmation of the presence of the Spirit. Both letters of recommendation and some sort of public display would enable the community to judge these "spiritual matters."[32] Now the antithesis of γράμμα/πνεῦμα has been set within this context. In contrast to Paul's distinct separation of πνεῦμα from γράμμα , it has been suggested that the Corinthians may not have been working on this disjunction. On the contrary, it would seem more probable, given Paul's strategy of argument, that the Corinthians have assumed that the presence of the Spirit is to be gauged by some confirmation of the competency of the bearer of the message. The γράμμα, then, could have been positively aligned with the πνεῦμα,[33] furnishing such a verification. Before we consider this positive association of πνεῦμα and γράμμα,[34] we must take into consideration the subsequent letter in this Corinthian correspondence to appreciate the depth of this issue of verification of the presence of the Spirit.

---

[31]See pp. 122-124 below. This public demonstration of his gospel must be connected to the need for letters of recommendation, another public confirmation of one's message.

[32]See p. 118 above.

[33]See pp. 124-128 below.

[34]Cf. Excursus above.

D. The Language of Opposition Continued: 2 Corinthians 10-13

The question of the objective verifiability of the presence of the Spirit is the underlying concern for this subsequent fragment in 2 Corinthians.[35] Indeed, the overarching irony behind this fragment is that the previous letter had been considered by both the Corinthians and Paul's opponents as an effective demonstration of the Spirit (10:10a). However, his subsequent appearance before the community did nothing to confirm this impression. On the contrary, a marked discrepancy evidently existed between his powerful letters and his personal presentation.[36] From the perspective of the community and the opposition, such a negative experience was an indication that Paul was not of the Spirit but was walking κατὰ σάρκα (10:2). His previous claims, even his impressive letter, could not be documented by anything other than his weak physical presence and worthless speech (10:10b). Without any objective verification of the value of his claims, Paul's position became subject to the charge that he was merely boasting (10:8), a matter of self-recommendation (10:12).

This charge of self-recommendation returns one back to 2 Cor 3:1ff. In other words, the ground of judgment employed by the Corinthians remains fundamentally the same. They have not seen his previous letter as a deflection of the summons for some objective verification, rather they have read it with their basic presuppositions intact. It is from this recognition of where the community stands that Paul begins his "apology".[37] The community evidently continues to

---

[35]Chaps. 10-13 do not connect well with the preceding chapters. There is a decided change in tone, style and topic. Certainly it is not a fitting conclusion to a plea for a collection. On the other hand, the issues as argued above resemble those of the first fragment, but with indications that relations are greatly strained, if not almost "lost".

[36]Cf. 10:11; 10:1; 11:6.

[37]For a treatment of the Apology of Paul, cf. H. D. Betz, *Der Apostel Paulus und die sokratische Tradition: Eine exegetische Untersuchung zu seiner "Apologie" 2 Korinthen 10-13* (Tübingen: Mohr, 1972).

exercise its "spiritual discrimination" (1 Cor 2:12ff.) in allowing missionaries to demonstrate their spiritual gifts (2 Cor 10:12b). In accepting this position, Paul notes, that in this warfare of the Spirit (2 Cor 10:3-6), he does not operate on such presuppositions. His standard of measurement (κανών) is not one of self-recommendation nor of comparison (10:12). Rather, it is intimately tied to the Corinthian community (ἐφικέσθαι ἄχρι καὶ ὑμῶν , vs 13). In criticizing those who would boast in the labors of others,[38] Paul points out that his κανών is the community's increase in faith.[39] It is not a matter of documenting one's accomplishments, which would emphasize the standard of the competent individual (10:18a), rather it is the upbuilding of the community (12:19b) which is at stake for him.

Nevertheless, the Corinthians' presupposition of some objective verification of the presence of the Spirit remains within the horizons of Paul's response. Accepting the charge of "boasting" in the ironic tradition of Socrates, he turns his "defense" into a comic affair.[40] The typical criteria of the spiritual individual, namely, grand accomplishments,[41] acceptance of well-deserved monetary reward,[42] and visions,[43] are parodied to the point of absurdity. The standard of the acceptable spiritual individual has been strategically presented in fool's

---

[38]10:15.

[39]10:15b; 12:19b; cf. also 1 Cor 4:6; 8:1; 10:23; 14:5.

[40]Cf. H. D. Betz, *Paulus und die sokratische Tradition*, chap. 3.

[41]11:23ff. This is a parody of aretalogies.

[42]11:7-11. Cf. 1 Cor 9:14. Paul's refusal to accept their money not only opened him up to the charge of deceit (12:16) but also prevented the community from expressing what they considered to be his spiritual worth.

[43]12:1-9. A parody of heavenly revelations, ending in a completely comic situation.

apparel.[44] By overturning what are considered to be basic criteria for determining the worth of the claims of a missionary, Paul is, in effect, disengaging the presence of the Spirit from such documentation. He has short-circuited the connection between the power of one's message and the typical verifications presupposed by the community. His message cannot be confirmed by an overpowering presence, nor by grand speech, nor by wonders nor even by ecstasies. The power of his message is found in the undocumentable life of the community itself. In short, Paul continues to speak out of the perspective which has already been indicated (2 Cor 3:1-6). This perspective, however, in light of its misinterpretation by the community and the much needed reinterpretation by Paul, would seem to be going very much against the basic cultural and theological grain, whereby the presence of the Spirit is radically associated with such objective documentation. It is time now to consider this understanding of Spirit in regard to the previous Excursus on Letter and tradition and the pioneering work of D. Georgi.

IV. The Opponents of Paul according to D. Georgi

What has emerged so far through an internal inspection of the fragmentary correspondence of 2 Corinthians, in regard to the need for an objective documentation of the presence of the Spirit, can be situated within the historical and theological dialogue of its time. Largely through the magisterial work of D. Georgi one can discern that the fundamental issues underlying the dialogue with the Corinthian community were part and parcel of the missionary sphere of the Hellenistic world.[45] Indeed, Georgi has argued that the opponents of Paul were not unusual; on the

---

[44]Cf. D. Georgi, "Folly", *IDBSup*, 340-41.

[45]D. Georgi, *Die Gegner des Paulus im 2. Korintherbrief.*

contrary, they represented perhaps a majority of the missionary groups in the ancient world.[46]

The contribution of Georgi has been to throw considerable light upon the lacunae of previous research. Most particularly Georgi attempts to deal with the issue of scriptural interpretation of the opponents in light of 2 Corinthians 3.[47] Moreover, in the course of his work, he has shown the connection of Spirit and Law, as well as uncovering the traditions and social situations wherein the titles designating the opposition have meaning.[48] Thus, according to Georgi, the opponents of Paul came out of the sphere of Hellenistic Jewish apologetic and sought to capitalize on the previous success of the Jewish mission.[49] These opponents represented a growing tendency within the early Jesus movement and enjoyed considerable prestige before they appeared on the scene in Corinth.[50] Furthermore they had a great feeling for tradition which focused on a pronounced pneumatic self-consciousness. In gathering the true power of the past, the opponents sought to demonstrate the power of the spirit in the present through such a breakthrough as to surpass the present existence.[51]

Now the locus for such a demonstration of the power of the Spirit in Hellenistic Judaism was synagogue worship wherein the exposition of Scripture was done.[52] Synagogue worship was the place of pneumatic

---

[46]Ibid., 218: "Die Gegner des Paulus im Zweiten Korintherbrief waren also keine singulären Gestalten, sondern Repräsentantem einer großen Gruppe von Missionaren der Urchristenheit, vielleicht sogar einer Mehrheit."

[47]Ibid., 14.

[48]Ibid., 31-82.

[49]Ibid., 205ff.

[50]Ibid., 301ff.

[51]Ibid., 114ff.

[52]Ibid., 94ff.

power within an almost theatrical setting.[53]   In such a situation the exegete of Scripture was considered a contemporary prophet.[54] Indeed, the competency or capability of the exegete was demonstrated in the worship service by bringing forth the divine power contained in Scripture. The interpretation of Scripture was the essential means of communication of the Spirit.[55] In proving themselves competent not only to open up the Scripture but also to enable their followers to likewise transcend themselves, the exegetes could lay hold of the tradition of θεῖοι ἄνδρες.[56] Thus, the issue of ἱκανότης which has been part of the investigation from the start becomes clarified. For the opponents of Paul, through their demonstrations of their competence, are inviting the Corinthian community to judge whether the pneumatic process was manifested through their powerful achievements.   The opponents, in effect, are continuing the tradition established in the Hellenistic Jewish mission.

Letters of recommendation likewise are part of the overall picture of this missionary advance.[57] For these letters once more document the competency of these men to bring forth the power of the Spirit. Letter, then, was a documentation of Spirit. Indeed, the entire tradition of the Jewish people, the text as well as the heroes, could be seen as the movement of the Spirit. The written Scripture especially was considered

---

[53]Ibid., 131ff.

[54]Ibid., 128; cf. Excursus, pp. 69-70.

[55]Ibid., 134: ". . . in den im Gottesdienst gezeigten Leistungen der besonders Befähigten sich die in der Heiligen Schrift erhaltene göttliche Potenz auf mannigfaltige Weise erschloßund aktualisierte. Die Schriftauslegung war das wesentliche Medium dieser Selbstdarstellung und Mitteilung des Geistes.

[56]Ibid., 168ff.

[57]Ibid., 241-45.

an effective container of the Spirit.[58] In fact, γράμμα used in the singular could stand for the entire tradition. The spiritual power within the tradition is so strong that it is necessary to contain it by a veil—the written text—and to control it.[59] Only a proper method used by competent people can tap and profitably employ this tradition for the well-being of the world and the individual. This method was that of allegorical exegesis.[60] The Letter and Spirit were not opposed but needed each other to bring about further progress in the Spirit.

It is in light of this understanding of tradition that the figure of Moses assumes enormous importance. Not only is Moses the θεῖος ἀνήρ par excellence, but it is he whose activity on Mt. Sinai becomes the paradigm for others to pass beyond human limitations. The Hellenistic Jewish tradition surrounding Exodus 33-34 shows no trace of a renewal of a broken covenant. Rather the text is treated as the climax of Moses' experience of God and the basis of the experience of transcendence in general.[61] By placing the figure of Moses and the material from Exodus 34 of 2 Cor 3:7ff. within this extended context, Georgi has argued that Paul is basically utilizing and glossing severely the method and materials of the opposition. He contends that for the opponents the turning of Moses to the Lord becomes a type of turning to the text to be allegorized. The opponents have equated the veil with the Letter of the text, that is, with the literal sense. The Spirit does not stand in opposition to the Letter, rather the Letter both covers up the Spirit and points the way to its disclosure. The Letter of the text for the allegorist is a mirror of the Spirit which makes possible the true vision.[62]

---

[58]Ibid., 265-73.

[59]Ibid.

[60]Ibid., 168ff.; cf. Excursus, pp. 65-70.

[61]Cf. Philo *Vit. Mos.* 2.70ff.; Josephus *Ant.* 3.99ff.

[62]Georgi, *Die Gegner*, 177.

What Georgi has done is to show that usually positive relation of Letter and tradition, which has been indicated in the previous Excursus, is fundamental to the self-understanding and mission of the opponents of Paul. In the Excursus it has been pointed out that the Letter was seen as the bearer or conveyor of tradition wherein one gained both self-definition as well as political or cultural power.[63] In getting to the roots of Letter and tradition it was found that the Letter could be seen as a means of entrance into the traditions of religion and culture.[64] The Letter, in short, becomes the means of advancement of civilization. Indeed, through the Letter one could come in contact with the basis of the cosmos, with the advance of history, with the preordained decrees of heaven.[65] The opponents of Paul, then, are very much in dialogue with this understanding of Letter. For them Letter is a positive means of entering into the arena of the Spirit. The missionary thrust of their modus operandi very much rests on this presupposition.

Another way of saying this is that through his opposition Paul has come face to face with the fundamental understanding of Letter and tradition. What has been seen already in the chapter on Galatians now becomes quite explicit. Paul must deal at point blank range with a lifeworld which is supported by an understanding of Spirit which is continuous with the world as it presently is and can be. Not only do the opponents of Paul have at their disposal this positive cultural momentum but also they can assert that their spiritual demonstration of the Letter can bring the Corinthians to the font of reality itself. More, their claims of objective demonstrations of their competence play upon the cultural presupposition that Spirit is conveyed and effected through such means. In short, the opposition seems to have Paul at quite a disadvantage.

---

[63]Cf. Excursus, passim.

[64]Cf. Excursus, pp. 55ff.

[65]Cf. Excursus, pp. 74ff.; 104ff.

V. The Lifeworlds of Letter and Spirit
A. The Pauline Difference

In light of the contribution of Georgi in regard to the self-understanding of the opponents of Paul, the antithesis of 2 Cor 3:6c becomes quite startling. However, this antithesis is not entirely unanticipated. An antithetical momentum has been underway from the outset of this fragment. Both in terms of language[66] and of content[67] a distinctive antithetical focus has been achieved. Moreover, the antithesis of 2 Cor 3:6b does not carry by itself the force of 3:6c. Indeed, according to Georgi's construction of the self-understanding of the opponents, the distinction οὐ γράμματος , ἀλλὰ πνεύματος could have been well employed by the opposition, inasmuch as this distinction is not exclusive but refers to the difference between the literal and spiritual understandings of the text. The spiritual level would be needed to complete the meaning of the literal.[68] Thus, the major difference of opinion between Paul and his opponents would appear to rest in 3:6c where the Letter, instead of serving as a positive step in the process of transcendence, takes on a deadly aspect. Indeed, the antithesis emphasizes precisely the activity and power of γράμμα and πνεῦμα. Not only does the γράμμα kill but πνεῦμα brings about eschatological

---

[66]Pp. 113-114 above.

[67]Pp. 114-115 above.

[68]The Letter (γράμμα) would not be seen in such a negative light; rather it would function as the first step in the search for understanding. Moreover, the phrase καινὴ διαθήκη could also have been used by the opponents, but not in any exclusive manner. The new covenant would not dismiss the former but would in fact be the depth of what had been given in the past. The new covenant could well take on the characteristic of an eternal covenant (cf. Qumran, pp. 77-81 above) which undergirds and grounds what has been given in history.

life.[69] The eschatological setting indicated already in 2:14ff. is continued here in the sharpest of terms.

The task of this section, then, is to investigate 2 Cor 3:7-18 in light of this dramatic antithesis. My contention is that 2 Cor 3:6c becomes the guiding or leading principle of interpretation for the following verses. This will be shown through an analysis of vss 7-18, whereby linguistic equivalents in these verses continue the momentum and the basic understanding proposed in 3:6c. What shall become clear is that Paul is once more concerned with the perspectives of two lifeworlds, the lifeworld of Letter and Spirit.

In order to assist this investigation, I shall employ the rule of thumb of Georgi in determining the possible position of the opponents of Paul within these verse. This will enable me to situate the language and ideas of Paul within the overriding cultural context of Letter and tradition. Paul will not be seen, then, as an isolated thinker but as someone engaged in this cultural dialogue wherein he takes a very different stance. Now Georgi's rule of thumb is this: in order to see what may well be due to the traditions of the opponents and that due to Paul's creative response we will consider all negatively critical remarks allotted to Paul, while definite positive assertions will be marked down to his opposition.[70] This rule of thumb is quite suggestive for this investigation since what seem at first glance to be but incongruous associations become very plausible connections within the operational horizon of the missionary opponents of Paul. In using this tool, one is able to see how the numerous jumps in associations of words, ideas and themes are basically occasioned by Paul's employment of the language and theological strategy of his opposition. By so disclosing the probable position of the opposition, one can see in very clear terms how greatly Paul transposes the entire score of the

---

[69]R. Bultmann, " ζωοποιέω κτλ ," *TDNT* 2. 874-75; cf. Chap. One above, pp. 46-47.

[70]Cf. Georgi, *Die Gegner*, 274ff.

argument. For Paul, in setting off the Letter against the Spirit, is definitely playing in another key.

B. Analysis of 2 Cor 3:7-18

The lifeworlds of Letter and Spirit are immediately set in opposition through three successive comparisons (vss 7-8, 9, 11). While each comparison argues a minori ad maius, in contrast to the balanced comparisons of vs 9 and vs 11, vss 7-8 present a rather disproportionate comparison. Why is Paul so concerned to spell out in such a heavy-handed fashion the lesser side of the comparison? Moreover, he characterizes the lesser ministry as ἡ διακονία τοῦ θανάτου as well as carved in γράμμασιν λίθοις . This last remark obviously refers back to ἐν πλαξὶν λιθίναις of vs 3. Further there is a change in tense from the aorist ἐγενήθη to the future ἔσται. Finally the phrase ὥστε μή . . . τὴν καταργουμένην apparently refers back to Exod 34:29ff.

However, when one reads Exodus 34, as well as the accounts in Philo[71]and Josephus,[72] the language of vs 7 becomes quite jarring. Both the description of the ministry (τοῦ θανάτου) and that of the glory from Moses' face (τὴν καταργουμένην) are quire unexpected. Moreover, the result clause ὥστε μή . . . provides more an interpretation than a description of Exodus 34. This language, on the other hand, is not surprising when one considers the preceding antithetical language (from 2:14ff.), especially that of vs 6c. If one, then, were to remove τοῦ θανάτου and τὴν καταργουμένην , along with εἰ δέ,[73] then vs 7 becomes very amenable to the self-understanding of Paul's opposition. The ministry of Moses would be seen as most glorious, the covenant carved in stone would be objective evidence of this

---

[71]Philo *Vit. Mos.* 2.70ff.

[72]Josephus *Ant.* 3.99ff.

[73] εἰ provides the sign of Paul's condition, δέ the connection with vs 6.

event, the peoples' inability to look on the face of Moses would be a further proof of the transcendent power. What we would then have before us is most likely the positive assertion of Paul's opposition to the effect that these missionaries stand within this tradition of Moses. There would neither be any negative indication nor any suggestion of a gap between the ministry of Moses and that of the opposition.[74] Rather, glory and continuity would be their watchwords. However, this is exactly what we find in vs 8 with not only the different description of ministry (τοῦ πνεύματος) but also of time (future rather than past). Thus, vs 8, demonstrating such an enormous break, would be ascribed to Paul. In sum, then, the disproportionate weight of the comparison in vs 7 is due to Paul's likely employment of his opposition's position, which he significantly transforms into his antithetical understanding. The ministry of Moses is linked especially with the Letter, but this ministry is characterized by death and transiency. The very appeal to the objective archive of the Mosaic tradition is situated within an understanding that sees no lifegiving future to it. On the other hand, the contrasting ministry of Spirit, by the force of the rhetorical question, conveys a lifeworld of both surpassing glory and future hope.

Verse 9 continues this comparison of two lifeworlds, but now under the eschatological terms of κατακρίσις and δικαιοσύνη .[75] This would immediately suggest the understanding of Paul. Moreover, the use of the explanatory connective (γάρ)[76] along with the rhetorical play of κατα κρίσεως δόξα . . . δικαιοσύνης δόξῃ [77] would further indicate Paul's hand. Thus, the eschatological understanding

---

[74]Cf. Georgi, *Die Gegner*, 274, 278.

[75]Such would certainly not be found in either Philo or Josephus; cf. nn. 71 and 72 above.

[76]Cf. also vss 10 and 11.

[77]While some texts read ἐν δόξῃ after δικαιοσύνης , both the lectio difficilior and the rhetorical play suggest simply δόξῃ .

developing from 2:14ff.[78] continues to nuance the ministry of Moses as well as shedding light upon the meaning of the ministry of Spirit.[79] The future dimension intimated in vs 8 becomes present in this verse.

The succeeding verse proves to be rather difficult. However, Georgi's suggestions are quite helpful. Thus, the οὐ would fall to Paul, as well as the qualifying phrase ἐν τούτῳ τῷ μέρει .[80] The preposition εἵνεκεν Georgi also sees as an explanation of Paul, thereby giving a purpose to the glorification of τὸ δεδοξασμένον and its subsequent fading away.[81] On the other hand, Georgi would allow the γάρ in this verse to be ascribed to the opposition, since it would connect with what has already been delimited above. Therefore, what would serve the opposition as a statement of the continued glory of the Mosaic tradition becomes in Paul's words an explanation for the dissolution of the former glory by the new lifeworld.

Verse 11 would fall to Paul for reasons similar to those given for vs 9. Two points in addition should be made. First, the use of the prepositions διά and ἐν with δόξα may well function to express the transitory duration of τὸ καταγούμενον as well as the present state of being of τὸ μένον.[82] Second, the use of neuter substantives is quite interesting. One also finds this usage in vs 10 (τὸ δεδοξασμένον).[83]

---

[78]Cf. pp. 110ff. above.

[79]Cf. Gal 3:21b-22, where limits of Law revealed in Christ event, p. 46 above.

[80]Cf. Georgi, *Die Gegner*, 275, 278.

[81]Georgi suggests that an ἐν or a διά could link τὸ δεδοξασμένον with τῆς ὑπερβαλλούσης δόξης ; cf. Georgi, *Die Gegner*, 278, 282.

[82]Cf. Smyth, 1685b; 1686b.

[83]In Exod 34:30 δεδοξασμένη , modifying ὄψις, is used. In changing the gender, Paul is also expanding the scope, implying the entire Mosaic tradition.

Should one interpret these as referring solely to the two ministries of vss 7-9 or is there a wider sense intended? It could well be that Paul is not only indicating two separate lifeworlds but also that he is linking them with πνεῦμα and γράμμα in vs 6. If this is correct, then one would have further confirmation that for Paul πνεῦμα and γράμμα are really seen as two different ages, which have specific temporal topographies.[84]

The next verse betrays Paul's hand in a number of ways. The assertion of confidence and freedom of speech breaks in as a conclusion (οὖν) to what has just preceded. Yet, this verse quickly moves[85] into a comparison (vs 13). Both the assertion of confidence and the use of the first person plural resume what was left off in vs 6. The verse functions as a resumptive clause much like others throughout this fragment (3:4; 4:1, 7, 16; 5:6, 11). The notion of freedom of speech recalls 2:17, as well as anticipating 3:18. The forensic situation already noted in 2:17ff. reemerges here. The hope which is based upon the appearance of the new lifeworld of Spirit becomes the reason for free speech.

Verse 13 features a negative comparison to what has been disclosed in vs 12. Again, while the reference is to Exod 34:33, 35, the negative aspects brought forward through οὐ and τοῦ καταργουμένου can be seen as Pauline interpretations. If they are removed,[86] then this leaves almost a repetition of vs 7. Both vs 7 and vs 13 provide an interpretation of Exodus 34: the first gives the result of the glory of such a ministry (ὥστε); the second provides a purpose (πρός). The veil (τὸ κάλυμμα) in this verse prevents the people from viewing the glory of Moses, that is, the final goal (τὸ τέλος). From the perspective of the opponents of Paul, this veil would not necessarily be seen in a negative light. On the contrary it would function as a safeguard to the great power of the spirit resident in the tradition of Moses. By responsibly using this

---

[84]See Chap. 1 above.

[85]An aposiopesis (Smyth, 3015); also Lausberg, 438-40.

[86]As well as καθάπερ which is due to the comparison with vs 12.

veil, one could become initiated into the mystery of this tradition.[87] However, in Paul's view the activity of Moses assumes a sinister aspect, whereby the veiling of his face becomes a "cover-up" of the "end" which is the process of fading away. Paul, therefore, from the lifeworld of the Spirit, provides the deeper intention behind the veiling by Moses.[88] His free speech (vs 12) from the new world of meaning allows him to expose this purpose. Moreover, such a negative comparison which Paul advances is a further indication that for him the lifeworld of the Letter, as that of the Spirit, is primarily a process or activity in which people discover their reason for existence.

The next verse begins with an explanation (vs 14a), which most likely comes from Paul. This thought is not found in Exodus 34 nor in Josephus or Philo. However, this sense of a fated condition already has appeared in 2:16 and is brought out again in 4:3 where the gospel is hidden from those fated to be lost.[89] In a certain sense the veil of Moses sets the fate of those whose minds were hardened. The objective or external situation is balanced by an internal or subjective veiling.

Verse 14b moves directly into the present time. The situation of the distant past is brought forward in time and space. The veil remains over the reading of the Old Covenant. This explanatory (γάρ) clause would easily fit in with the opponents' position, following directly from vs 13. The claim underneath this bringing forward of the text is that the

---

[87]The use of the imperfect ἐτίθει instead of the aorist (Exod 34:33, 35) is significant. From the viewpoint of the opposition, this could refer to the process begun by Moses which they carry on. From Paul's perspective this would take on the notion of a repetitive fate, which cannot be understood except from the perspective of the Christ event; cf. vss 14, 16-17. For the positive interpretation of the opponents' use, cf. Georgi, *Die Gegner*, 275, 279.

[88]Cf. Gal 3:22, where the true purpose of ἡ γραφή is revealed. Also cf. Gal 3:19, where Moses functions as μεσίτης but in a hindering light, preventing immediate transcendent experience.

[89]We should take into account 1 Cor 10:7-11. Here Paul is obviously aware of the sin in the desert tradition (Exod 32:4, 6). But here the fated condition seems less determined by the sin of the people than the veiled condition.

power of the Spirit inherent in the text is still effective for those who continue to read and penetrate the meaning of the text. Apart from vs 14a, vs 14b need not be seen in a negative light, for, from the perspective of the opposition, it would provide in the act of reading and interpretation of the text the means of entering into a living tradition. As Georgi has pointed out,[90] the term ἡ παλαία διαθήκη would hardly be seen as negative but would on the contrary carry a most positive weight. To interpret correctly would enable one to enter this Covenant. This positive understanding is immediately negated by vs 14c. The veil is μή ἀνακαλυπτόμενον , despite what the opponents would claim. Moreover, it is not a question of penetrating the veil since it has been destroyed in Christ. The causal clause resumes Paul's preoccupation with a Christological understanding (from 2:14ff.), as well as the usage of καταργεῖται (vss 7, 11, 13). Thus, the fated condition indicated in vss 13 and 14a actually continues without reprieve, a further instance of the lifeworld of the Letter, while from the situation ἐν Χριστῷ Paul can speak freely, commenting on how this determined condition has been destroyed. Therefore, it is not a question of a better or deeper interpretation which would penetrate the veil of the Old Covenant; rather, it is a matter of an entirely different condition brought about in Christ.

The next verse, while appearing to repeat vs 14b, is very much a gloss by Paul. The most substantial one appears to be κάλυμμα ἐπὶ τὴν καρδίαν αὐτῶν κεῖται . This repeats what we have seen in vs 14a and can be ascribed to Paul. On the other hand, ἀλλ' ἕως σήμερον ἡνίκα would easily come from vs 14b. Indeed, without the major gloss just excised there appears to be a run on to vs 16. If ἂν ἀναγινώσκηται (vs 15) and the repetitive ἡνίκα δὲ ἐάν (vs 16) are removed[91] then Moses becomes the subject of vs 16, which would be in line with Exod 34:34. Again, as has been noted above, this would not

---

[90]Georgi, *Die Gegner*, 279.

[91]Georgi, *Die Gegner*, 280.

be a literal rendering of Exod 34:34. On the contrary, the changes in mood and tenses would indicate that the text is still seen as effective for those wishing to participate in the Spirit. The true heirs of Moses can turn to the text and the veil of non-understanding will be uncovered. The emphasis on the veil as the threshold of understanding which was noted in vss 13, 14b becomes quite direct here. Indeed, Moses does not remove the veil, rather it is removed, indicating a possible divine transformation.[92] However, from Paul's perspective, which one gleans from the glosses, the possibility of such a transformation is non-existent since the veil of non-comprehension remains. In short, the activity of interpretation carried out by the opposition continues to revolve in the frustration of the lifeworld of the Letter. The apparently progressive cultural vehicle of transcendence remains a stillborn exercise.

Reading instructions for vs 16 are given in vs 17a. The δέ apparently functions as an explanatory connective. Thus, one should read τὸ πνεῦμα for ὁ κύριος. The Spirit would provide the means and the power for entering into the tradition of the Spirit. Through such an allegorical interpretation, the opponents of Paul could well find vs 16 meaningful. By this discovery of meaning, the readers or exegetes of the text can enter the tradition Moses has prepared for them (cf. vs 13). The difficulty with this verse lies in the second part. Is this a later gloss? Or is this another one of Paul's comments? There is little textual evidence to support the first possibility,[93] whereas it has been suggested throughout this present analysis that Paul has been "glossing" his opponents' understanding of Exodus 34. Moreover, the introduction of ἐλευθερία does tie in with the argument Paul has been pursuing since 2:14ff. The forensic aspect of the fragment which has been noted, where freedom of speech is characteristic of the lifeworld of the Spirit, now reasserts itself in this word. Paul, then, is not simply continuing to allegorize according to the format of the opposition; rather, he is transposing the entire basis

---

[92]That the passive stands for divine action is confirmed in vs 17a.

[93] ἐκεῖ has been inserted before ἐλευθερία in D[1], F, G, and Ψ.

for the action of interpretation. The lifeworld of Spirit provides the ground for understanding that the Spirit is the spirit of the Lord[94] and that this situation is one of freedom.

Finally, vs 18 continues this reinterpretation by Paul. πάντες presents the first difficulty. This would not be a logical consequence for the opponents of Paul. Only those initiated into the mystery of the text could bear the weight of glory. Further, it is not the people but the text which is to be unveiled. On the other hand, πάντες carries the inclusive sense used by Paul throughout this fragment, notable by his use of the first person plural. Indeed, Paul has already in his opening remarks included the Corinthian community within the revelatory sphere of the Christ event. They function in their communal existence as a heavenly letter, manifesting the Spirit. Next the phrase ἀνακεκαλυμμένῳ προσώπῳ appears to be connected with vss 14a, 15. The unveiled face is precisely the reversal of the condition noted in these two verses. It seems that Paul is playing an exegetical game which out-gnosticizes even his opponents.[95] For the enlightenment which is present to all does not come about through the allegorical method but has been present already in the community as they reflect the glory of the Lord. Indeed, the phrase τὴν αὐτὴν εἰκόνα not only carries Christological meaning[96] but brings the community in its mutuality to the action of Creation itself.[97] The glory of the Lord is not found by those who fall under the sway of the Letter but is recognized by those who already possess this glory through the outpouring of the Spirit. The lifeworld of the Spirit does not limit the act of interpretation to the unlocking of a text. Rather, all time and space which fall under the

---

[94]That is, the Christ; cf. Gal 3:22.

[95]Note 2:14-15; 3:3; 4:3-6.

[96] Κυρίου in vs 18 is tied to vs 17b; cf. 4:4.

[97]Cf. 4:5-6; Gen 1:26.

dominion of the triumphant Christ are now part of the creative reinterpretation in the Spirit.

The foregoing analysis has shown that the antithesis of 2 Cor 3:6c is a guiding interpretive principle for the entire section. The lifeworlds of Letter and Spirit come to light through this extended comparison, which focuses on the activities, results and destinies of each lifeworld. The Letter, standing for the entire momentum of the Mosaic tradition, is found to be lethal. Those who would enter into this lifeworld must face the prospect that this world, featuring the culturally desirable objective documentation, is from Paul's perspective a world of death, transiency, deception, unenlightenment and frustration. On the other hand, the world of Spirit brings righteousness, permanency, mutual enlightenment and freedom.

C. The Task of Interpretation

To understand why Paul would set up this extended argument, one should consider the situation before him. As it has been noted above, the position of Paul's opponents rested upon some of the most cherished presuppositions of the ancient world. Their claims of authority, competence and objective verification would seem to place Paul at quite a disadvantage. From what one can gather from the correspondence, the Corinthian community was greatly swayed by such an understanding. Thus, Paul's response is dictated by this double aspect: the understanding of his opposition and the situation within the Corinthian community. In order to regain his relationship with the community he must deal with the lifeworld brought out explicitly by his opposition. Thus, the fragment under investigation can be seen, from the outset, as an attempt to persuade the Corinthian community to reexamine, and thus reinterpret, their own understanding of the situation before them. It has been necessary, then, to use the research and suggestions of Georgi in order to perceive how Paul takes up the language and understanding of his opposition. But, in so doing, one finds that Paul has significantly changed the basis for their position. His effort at persuading the Corinthian community becomes an act of reinterpretation of his opposition's position in light of a different horizon.   For Paul the task of reinterpretation is quite unlike the interpretive activity of his opposition. He does not see tradition (Letter) as a transcendent source which needs to be tapped for present application. He does not buy into the presupposition that transcendent experience can be brought forward in a continuous line. Paul's position, rather, takes its lead from the eschatological event in Christ, whereby an unexpected future breaks in, throwing every cultural and religious presupposition into a new and critical light. Thus, from Paul's standpoint, the advantage of his opposition is hardly that at all. On the contrary, because their position does not understand the implications of the Christ event, it is locked within a lifeworld which can promise nothing more than death.   The claims of objective verification and demonstration, of wonder-working and privilege, which presuppose the lifeworld of the Letter, of cultural continuity, and thus of ignorance of the reality of the Christ, when thrown up against this future dimension and perspective, fade along with this lifeworld into insignificance.   However, this does not mean that this fading lifeworld does not possess any power. Indeed, the real power of this lifeworld is finally seen for what it truly is: a deadly and deceitful force.

On the other hand, Paul has encouraged the Corinthian community from the outset of this fragment to align themselves to the lifeworld of the Spirit. He anticipates vs 18, where all mutually reflect the glory of the Lord, with his remarks in vss 2-3. His strategic *captatio benevolentiae* invites the community to enter into this process of self-interpretation, of recognizing the revelatory power of the Spirit in their midst. Further, this revelation through the community is a participation in the universal triumphal procession in Christ (2:14-16). Thus, the antithesis of 3:6c becomes for the community a leading principle of self-understanding and interpretation. The points which he makes concerning the two distinct lifeworlds of Letter and Spirit are set forth before their eyes and ears. In reinterpreting the opponents' probable allegorization of Exodus 34, Paul undercuts the opponents' claim that the fullness of the Spirit can only come through this controlled use of tradition. Indeed, he suggests that the lifeworld of the Spirit is already present in its fullness to the community.

It is then not a matter of calling into question his oppositions' credentials as it is a matter of undermining the very basis for such a quest for objective verification. If proof is to be given by Paul, it is found already lodged within the Spirit-filled experience of the Corinthian community. Thus, Paul's strategy in opposing the notion of the archive of the Spirit is to bring the Corinthians to the awareness that the living deposit of divine life already is at work in their midst. Indeed, if the community agrees with his line of interpretation then vs 18 confirms the process which is already at work. Paul then would succeed at demonstrating that he has no need to perform any demonstration! If this analysis is correct, then the history of interpretation of 2 Cor 3:6 has, for the most part, fallen in the footsteps of Paul's opponents. The distinction of literal/spiritual or external/internal is precisely the distinction upon which the opponents hinge their methodology. Of course, what most of the history of interpretation has missed, even from the opponents' perspective, is the cultural relationship presupposed by Letter and Spirit. Moreover, in limiting the meaning of Letter/Spirit to the matter of reading and interpreting a text, subsequent exegetes have failed to appreciate the revolutionary position of Paul. For Paul is concerned with an entirely new perspective, not simply in regard to understanding Scripture, but in regard to the entire momentum of history. From his vision of the world-shattering event in Christ, Paul is compelled to reinterpret even the most basic presuppositions of his time. Hence, just as the Corinthian community forms part of the revelatory process in Christ, so too does this letter of Paul. It functions basically to further the momentum of the triumphal drive of Christ as it impinges upon the consciousness of the Corinthian community.

This means that for Paul interpretation is no longer a controlled activity performed only by experts and appreciated only by initiates. Rather, interpretation becomes the way in which one stands and moves in the momentum of the lifeworld of the Spirit. The future horizon of the Christ event calls each member of the community to enter into this activity of interpretation. Indeed, as one is caught up in the triumphal progress of the revelation in Christ the act of interpretation takes on the character of re-creation. The future horizon calls its interpreters to bring to light what is the true intention of creation itself (4:5-6). Interpretation is, then, not of the Spirit if it does not enter into the historical situation of the believing community and if this activity of interpretation does not take its leading sense from the world-shattering vision of the Christ. Otherwise, the act of interpretation falls back into the lifeworld of the Letter, aloof from mutual engagement and enlightenment and determined to a fate, where there is no surprise but only the illusion of transcendence.

VI. Conclusion

In conclusion, one can note that Paul has gone beyond the contemporary understanding of the Letter/Spirit relationship in an effort to win back the Corinthian community who shared with Paul's opponents much of the contemporary understanding of Letter and Spirit. Cohen was certainly correct to declare that Paul had eschatological grounds for his understanding of Letter/Spirit; but he was off the mark in ascribing this to a mere rhetorical flourish. Paul was deadly serious in making this creative distinction. For him the condition for human existence had dramatically changed in Christ. And he saw in the very life of the Corinthian community a furtherance of this process of revelation. In that light he employed his famous antithesis to help interpret the chasm which exists between the two different lifeworlds of Letter and Spirit. In so doing, Paul was battling with basic preconceptions of history and tradition. This debate with his opposition actually causes Paul to widen the dualism which has been uncovered in the chapter on Galatians. Furthermore, the very act of interpretation comes dramatically into focus here. Interpretation becomes the task of understanding human activity and history in light of the unexpected future of the Christ. As this investigation moves on to the pertinent sections from Romans, it will be necessary to see whether Paul widens this dualism and whether he continues on this line of creative reinterpretation.

CHAPTER FOUR

Spirit and Letter in Romans

I. Introduction

The radical understanding of Letter and Spirit found in 2 Corinthians not only continues but is even greatly expanded in Romans. In order to see this, I shall deal with the ways in which Paul reexamines traditional categories which constitute human existence. From the eschatological perspective of the Gospel, such traditional understandings of human existence are brought into question and realigned. What emerges from Romans 2 and Romans 7-8 is a further instance of Paul's tendency to make interpretation subordinate to and instrumental of the fundamental understanding of the powers and forces of human history and society, rather than just a matter of scriptural interpretation. Through a perspective molded from apocalyptic, wisdom, and popular philosophical influences, interpretation becomes for Paul a universal enterprise, so much so that what is found in from 7:7ff., growing out of the hermeneutical thesis of 7:6, is nothing less than a re-creation of human history and society under a radically new perspective, cast in existential terms.

Once again close attention will be paid to the movement of language, especially as it throws light on the manner in which Paul makes use of tradition and the various possibilities of lifeworlds suggested by tradition. In this investigation of Romans, it will become quite evident that the language used is very much in motion and conflict. The clash of language forms is a primary indication that different lifeworlds and their powers have been set in motion, disclosing to the reader that the act of interpretation is a matter of striving to uncover what is true. In laboring to bring forth his understanding of Letter and Spirit, Paul has chosen linguistic conventions which break down attempts to keep the truth of human existence at a distance.[1]

My first consideration, then, will be to investigate Romans 2:29 as to its function and context. It is essential to find out why Paul placed this antithesis of Letter/Spirit in the block of material from 1:18 to 3:20. If, as has been argued so far, this is such a critical phrase, why does Paul wait so long to employ it? He did not do so in 2 Cor 3:6, where it provides a thematic lead-in for 2 Cor 3:7ff. Moreover, the language surrounding vs 29 seems far removed from what has been encountered in Galatians 3 and 2 Corinthians 3. We are not dealing with a reinterpretation of a text. Moreover, does the decided use of diatribal elements as well as categories from popular philosophy in Romans 2 influence, modify or in any way alter the meaning of the Letter/Spirit antithesis? Finally, what significance has the eschatological perspective (under which this large block of material stands) for an appreciation of the antithesis?

My argument for the remaining part of this chapter will be that what is discovered in Romans 2 will be decisive for the resumption of the antithesis of Letter/Spirit in Romans 7:6. The meaning unearthed in chap. 2 will provide a promising basis on which 7:6 operates. Moreover, it will be argued that 7:6 and what follows this hermeneutical thesis in fact explore the meaning developed in chap. 2, proceeding to fill out its significance in existential terms.

---

[1]Thus, in from 7:7ff., for example, we shall see how Paul, in bringing the condition of alienation right into the structure of the "I", shatters this self-alienating situation by the power of the Spirit, which allowed him in the first place to bring the thraldom of the "I" into interpretive focus and light (8:2ff.).

II. Romans 2:29

A. Introductory Remarks

Any attempt to resolve the meaning of Romans 2:29 must be made in light of its surrounding context. As noted above, the presence of the antithesis of Letter/Spirit at the apparent conclusion of the argument in chap. 2 seems to be in direct contrast to the employment of the antithesis in 2 Cor 3:6, where it functions as a leading thesis for the subsequent interpretation. Furthermore, concern for the immediate context is warranted, since the language surrounding the antithesis of 2:29 also uses similar rhetorical conventions.[2]

The display of such rhetorical conventions has caused many commentators to consider the relationship of the language of chap. 2 with that of the form of the diatribe.[3] However, before such rhetorical conventions can be assessed, it is imperative to place vs 29 (as well as chap. 2) in a wider frame of reference by noting the position of 2:29 within the material from 1:18 to 3:20. For it is from this enlarged perspective that the use of such rhetorical elements gains significance and force.

---

[2]The second chapter is filled with similar rhetorical conventions. Thus, the antithesis of Letter/spirit is part of the antithesis ἡ ἐν τῷ φανερῷ ἐν σαρκὶ περιτομή/περιτομή καρδίας ἐν πνεύματι οὐ γράμματι, which balances ὁ ἐν φανερῷ ᾿Ιουδαῖος/ὁ ἐν κρυπτῷ ᾿Ιουδαῖος (vss 28-29). Verse 13 also supplies a significant paradox: οἱ ἀκροαταὶ νόμου/οἱ ποιηταὶ νόμου. Paradoxes abound. Verse 3 presents the paradoxical position of those who judge and yet do what they condemn. Verse 14 presents the paradox of those who do not possess the Law yet perform it. Verses 26-27 indicate how the uncircumcised actually are counted as circumcised and even judge the circumcised transgressor. Finally, a major contrast occurs between vss 14-15 and vss 17-24.

[3]Cf. E. Käsemann, *Commentary on Romans* (Grand Rapids: Eerdmans, 1980) 53ff.; Stowers, *Paul and the Diatribe*, 144ff.

B. 1:18-3:20: The Apocalyptic Setting

Before one can consider the clash of language in chap. 2, the language
worlds of 1:18ff. must be taken into account. For here we have a
combination of two linguistic traditions, that of apocalyptic and that of
Hellenistic Jewish apologetic. The effect of such a combination is quite
startling, since the apocalyptic perspective appears to realign the language
which Hellenistic Judaism has taken from popular philosophy. In
bringing to light the present situation, Paul disengages the truth of this
situation from any sense of continuity which Hellenistic thought assumes
between the knowledge of the world and the divine.[4]

While one can rightly note the affinity that certain terms and
theological topoi have to the apologetic activity of Hellenistic Judaism,[5]
Bornkamm is correct in arguing that this section can hardly be called an
apologetic excursus,[6] whose goal is to lead the listener away from
ignorance and into a right knowledge of God. Instead of assuming the
common starting point that the knowledge of God is in harmony with a
reasonable understanding of the world, Paul dramatically changes the way
in which this "knowledge" is understood. This change is effected through
the thoroughgoing apocalyptic perspective adopted right from the
beginning.[7] Romans 1:18-3:20 is, in Bornkamm's words, a "penetrating
accusation that 'all are under sin' (3: 9, 10ff.)."[8] It is precisely the

---

[4]Cf. Excursus, pp. 55-64 above.

[5]Thus, such terms as τὰ ἀόρατα αὐτοῦ , ἥ τε ἀίδιος αὐτοῦ
δύναμις καὶ θειότης (1:20) suggest a common tie with Hellenistic
Jewish apologetic; cf. Käsemann, *Romans*, 39. Τὰ καθήκοντα (1:28), as
well as the asyndetic lists (1:29f.) also give some link to popular philosophy;
cf. Käsemann, *Romans*, 49-50. Bornkamm has noted ("Revelation", 50ff.) four
common theological propositions which come from the same theological
tradition as that of Hellenistic Judaism.

[6]Cf. Bornkamm, "Revelation", 50-54.

[7]Cf. 1:18; also Zeph 1:18; Dan 8:19; Enoch 91:7.

[8]Bornkamm, "Revelation", 61.

knowledge of God which forms the basis of the accusation against the ungodly world.[9]   Humanity already has the Truth, although it has suppressed it in injustice (vs 18).   Knowledge of God has not occasioned praise or thanksgiving (vs 21), nor any attempt to prove the worth of this knowledge (vs 28).   Instead, humanity has refused to acknowledge God, changing the truth of its existence into a lie (vs 25).   Indeed, this human action establishes its own destiny.   For God gives up the disobedient to their own wish for autonomy (vs 24).   The very lifeworld of the gentiles becomes revealed as a cursed condition,[10] as God hands them over to their fate (vss 24, 26, 28).[11]   It is this inverted existential relationship which is exposed from 1:18ff.   For what is at stake is not the disclosure of the divine nature but the exposition of how humanity stands before God.[12]

Moreover, in contrast to the Hellenistic Jewish strategy of viewing religion as the pinnacle of human possibility,[13] religion, through the traditional critique of idolatry,[14] becomes the manner in which humanity's error is most explicit (1:23, 25) and, in fact, the cause of the subsequent anarchy of moral life.   The turning away from God by the world to seek its own illusory autonomy ends in the grostesque idolatry of paganism.[15]   The apocalyptic wrath (1:18) has already taken place insofar

---

[9]Cf. vss 19, 20, 21, 28, 32.

[10]Cf. Käsemann, *Romans*, 43.

[11]Cf. W.S. 14.8-31.

[12]Cf. Bornkamm, "Revelation", 56; Käsemann, *Romans*, 51.

[13]Cf. Excursus, pp. 64-66.

[14]E.g., W.S. 13.1-15.17.

[15]Schiler, quoted by Bornkamm, "Revelation", 58.

as God gives humanity up to this "possibility of an autonomous life"[16]
which is actually the "constraint allotted to them by the brazen necessity
of a powerless death."[17] Thus, the unfolding of this passage, detailing
the knowledge of God, the folly of idolatry, the error of moral life and the
consequent death sentence, is not a starting point leading to a deeper
disclosure of God's being but an exposé of humanity's fate as it stands
under the eschatological light of God's wrath.[18]

       If one moves to the section 3:1-20, one can see that this accusation
that all are under God's wrath is maintained. The objection raised by the
imaginary Jew about his advantage as a Jew takes on a different
perspective in Paul's opinion. The presumed advantage of the Jew's
positive religious tradition becomes an indication of God's faithfulness
despite the unfaithfulness of the Jew.[19] Indeed, the Law itself (3:19),
speaking to those ἐν τῷ νόμῳ, declares that no one has an advantage,
no one is justified (3:10-18, 19-20). The knowledge which comes
through the Law reveals that both Jew and Gentile stand under the
darkened eschatological vision of God's wrath.

       This last point about the negative knowledge given by the Law has
already been brought out in my analyses of Gal 3:16ff., 21 and 2 Cor
3:6ff. In the chapter on Galatians the reliance upon the lifeworld of the
Torah was disclosed as resulting in bondage. Moreover, in the
investigation of 2 Cor 3:6ff. we saw that the power of γράμμα was
essentially death-dealing. In both instances the way in which the lethal
limitations of the tradition of γράμμα were revealed was through the
insight gained through the positive revelation that the power of this cursed
condition ended in the death of Christ (Gal 3:13; 2 Cor 3:14). It is also

---

[16]Bornkamm, "Revelation", 58.

[17]Ibid.

[18]Cf. 2 Bar 54:17ff.

[19]3:3-4. This repeats what he argues in 1:18, where God is faithful despite the
gentiles' refusal.

the case in Romans, for the entire section 1:18-3:20 is ringed with the positive verses 1:17 and 3:21-26. Through the revelation of the righteousness of God, the world comes to the awareness that the crucial time has arrived. Through the illumination by this "final event" the confinement under sin can be revealed in its grimmest aspect;[20] this perspective allows all to see the shadows and limited power of the confined and cursed world. Moreover, we should also see in Romans that Paul is moving beyond the ἔργα νόμου and γράμμα as representative of the power of the Jewish tradition. He enters more overtly into the fray with the very forces and powers of history and society. In using critically the language of Hellenistic Judaism's universal apologetic, Paul widens the scope of his interpretive vision. Now, right from the outset in Romans, his tendency is to consider humanity, Jew and Gentile, in its most universal and deepest aspect. And it is under the fire of his eschatological perspective, where the Gospel extends to all who believe (1:16) that this interpretation of the forces of history takes place.

C. Romans 2: An Analysis

The language of accusation is broken abruptly by 2:2.[21] An interesting change in focus is immediately brought about by this sudden turn and

---

[20]Cf. Gal 3:10ff., 22; 2 Cor 3:7-11.

[21]I regard both 2:1 and 2:16 to be glosses in the text. Bultmann has argued that 2:1 might well be an early marginal gloss which drew its conclusion from the rhetorical question in 2:3. Moreover, διό at the beginning of the sentence is rather difficult to explain (the suggestion of Fridrichsen notwithstanding ["Conjectures", 439ff.]). Finally the πᾶς ὁ κρίνων is hard to accommodate, for it not only adds a possibly unnecessary generalizing trend but also turns the emphasis away from the eschatological light exposing the contradictory actions to that of the act of judging. 2:2, on the other hand, quite fittingly comes after 1:32, while at the same time changes the direction of the passage. The best objection raised against Bultmann's theory is that of Stowers, who argues that Bultmann contradicts himself by first noting the diatribal characteristics of vs 1 and then removing the verse from the subsequent diatribal verses by declaring it to be a gloss (*Paul and the Diatribe*, 127ff.). Stowers, following Dahl et al., sees a line of continuity from 1:32 to 2:1, noting that

interruption. Moreover, the use of the first person plural with a verb of knowing is quite characteristic of the diatribal form which presents thereby what seems to be a generally agreed upon assumption. In fact, this reaches back to 1:32a and reinforces the position of those included in the οἴδαμεν who can assent to the claim that the judgment of God falls upon those who do "such things." The effect of this verse is to distance momentarily the "we" from those objectified under God's wrath in 1:18ff. It also continues the theme of "knowledge" established in 1:19, 20, 21, 28, 32. Yet, on the strength of this assumption in 2:2 there seems to be a "knowing" which can separate those under the wrath from those who know about the judgment. This position would not be unlike that found in apocalyptic literature.[22]

However, the assurance of vs 2 is broken completely by vs 3. An indicting rhetorical question directly addresses the ἄνθρωπος in the

---

Paul is speaking to both Gentile and Jew in 2:1-5 (pp. 128ff.). However, Stowers' main point that 2:1-5 is constructed in diatribal fashion is not lost when 2:1 is removed. Indeed, he even notes that it is common to see first an expression of common ground which is then followed by an apostrophe (p. 145 n. 65; cf. Epictetus *Diss*. 2.6.16; 3.22.80, 81; 2.16.11-28; 1.1.14-17). Furthermore, Stowers does not take into account the loss of eschatological focus which is present throughout 1:18-3:20 and which is not apparent in 2:1. This loss becomes explainable if 2:1 is a gloss from a later hand which understood the notion of inconsistency employed by Paul in chap. 2. As for 2:16, it appears to be a foreign body in the text. It turns back to a future perspective from the present established in vss 14-15. There also could be some influence by 1 Cor 4:5 (with its future emphasis). Most telling is εὐαγγέλιον μου which is nowhere found in the genuine Pauline corpus (cf. Romans 16:25, itself a probable gloss; 2 Tim 2:8). Instead we find in the Pauline corpus εὐαγγέλιον ἡμῶν (cf. 2 Cor 4:3; 1 Thess 1:5; in the former we have a polemical distinction, in the latter a collective understanding; cf. R. Bultmann, "Glossen im Romerbrief." in *Exegetica* (Tubingen: Mohr, 1967), pp. 197-202). While I removed 2:1 because of the loss of its eschatological nuance, I cannot retain 2:16 simply because of its future reference. It appears that it picks up the notion of "hiddenness" of vs 29 and applies its eschatological vision to finish what apparently seemed an unfinished sentence (2:15).

[22]Cf. 2 Bar 84:7ff.; 85:9; 4 Ezra 7:34ff; also W.S. 15.1-2.

second person singular, once more turning the language around with this sudden interruption. Here is a sarcastic, ironical question exposing the inconsistency of the one who does what he has condemned. Moreover, this self-contradiction is brought together with the eschatological judgment of God. It is not simply a matter of inspecting the inconsistency of the judge but of bringing out the impossibility of that judge to remain aloof from transobjective judgment which has been established from 1:18ff. In employing such a diatribal speech pattern,[23] Paul is historicizing even more concretely the apocalyptic vision brought out in chap. 1. I have already noted that an overriding theme for 1:18-3:20 is that the judgment of God is upon all. But, here, one can see that the assumption of 2:2, that some can distance themselves from this fateful circumstance, has been gravely disturbed.[24] This concretizing of the eschatological event of God is quite in line with Israel's prophetic tradition.[25] The future aspect of the judgment of God is even more embedded in the very present action of judgment by those mentioned in vs 2. The self-contradiction of the ἄνθρωπος in vs 3 resembles the inverted fate of the gentiles in chap. 1.

Verse 4 continues the heavy-handed irony by a second rhetorical question, once more using a verb which indicates a lack of perception (ἀγνοῶν).[26] While the language here is reminiscent of the Wisdom of Solomon,[27] the point is quite opposite. The ἄνθρωπος is charged with scorning the patient kindness of God because he is ignorant that this is meant for his repentance. Knowledge about the richness of God's mercy alone is not enough to keep the ἄνθρωπος from being included in the judgment. In contrast to the forbearance of God (vs 4), a warning to the

---

[23]Cf. Stowers, *Paul and the Diatribe*, 144ff.

[24]Cf. Enoch 52:7.

[25]Cf, 2 Sam 12:7; Isa 3:13-15.

[26]Cf. Stowers, *Paul and the Diatribe*, 146.

[27]Cf. W.S. 11.23; 15.1-3.

hard and unrepentant heart is given in vs 5. This warning is characteristic not only of the prophetic tradition but also of the diatribe.[28] The future day of wrath and judgment is directly tied to the fundamental condition of the human. The self-contradiction brought out in vs 3 is now seen as a symptom of the unrepentant heart. To this warning is added a quotation[29] adapted for his argument.[30] This continues to emphasize the inclusion of the future world of judgment while simultaneously directing the judgment towards the individual in his concrete existence (ἑκάστῳ κατὰ τὰ ἔργα αὐτοῦ).

The following section (vss 7-11) brings out not only the future lines of this world of judgment but also the very explanation of the basis of this judgment (vs 11). Through these verses the future world of wrath and reward impinges even more directly upon the present conversation. In vss 7-8 we have a contrasting parallelism, delivering the appropriate destinies to those who in their earthly existence already prefigure them. Verses 9-10 not only extend this parallelism but even form a rhetorical chiasmus with vss 7-8. Significantly, Paul has used the phrase Ἰουδαίου τε πρῶτον καὶ Ἕλληνος (vs 9)/ Ἰουδαίῳ τε πρῶτον καὶ Ἕλληνι (vs 10) for the first time since 1:16. The universality implied in vss 6, 7-8, is now characterized by what appears to be a standard distinction in Hellenistic Jewish speech. Certainly there would be no difficulty for Philo or Josephus to use such a phrase. One

---

[28]Cf. Epictetus 2.8.11-14.

[29]Either from Ps 62:13 or Prov 24:12; in either case Paul has changed either the person from second to third or the tense from present to future.

[30]Cf. Stowers, *Paul and the Diatribe*, 147.

can even trace this thinking back to Isaiah.[31]   Neither would the impartiality of God as the ground of the judgment be debated.[32]

What is a matter of debate is whether this universal judgment gives any clue to the identity of the ἄνθρωπος in vs 3. Some have argued that while there is a change in style there is no change in the intended direction of Paul's words. Thus, Paul is including both Jew and Gentile in his apostrophe.[33] The section following vs 6 would seem to support this opinion. Is not Paul revealing a universal perspective, where judgment falls upon all? The difficulty with this position is that it fails to take into consideration the strategy for this change in style. In presenting vs 2 and then interrupting it by vs 3, Paul forces us to ask who could make this agreement in vs 2, while coming into criticism in vs 3? In my judgment it can only be a Jewish self-understanding which would be brought into question. For it was precisely the Jewish understanding that one's knowledge and possession of the Law removed one from the wrath to come.[34] Moreover, the language used in vss 4-5 comes out of the Hellenistic Jewish and prophetic traditions. Not only would this language be understandable to those coming from such traditions, but it would call into question the "natural" advantage these traditions provide for the Jew. In essence, what Paul seems to be doing[35] is shaking up the very language of the Jewish tradition by focusing it under the light of another part of Jewish tradition, namely, apocalyptic. Those who see a universal

---

[31]Cf. Isa 66:18ff.

[32]Indeed, one can find this also in Epictetus 4.8.17 and Pseudo-Heraclitus 9.2. See also the universalism of God's judgment in the Wisdom tradition, e.g., Sir 32.35.

[33]Cf. Stowers, *Paul and the Diatribe*, 128ff.

[34]Cf. p. 144 n. 1.

[35]Or more precisely, "de-objectifying".

understanding of ἄνθρωπος [36] are not altogether far from the point Paul
eventually will make. But first his concern is to make some inroad into
the basic assumptions of Jewish understanding. The result of vss 7-11 is
to democratize the coming judgment. But this is in no way clear from the
assumption presented in 2:2. If, however, I am correct in taking
ἄνθρωπος as an apostrophe to the Jew, why is the title Ἰουδαῖος
kept back until vs 17? The answer to this question can only be made in
light of an analysis of vss 12-15 and their relationship to vss 17-24.
Therefore, let us continue the analysis.

It is quite striking that Paul continues to speak of the parties
involved in the coming judgment. If, as some would argue, Paul is
chiefly interested in assigning all under judgment, then the remaining
section of chap. 2 becomes quite difficult to explain. In order to get
around this, it can be suggested that Paul first presents a general ground
and then substantiates this in regard to the gentiles and then the Jews.
This would then turn vss 12ff. into an exemplum of the preceding verses.
However, this does not meet adequately the reason for vss 12-15, 17-24,
not to mention vss 25-29 where we seem to have a collision of the
previous two sections. If this is but an expansion, why do vss 14-15
indicate a positive image of the gentiles, while vss 17-24 demonstrate the
inconsistency of the Jew? Moreover, why are these two images exploited
in such paradoxical fashion in vss 25-29? Finally, if this concluding part
is an expansion of the final scene of judgment, why is there such an
emphasis on the present?[37]

Verses 12-15 present a series of explanations, which is actually
begun in vs 11. The impartiality of God is now explained (γάρ) by the
parallelism of vs 12. By itself it provides no difficulty for Jewish ears.[38]
Indeed, this continues in the vein (somewhat chiastically) of the future

---

[36]Abetted by the gloss in 2:1.

[37]Vss 14-15, 17-24, 25, 27(?), 28-29.

[38]Cf. 2 Baruch 48:47.

fate meted out to the Jew and to the Gentile (vs 9). At the same time, however, it returns to the notion found in vs 6, that the standard of judgment is based upon one's own deeds. Here, of course, in vs 12 the emphasis is on the failure of each one.

In vs 13 we find a further distinction based on the antithesis οὐ οἱ ἀκροαταὶ νόμου/ἀλλ' οἱ ποιηταὶ νόμου. This verse is not in direct parallel with the previous verse. At the same time, this verse does represent a further explanation (γάρ) of the judgment of God. The effect of this verse is to drive a deeper wedge into the basis for God's judgment. Verse 13 cannot be taken simply with vs 12b, thereby referring to those who know the Torah. For this is precluded by what follows in vss 14-15. Moreover, the force of the Torah is even seen in vs 12a where the Gentiles are described negatively in reference to the Torah (ἀνόμως). The distinction is one quite at home in Hellenistic Judaism.[39] For what is at stake here is the notion of authentic human performance or praxis. It is such authentic action which becomes the basis for the eschatological judgment of God.[40] Already in this investigation we have encountered this in the figure of Abraham who fulfilled the Law through following the unwritten law, taught, as it were, by unwritten nature. We have noted also that Abraham, became a κανών for Gentile and Jew, the embodiment of the Hellenistic ideal of the νόμος ἔμψυχος.[41]

It is, therefore, not totally surprising for vss 14-15 to follow vs 13. Bornkamm has correctly pointed out the probable connection of these verses to the tradition of the Unwritten Law in Greek thought.[42] The concern of Käsemann that φύσει (vs 14) may be taken as support for a Natural Law or that the Gentiles have the same law as the Jews but in a

---

[39]Cf. Philo *De praem. et poen.* 79ff.

[40] δικαιωθήσονται, vs 13.

[41]Cf. Excursus, pp. 55-60 above.

[42]Cf. G. Bornkamm, "Gesetz und Natur," *Studien zu Antike und Urchristentum* (Munich: Kaiser, 1959) 93-118.

different way is misplaced.[43] Paul is precisely bringing forward into the
discussion the language of Hellenistic Judaism, taking advantage of the
tradition which sees a fundamental link between the Law of Nature and
the Torah.[44] None of the verses in this section (vss 12-15) runs counter
to what we have discovered in the Excursus. Indeed, we can even find
apocalyptic thought supporting such a link between Law and the Torah.[45]
However, unlike most apocalyptic texts, Paul is presenting a positive
image of the Gentiles actually doing τὰ τοῦ νόμου (vs 14).[46] Indeed,
this positive image is based upon the long-standing hope within the
Hellenistic world for the truly autonomous individual[47] who could, in
living according to nature, fulfill the divine law.[48] Paul is bringing under
the light of the eschatological perspective this very hope of the Hellenistic
world for authentic human existence. Moreover, it is under the pressure
to understand the basis for the eschatological judgment that this primordial
figure is brought forward for inspection. The exemplar of true human
promise,[49] of genuine religion is the one who is a law unto himself (vs
14). Furthermore, we should wonder if vs 15, τὸ ἔργον τοῦ νόμου
γραπτὸν ἐν ταῖς καρδίαις αὐτῶν , is not effected either by a
reminiscence of Jer 38:33[50] or more directly by Paul's own thought in 2

---

[43]Käsemann, *Romans*, 63-64.

[44]Cf. Excursus, pp. 63-66 above.

[45]Cf. 2 Baruch 57:2.

[46]Cf. the contrast in 2 Baruch 48:38, 40, 47; 4 Ezra 7:72.

[47]Cf. Excursus, pp. 86-92.

[48]Epictetus 2.19.24-28.

[49] ἐπαγγελία ; cf. Epictetus 2.9.19-22.

[50]Bornkamm, "Gesetz," 107.

Corinthians 3. In either case, the notion of the ἔργον being written in the heart would bear an eschatological nuance.

One final point must be made. There is a significant change in time from vs 13 to vs 14. Whereas vss 12-13 are written in light of the future, vss 14-15 stand boldly in the present. An immediate objection to this observation is that this seems impossible, since 1:18ff. have completely demolished any possibility that the Gentiles can stand justified before God. This objection, however, misses the point of these verses. Paul is not interested in discovering any particular Gentiles who can stand in the Judgment; rather, he is concerned with exploring the basis upon which the Judgment is given. The series of explanations (vss 11ff.) is precisely given for that reason. The use of the present tense is a functional indication that the primordial possibility of human authenticity has been exposed by the light of God's judgment. In doing so, we find that the criterion of judgment is not determined by convention, or outwardness, but is uncovered in one of the deepest hopes of the Hellenistic world. Thus, Paul continues to use the diatribal structure of moving from superficial pre-conceptions to that which is the true basis for judgment; from what is a matter of public evidence to that which is known solely by oneself and God.[51] At the same time, this movement towards a genuine self-understanding is brought about by the fundamental eschatological perspective in which everything becomes patent. The stage set in 1:18ff. now features the figure of the primordial human. Or, in more technical terms, the figure of the Urzeit has been disclosed and established by the reality of the inbreaking Endzeit.

Interrupting this disclosure of the ground of judgment, vs 17 begins a section (vss 17-24) quite telling in its rhetoric. Through the use of diatribe and especially the anacoluthon at the end of vs 20, Paul stylistically demonstrates the discrepancy between the claim and the performance of his addressee. As was the case with the beginning of chap. 2, Stowers has shown that vss 17-24 exhibit diatribal

---

[51]Cf. Epictetus 4.8.10ff.

characteristics. Thus, we rapidly encounter (1) the use of the second person singular pronoun in direct address; (2) the sudden turning to address an opponent; (3) a series of indicting rhetorical questions; (4) the use of vices in an apostrophe; (5) statement-question pattern; (6) the use of supporting quotation.[52]   Perhaps most dramatically effective is the anacoluthon, which breaks up the apodosis of vss 17-20 with a surprising series of rhetorical questions (vss 21-22).

Indeed, so typical are both the format and the accusations which Paul employs that Stowers has justly observed that if the title "Jew" were changed to "Stoic" and if the specific Jewish references (vss 22b, 24) were eliminated, then what one would find would be a clear example of the indictment of the pretentious philosopher.[53] The functions mentioned are also those of the Cynic/Stoic philosopher who is a "guide to the lost,"[54]   an   instructor   of   the   foolish,[55]   claiming   to   discern (δοκιμάζειν) right impressions from wrong as a basis for ethical choice.[56] The characterization of the figure addressed is not simply that of a pretentious person but of a pretentious moral and religious teacher.[57]

Now Paul has in vss 17-20 brought forward what would at first blush appear to be a rather positive image of the Jewish teacher/missionary.[58] The five verbs in vss 17ff. characterize the attitude brought about by the possession of the Torah.[59] The participial phrases

---

[52]Cf. Stowers, *Paul and the Diatribe*, 149-51.

[53]Cf. ibid., 173-75.

[54]Epictetus 2.12.3.

[55]Epictetus 3.22.17.

[56]Ibid., 1.20.7; 2.12.20.

[57]Cf. Stowers, *Paul and the Diatribe*, 174.

[58]Cf. Käsemann, *Romans*, 70.

[59]Ibid., 69.

(vss 18c, 19a) continue to build on this characterization, with the latter participial phrase introducing a list of titles (vss 19ff.) which are followed by another participial phrase providing the basis for these self-predications. Up to this point the confident boasting and self-predication which appear to follow are basic prerogatives for the knowledge and possession of the νόμος.

This conditional address is rudely shaken by vss 23ff. A series of indicting rhetorical questions[60] renders the addressee inconsistent. The public claim and image is upset by the discrepancy of human praxis.[61] The μόρφωσις (vs 20c) which at first seems quite positive now becomes a mere appearance without substance. The figure of the "Jew" cannot hold up under the disclosure of his self-contradiction. Verse 23, summarizing this inconsistency, shows how the initial understanding of καυχᾶσαι in vs 17 is radically undermined by this development. Now the boasting turns to a bragging about what one does not truly possess.[62] The apparent advantages turn out to be evidence of the self-indictment, for the "Jew" does not fulfill what his titles and image promise.

This disclosure of the self-contradiction of the "Jew" is quite significant for our investigation. Not only does Paul utilize the structure of the diatribe here but he makes use of language which is common to Hellenistic Judaism. In essence he has brought forward into this discussion language through which the basic contemporary self-understanding of the Diaspora Synagogue was constructed.[63] Paul turns upside down the image understood in Hellenistic Judaism.[64]

---

[60]Cf. Seneca *Ep*. 77.17; Epictetus 2.1.28.

[61]Cf. Epictetus 2.9.19; 2.19.24-28.

[62]Cf. Bultmann, " καυχάομαι κτλ ," *TDNT* 3. 645-54.

[63]Cf. Käsemann, *Romans*, 69-70; E. Norden, *Agnostos Theos: Untersuchungen zur Formengeschichte religioser Rede* (Stuttgart: Teubner, 1956) 296ff.

[64]Cf. W.S. 18:4; Sib.Or. 3.195; Josephus *Contra Ap*. 2.293.

Furthermore, in bringing to light the lifeworld created through this language, Paul juxtaposes this figure of the acme of present Hellenistic Jewish understanding with the figure of the Urzeit discovered in the previous section. Indeed, the very basis for determining the self-contradiction of the "Jew" is found already in vs 13. The effect of this section, then, is not simply to discern this self-contradiction but to view it in light of the criterion unveiled through the eschatological understanding of the preceding verses. The judgment against the "Jew" is made not simply by observation but from the perspective gained through the revelation that God's judgment is now upon all. The quotation from Isaiah 52:5 (LXX) confirms this sense of eschatological judgment (vs 24).[65]

In returning to the question asked earlier about the "identity" of the ἄνθρωπος in 2:2, one can see that the reason why Paul does not begin with calling this ἄνθρωπος 'Ιουδαῖος is due to his understanding that 'Ιουδαῖος represents a title but not the essence of what it means to be a "true Jew". Moreover, his strategy was to determine a basic criterion which a Jew could agree upon as constituting authenticity before he exposed the worth of the title. For through this diatribal format Paul is attempting to move away from given preconceptions to that which has a genuine basis. To delay even the title 'Ιουδαῖος causes the Jewish self-understanding to pause, giving Paul the opportunity to lay the basis for his argument.

The final verses of chap. 2 graphically present a collision of lifeworlds. The contemporary self-understanding of the Jew is brought together with the figure of the Urzeit in a critical confrontation. Now the symbol of sharing in the Covenant of God with Israel, circumcision, is

---

[65]Paul here changes the meaning of this verse into its opposite. What causes the Gentiles to blaspheme is no longer the suffering of the Jews but their inconsistent behavior. This verse, as Käsemann suggests, could well have been a missionary polemic (*Romans*, 71), although I do not see that it necessarily has to be a primitive Christian one.

mentioned for the first time. Yet, the criterion of true performance (vs13) determines how one looks upon this rite. Its worth is subject to the criterion of usefulness (vs 25a). What matters really is genuine performance,[66] thereby rendering circumcision one of the external advantages enumerated in vss 17-20. Far from guaranteeing an assured position, circumcision is subject to the paradoxical situation that transgression of the Law renders it uncircumcision. In continuing to address the apostrophied "Jew", Paul exposes the paradoxical situation by first rhetorically asking whether the uncircumcised who keeps the Law (cf. vss 14-15) will be accounted as circumcised (vs 26) and then by declaring that the uncircumcised who carries out the Law will judge the circumcised transgressor of the Law (vs 27).

Verse 27 is extremely important for this investigation. For here, at last, γράμμα is introduced into the dialogue. Moreover, the relation of γράμμα to περιτομή and to φύσις must be considered. There appears to be a contrasting parallelism set up. Ἡ ἀκροβυστία judges the Jew directly addressed (σέ). Further, ἐκ φύσεως modifies the former, while διὰ γράμματος καὶ περιτομῆς the latter. The first fulfills the νόμος, the second transgresses it. Without γράμμα the sentence follows directly, if not surprisingly, from what has been shown above. The eschatological perspective actually inverts what was the original assumption of the "Jew" (vs 2). It is the "Gentile" who judges the "Jew", contrary to the assured position of those who "know". The uncircumcised acting ἐκ φύσεως [67] is set off against the "Jew" who relies on external assurances.[68] Why, then, has γράμμα been introduced? So far in this investigation of Letter/Spirit we have seen how γράμμα carries in its realm of significance the understanding that there exists a way in which tradition can be embodied and objectively assessed.

---

[66] ἐὰν νόμον πράσσης , vs 25a.

[67] Cf. vss 14-15.

[68] Cf. vss 25, 17-24.

In the chapter on Galatians, I have argued that Paul sees any reliance upon circumcision and works of the Law as a retreat into a deadly lifeworld. The analysis of 2 Corinthians 3 has further shown how the lifeworld of the γράμμα was drastically criticized through the eschatological event in Christ. Paul refused any attempt to assure objectively his position. And here in this chapter, one can see that the issue has come down to that of true performance and external reliance. Thus, in bringing γράμμα into the discussion, Paul is indicating that he continues to work within the cultural horizon opened up in Galatians and explored even further in 2 Corinthians. Indeed, we can see this employment of γράμμα in vs 27 as a further expansion of his intellectual conversation, since, in opposing γράμμα to φύσις, Paul is juxtaposing the use of tradition, insofar as it stands for an external self-understanding, with the primordial, mythic possibility of the Urzeit figure. He is setting the longed-for promise of the "natural" human (seen in an eschatological perspective) against the contemporary cultural figure of what most would regard as genuine religion. In short, the cultural bases and associations unearthed so far in this investigation of the Letter/Spirit now take on through this apocalyptic setting a universal, if not mythic, significance. In facing the "Jew" in his highest cultural embodiment (and his greatest self-contradiction) Paul is questioning the very basis of *homo religious*. We have had indications of this in chap. 1.[69] Now the apparent embodiment of true religion and thus of human hope is put into question. And the means (διὰ γράμματος καὶ περιτομῆς) whereby this ideal can be effected are now seen in radical opposition to the possibility of fulfilling this human drive.

The final two verses, bristling in antitheses, bear out this line of thought. Again, taking his rhetorical patterns from diatribal speech, Paul distinguishes the public Jew from the hidden Jew. Verse 28 makes it quite clear that the true "Jew" has no public ground of support. The external rite of circumcision has as little ultimate worth as the title of

---

[69]Cf. p. 5 above.

"Jew".[70] The antithetical contrast in vs 29 finally brings to light the guiding principle for the entire dialogue. The true "Jew" is hidden, whose circumcision is of the heart, whose praise is from God and not from men. The use of περιτομή καρδίας not only is in direct opposition to ἐν σαρκί περιτομή (vs 28b) but also takes in the import of vs 15 as well as the eschatological association of vs 5. Indeed, Paul is going beyond the Cynic-Stoic distinction of inauthentic and authentic praise.[71] by placing this distinction within his eschatological focus. Thus, the public/hidden distinction does not refer simply to the distinction between appearance and reality or between material and spiritual but to two different lifeworlds. Käsemann has rightly noted that Paul is not referring to any external/internal motif, as could be found in 1 QS 5:5.[72] Rather, in applying the antithesis ἐν πνεύματι οὐ γράμματι to περιτομή καρδίας , Paul brings forward the Jewish eschatological tradition[73] as well as his own prior use of γράμμα/πνεῦμα (2 Cor 3:6), making it clear that the mythic *incognito* of human hope is realized not through the powers of the present age but by the eschatological power of the Spirit. The transcendent force associated with either term of the antithesis allows Paul to place this diatribal examination upon a universal level.

Lastly, we must be concerned with a matter of time. Verse 29 does not contain any explicit verb. Are we to read in the present tense, as in vs 28, or do we follow the lead of vss 26-27 and supply an understood future? If Paul is concerned with an eschatological perspective, it would seem that the latter possibility is warranted. However, there seem to be compelling arguments to the contrary. First, we have noted throughout

---

[70]Both of which are predicates in vs 28.

[71]Cf. Epictetus 4.8.17.

[72]Käsemann, *Romans*, 75.

[73]Cf. Jer 4:4.

the interplay of future and present. Indeed, what we have observed is that Paul is bringing the future to bear and cast light upon the possibilities of the present. Second, the tense of κρίνεῖ in vs 27 is itself a matter of dispute. Thirdly, the constructed antithesis with vs 28 would argue for a continuance of the temporal sense. Lastly, one must consider the strategy of the entire diatribal dialogue which has been investigated. The concern of diatribe is to come to the truth, especially insofar as it concerns one's present understanding. Verses 28-29 present us with a decisive statement of what constitutes genuine existence in the eyes of God. Indeed, the future light shines directly into the present dialogue. Moreover, the wished-for ideal, the figure of the Urzeit, is now seen as a reality effected through the lifeworld of the Spirit. There is a future note, but it is not indicated by the missing verb. The future is found in the figure of mythic possibility which is now grounded in the present.

Thus, a detailed analysis of chap. 2 has shown that Paul uses a diatribal format to bring to light the genuine basis for self-examination. Within his apocalyptic horizon Paul has brought into radical questioning the contemporary assumptions of what constitutes the human project. In bringing the "public Jew" into self-examination, Paul has exposed within the Jewish tradition as well as in that of Hellenism the abiding, mythic figure of the "natural" human as the projection of what is authentically human. He has set two lifeworlds in opposition under the light of God's eschatological action and has allowed his audience to conclude with him that the hope of the Urzeit has come true ἐν πνεύματι . Moreover, through the use of the antithesis γράμμα/πνεῦμα , Paul has shown that his own intellectual journey comes out of his previous discussions and that it is now expanding on a universal scale to deal with the issues of human history and society.

III. Romans 7:6

A. Preliminary Remarks

The surprising reappearance of Letter/Spirit in Romans 7:6 once more brings up the question of the position and function of this verse within the context of the epistle. It has already been pointed out[74] that 7:6 presents a likely summary of the main theme of chaps. 7-8. In noting the oddity of this verse along with vss 1-5 in regard to the preceding material, Käsemann has suggested that this verse may well be an introduction of Paul's own theological reflection (coming from the conflict in 2 Corinthians 3), going well beyond the application of baptismal exhortation.[75] While I find myself in agreement with this suggestion,[76] I am not at all certain that 7:1ff. represents an entirely new turn in the movement of the epistle, where Paul once more faces the issue of the Law. Rather, what I shall try to demonstrate is that Paul works precisely out of the lifeworlds disclosed in chaps. 5-6 and that in 7:6 we have a hermeneutical thesis which not only serves as a basis of expansion for the subsequent chapters but also explicitly distinguishes the lifeworlds already brought out. Further, in employing the antithesis of Letter/Spirit in 7:6 Paul not only brings back into the conversation the issues disclosed in 1:18-2:29 but continues to enlarge the scope of these issues. Thus, it will be argued that 7:6 serves as both a summary and a leading transition. Using what has been brought out in regard to the central focus of significance of the death of Christ and the subsequent question of δουλούειν, it provides the governing themes for chaps. 7-8.

---

[74]Cf. Bornkamm, "Sin, Law and Death," in *Early Christian Experience*, 88; Käsemann, *Romans*, 190.

[75]Cf. Käsemann, *Romans*, 190-91.

[76]As well as with the claim that 7:7ff. does not serve as an excursus or apology for the Law; cf. Käsemann, *Romans* 192, note list.

B. Romans 7:6 and Its Context

The language in which the antithesis of Letter/Spirit is embedded demands
an appreciation of the preceding context. Indeed, if 7:6 is taken by itself
one can see that each part of the verse is fraught with possible questions
and difficulties:

7:6a) νυνὶ δὲ κατηργήθημεν ἀπὸ τοῦ νόμου,

7:6b) ἀποθανόντες ἐν ᾧ κατειχόμεθα,

7:6c) ὥστε δουλεύειν ἡμᾶς ἐν καινότητι πνεύματος

7:6d) καὶ οὐ παλαιότητι γράμματος

In order to clarify the meaning of the antithesis one must take into account
the   temporal   aspect   introduced   both   by   the   terms
καινότης / παλαιότης   and by indication of a past situation which
now no longer obtains (νυνὶ . . . κατειχόμεθα).   The present
situation (νυνί) is set off against the past situation given in vs 5 (ὅτε .
. .).   Secondly, the presence of νόμος raises still further questions as to
its relationship to the new situation as well as to the old.   Thirdly, the
meaning of 7:6b is hardly clear.   What is the sense of the clause
introduced by the phrase ἐν ᾧ? How is this latter prepositional phrase to
be taken? Does it refer simply to the situation of being ὑπὸ νόμον
(6:14), or is there more implied?   Lastly, what is the significance of
δουλεύειν   in 6c? I have argued that πνεῦμα is associated with
freedom; why now does Paul link the new epoch of the spirit with
slavery? Is this not a contradiction?

The antecedents of the issues underlying the language of 7:6 can be
found in the two preceding chapters. In these chapters Paul expands the
horizon of his discussion to take into account the life and death forces
which undergird not only the present situation but all of history, past and
future. Thus, after establishing the claim that the death of Jesus grounds
the confidence of those ἐκ πίστεως (5:1-11), Paul expands the
perspective of the meaning of Christ's death by bringing in the mythic
figure of Adam as a type of the one to come (5:14). Using the type of
Adam, Paul is able to explore the lifeworld which has come into existence
through this prototype. Through Adam's trespass, sin and death become
dominant forces in human history (5:12, 14, 15, 17, 19, 21). The

relationship established from the beginning is hardly the promise of a Golden Age; rather, humanity is locked into a deadly fate. The future is quite grim: only condemnation awaits (5:16, 18). Now it is in this mythic account of history that Paul includes the Law. Consistent with his argument in Gal 3:17ff., Paul notes that the Law is limited in its temporal appearance. However, the negative force of the Law becomes abundantly clear. For only with the Law does sin become accountable (5:13). Indeed, with the coming of the Law the fatal situation is exacerbated not relieved (5:20). Sin's grip on humanity through death is thus viewed as a complete stranglehold (5:21).

Of course, this revision of human history is done through the perspective of what has been brought about through the death of Christ. Indeed, the death of Christ was the occasion and the stimulus for casting the mythic net of understanding wide enough to include even the primordial past. It is the present effect of the death of Christ which allows Paul not only to view the fated destiny of humanity but to envision the overcoming of this desperate condition (5:15, 16, 17, 18, 19, 21). The death of Christ establishes the possibility of another lifeworld which both illumines the deathworld of Adam and indicates its limits. The cursed lifeworlds found in Galatians and 2 Corinthians have been radically expanded here in Romans by Paul. But, as in the two previous cases, the eschatological action of God in Christ is the cause for this interpretation.

This mythic expansion and revision by Paul in chap. 5 is then brought up short by the rhetorical questions in 6:1. The implications of such a vision are sought once more through an anonymous interlocutor, who brings out some existential possibilities of the new situation. While the questions are easily exposed as misunderstandings of the situation (6:2, 3), they are the lead-in for Paul to ground the present condition of his audience in a radical appreciation of their own baptismal experience (6:3). This experience becomes the basis for an exhortation to live in the newness of life (6:4). Their past and future now take on the fate of Christ. Just as they have grown into the likeness of his death, so they will grow into the likeness of his resurrection.[77] The inclusion into the death of Christ means not only a sacramental link but a destruction of the lifeworld in which the believers had previously existed. The "old man" is crucified (6:6), death and sin no longer are the dominant forces of existence (6:6, 7, 9). This new appreciation of the forces and powers at work in the believers' lifeworld allows Paul to exhort the believers to live the resurrected life already in the present (6:12-23). The believers are enabled through the new powers to actually live beyond the fated conditions to which they were heir.

Now it is this new situation which gives rise once more to the problem of antinomianism (6:15). Does not this new freedom actually mean that the believers are able to give into their instincts and desires? Are they not empowered to finally fulfill the sophistic dream of the instinctual man who knows no convention, no law, no custom?[78] In giving up the Law (6:14), which is part of the fated epoch, are they now liberated to pursue their own desires?

It is in answer to these concerns that Paul brings in the language of slavery. For Paul there is no such thing as an isolated or autonomous existence. Rather, one is either under the sway of death or of life. One is fundamentally *related*. Thus, liberation from the powers of sin and death implies simultaneously service for God (6:16, 19, 20, 22). Here Paul shares a common assumption with both Stoic and Cynic thinking.[79] However, the telling difference is that for Paul this liberated condition is effected through the perspective of the believing community.[80] In no way

---

[77]6:5. This "growing together" is of capital interest since it recalls one of the ways in which the primordial humans lived with the gods; cf. Dio Chrysostom 1.27ff.

[78]Cf. Excursus, pp. 82-84.

[79]E.g., Epictetus 3.22.2-3.

[80]Cf. pp. 187ff. below.

is it a matter of the liberated individual who is privately related to God.[81] Lastly, we should note that, while Paul presents the effective reality of the new lifeworld in the midst of the daily lives of the believers, he does not say that the former lifeworld of sin and death has been completely removed from the stage of human affairs. The force and the language of 6:12ff. indicate precisely the opposite, namely, that the believers are part of the new age which has established a beachhead in their midst against the still present, though ultimately defeated, powers of the world of Adam.

It is in light of these two chapters which disclose the lifeworlds of death and life that 7:1ff. should be read. This section begins once more with a direct address to those who "know the Law." In typical diatribe style we have a verb of thinking, used ironically (ἀγνοεῖτε)[82] along with an agreed upon assumption (ὅτι . . . ζῆ). It has been pointed out that this general proposition could be understandable to both Jew and Gentile alike.[83] Indeed, from what we have discussed so far the concern for the threat of antinomianism (6:15) carries significance not only for the Jew but also for those pagans who found law to be ultimately linked with the possibility of order in the cosmos.[84] Moreover, the example advanced in vss 2-3 would fall under common legal experience. In vs 4 we have an application of the example to the present situation of the community, providing an exhortation implied in the interpretation of the believers' relation to the Law and the death of Christ. Finally, vss 5-6 bring out the temporal horizon of the situation quite explicitly, as well as further describing the lifeworlds of existential option. The fittingness of the example produced by Paul can be seen when one considers the aspect

---

[81]Contrast Epictetus 4.8.18.

[82]Cf. Stowers, *Paul and the Diatribe*, 138.

[83]Cf. Käsemann, *Romans*, 187.

[84]Cf. Excursus, passim.

of existential relatedness which has been mentioned above.[85]   The
complex comparison of wife to husband under the Law brings out a
number of points. First, it ties in the issue of relatedness coming from
6:16ff. Second, it articulates the distinction between a primary relation
and the overriding condition (the Law). The force of the Law is seen as
effective only insofar as the relationship to the husband exists. Thirdly,
this comparison allows Paul to build on it in terms of "bearing fruit" (vs
4). Fourthly, the point of death becomes the determining factor for both
the "bound" (δέδεται) and free (ἐλευθέρα) conditions of the
woman. And, as we have just seen, it is the death of Christ which has
been the operating basis for the discussions of past and present existence.
Thus, the conclusion from the example (vs 4) once more reiterates what
Paul has attempted to establish in chaps. 5-6. Furthermore, the personal
relation inherent in the image of vss 2-3 forces the meaning of the
relationship brought out in vs 4 to take on equally personal overtones.[86]

        The following two verses (5-6) provide a further elucidation of the
past and present conditions. Already noted has been the temporal
emphasis (ὅτε . . . νυνί), which corresponds to the time the woman
was under the force of the Law and when she becomes free. In vs 5 we
see how the past condition for ἡμεῖς is a concretization of the mythic
fate outlined in chap. 5. Indeed, through the Law the παθήματα τῶν
ἁμαρτιῶν ἐνηργεῖτα ἐν τοῖς μέλεσιν ἡμῶν .[87] The
product of this existential condition is the same as that found in Adam's,
namely, death. The sixth verse, then, picks up the notion of liberation
from the law.[88]   7:6b becomes understandable also in light of what
precedes. "We" have "died" picks up the implications of the baptismal

---

[85]P. 168ff above.

[86] εἰς τὸ γενέσθαι ὑμᾶς ἑτέρῳ ; cf. 6:10; Gal 2:19-20.

[87]Cf. 5:20; 7:23.

[88]Cf. 7:2c, 3d.

language in 6:3ff. The emphasis is upon the death of the condition in which "we" existed (cf. 6:6). Ἐν ᾧ κατειχόμεθα thus means not simply the Law but the conditions under which the Law has had binding effect, namely, the fated lifeworld of sin and death. The conclusion that service is now the present condition (δουλεύειν) thus touches both the relatedness brought out in 7:2-3 and that found in 6:15ff. It is easily noted that the comparison which Paul uses in 7:2-3 does have a particular flaw. If the woman, freed from the force of the Law, marries again, does she not bind herself once more to the very Law which has confined her? While no comparison usually walks on all fours, Paul is not unaware of the force of this figure. His primary purpose was, of course, to provide an example of how one can get out of a legal bind. Further legal speculation is not required. Yet, he is aware of the related aspect which he continues to use in vs 4e. However, the condition of this relatedness is radically changed in Paul's perspective, and this is brought out by the modification of the "new" slavery by the antithesis ἐν καινότητι πνεύματος καὶ οὐ παλαιότητι γράμματος . In using this antithesis, Paul brings to bear the temporal horizon which he has established in chaps. 5-6, especially as it relates to the new vision of the believers' present situation (cf. 6:4). Moreover, by introducing the Letter/Spirit antithesis at this point, he expands the meaning and dimension of this association. We already have mentioned that in 2:29 Paul has extended the horizon of this antithesis to take in the more universal or mythic condition of human existence. Now, the lifeworlds of chaps. 5-6 are revealed as the epochs of Letter and Spirit, encompassing the history and the future of humanity. Moreover, in each instance one can see that Paul employs this antithesis in a discussion which is trying to work out the conditions of human existence. As we have seen in Galatians and 2 Corinthians, the Letter/Spirit antithesis comes into play as a way of distinguishing authentic from inauthentic existence. Thus, 7:6 provides a more than adequate summary of the preceding chapters, especially since it situates the existential possibilities of the believing community within the overarching forces of death and life. The introduction of γράμμα and πνεῦμα, already providing a universal thrust in 2:29, now with the

additional mythic reappraisal of history, establishes a fundamental
hermeneutical basis for understanding human existence. In the following
sections, I shall argue that 7:6 provides the leading thoughts for the
exposition of the epoch of the Letter (7:7-25a) and the epoch of the Spirit
(8:2-25). In each instance the two opposing lifeworlds will be seen even
more explicitly, as Paul continues to discover the limits and depths of
these lifeworlds.

IV. Romans 7:7-24

A. A Question of Strategy

What follows Romans 7:6 is not only dramatic in its own right but has
long been a matter of contention in the history of ideas. Both format and
content have been subject to perennial debate and exegesis. Indeed, 7:7-
24 has been seen usually as a Pauline digression permitting the writer one
more chance at explaining his understanding of the Law. Of course, the
"I" of this section has given rise to a plethora of interpretations.
However, since Kümmel's monograph,[89] it has been generally agreed
that the "I" must be distinguished from either an autobiographical usage
or some aspect of Christian existence. It has even been argued that
Romans 7:7ff. deals so specifically with a historical situation between
Jews and Gentiles that any attempt to generalize from this text would be a
misapplication of the material.[90] Nevertheless, the task of interpretation
of these verses must once more be undertaken in order to find out how the
hermeneutical thesis given in 7:6 is borne out by Paul. In this part of the
investigation I shall concentrate precisely on the breaks, changes and
surprises in the text so as to discover what kind of lifeworld Paul is
speaking of with his audience.

---

[89]W. Kümmel, *Romer 7 und die Bekehrung des Paulus* (Leipzig: Hinrichs,
1929).

[90]K. Stendahl, "The Apostle Paul and the Introspective Conscience of the
West," in *Paul among Jews and Gentiles* (Philadelphia: Fortress, 1976) 78-96.

To disclose what kind of lifeworld Paul is speaking of it will be necessary to focus sharply on the use of the "I" in 7:7ff. The phenomenon of the "I" embedded in an array of diatribal conventions suggests that, in determining the strategy employed, one might gain a hermeneutical clue to the lifeworld at issue. Finally, what must not be lost in this task is the place of the audience in regard to the text. What has usually been overlooked in the history of interpretation is that Paul is speaking to people who may well have been challenged by what he brings forward.

First of all, then, in regard to the literary format as a whole we find that diatribal characteristics are quite evident. These are: the posing of an imagined objector's questions (7:7, ὁ νόμος ἁμαρτία ; 7:13, τὸ οὖν ἀγαθὸν ἐμοὶ ἐγένετο θάνατος ;); a short citation from authority (7:7, ὁ νόμος ἔλεγεν); the use of paradox (7:9-10); the presentation of internal contradictions (7:15, 17, 18b, 19, 20a); antitheses (7:9, 10, 15, 17, 18,19, 20, 22-23); statement of assumed agreement (14a); a dramatic or rhetorical question, emotionally charged (7:24); an expression of thanksgiving (7:25a); the use of personification (νόμος, 7:7, 14(?), 22(?); ἁμαρτία , 7:8, 9, 11, 13, 17, 20 23?).[91] And, of course, throughout 7:7-25a we have the use of "I", within a movement of increasing self-judgment.

Now it is the use of the first person singular which is both striking and perplexing in this section. In the preceding two and one-half verses (4d-6) we find the first person plural, indicating Paul's deliberate identification of himself and his audience. In fact, vs 7 begins with another first person plural, suggesting a possible conclusion to his argument. The latter use, however, clearly indicates a different "voice"[92] which is immediately answered (μὴ γένοιτο) by the first person speech in vs 7b. In attempting to clarify the relationship of the Law to sin Paul has moved from the mytho-historical language of chap. 5. Indeed,

---

[91]Cf. Stowers, *Paul and the Diatribe*, 133ff.

[92]Such as the objectors in 3:9; 4:1.

we have already noted that the mythic thinking of chap. 5 has been altered in chap. 6 and 7:1-6 as Paul applies the meaning of this thinking to the life of the community he addresses. The issue seems no longer to be sketched broadly against the backdrop of the universal forces of history but concentrated on a smaller scale. In fact, the issue becomes located within the perimeter of the "I". It remains to be seen, however, whether the forces uncovered in chaps. 5-6 have actually disappeared from the scene altogether.

Yet, the question as to why Paul employs the "I" at this point remains unanswered. Scholars since Kümmel have noted that this "I" should be distinguished from an autobiographical sense or from a representative of Christian existence. But, why the first person singular has been employed and not, for example, the second person singular (as in chap. 2), or even the third person singular, in apostrophe, still remains a puzzle. For if the "I" is embedded in such diatribal elements, why does this form appear and not others?

B. "I" as Persona

A possible avenue towards a resolution of these questions comes through asking what possible lifeworld is disclosed through this expression of the first person singular. For it is simply not a matter of identifying the "I" but of placing the "I" within the lifeworld of which the "I" is a concrete articulation. In addition, the employment of diatribal convention by Paul may give us a clue as to interpreting this lifeworld. For the "I" understood by the Cynic tradition is very much a dramatic figure. Indeed, the comparison of the true Cynic with that of an actor in a play is a commonplace. In Ench. 17, for instance, we have a remarkable summary of the interpretation of authentic existence in terms of a dramatic role:

> Remember that you are an actor in a play, the character of which
> is determined by the Playwright: if He wishes the play to be
> short, it is short; if long, it is long; if He wishes you to play the
> part of a beggar, remember to act even this role adroitly; and so
> if your role be that of a cripple, an official, or a layman. For

> this is your business, to play admirably the role assigned to you; but the selection of that role is Another's [93]

In a fragment from a homily of Arrian we have a reiteration of this:

> And then shall the man of noble nature make a poorer showing than Polus, and not play well any role to which the Deity assigns him?[94]

Indeed, when a person becomes aware of his true relation to the universe and to God, he becomes free from fear and can enter into the drama of life. Thus, in Epictetus 4.7.12ff., we find such an attestation of this free human:

> "Would you have me bear poverty?" Bring it on and you shall see what poverty is when it finds a good actor to play the part. "Would you have me hold office?" Bring it on. "Would you have me suffer deprivation from office?" Bring it on. "Well, and would you have me bear troubles?" Bring them on too. "Well, and exile?" Whenever I go it will be well with me.[95]

In Teles' Περὶ αὐταρκείας we have perhaps the most explicit working out of this comparison. Just as a good actor must perform properly whatever role the poet assigns, so too the good man must perform whatever Tyche assigns. Quoting Bion, Teles explains:

> For she (Τύχη), like a poetess, sometimes assigns the role of the first-speaker, sometimes that of second-speaker; and sometimes that of king, sometimes that of vagabond.[96]

This explanation is then concretized by a monologue on Bion's part:

---

[93]Ench. 17 (Loeb trans.).

[94]Frag. 11(174), Stobaeus 4.33.28 (Loeb trans.).

[95]Epictetus 4.7.12 (Loeb trans.).

[96]Teles Περὶ αὐταρκείας (5H), trans. E. O'Neil, in *Teles* (Missoula: Scholars, 1977) 7.

> You rule properly, and I obey, he says; and you are the leader of
> many, but I of this one alone; and you, since you are wealthy,
> give freely, but I receive from you confidently, not submissively
> or like a low-born man with grumbling. You enjoy many things
> properly, but I just a few.[97]

Indeed, the use of the dramatic role (πρόσωπον) can also be envisioned for conditions or affairs. Teles quotes Bion again who personifies Poverty in an attempt to cause people to give up their assumption that it is Poverty's fault for human unhappiness:

> Why do you fight me? You aren't being deprived of any good
> because of me are you? Not of wisdom, are you, not of justice,
> not of courage?[98]

The point of this brief excursion into the dramatic mode of speech within the diatribal tradition is this: that the expression of the "I" can be viewed as an articulation of a πρόσωπον , a role in which the self-understanding of that role is tied to forces or powers which engender that particular role. The "I" is not simply an isolated individual but is related to the powers which have assigned its fate. In other words, in choosing to use the "I" the writer is indirectly disclosing the lifeworld which gives meaning to the "I". Furthermore, if Paul is using the "I" within a diatribal strategy, then he may be exhibiting this "I" in order to display before his audience a persona which speaks for and to the preconceptions of that audience. In using the "I" Paul is presenting the possibility that the audience can recognize itself in the "I" and becomes its own accuser.[99] For the very nature of this language calls for participation and self-critique. The use of the "I" asks the unspoken questions: where does this "I" come from and why is it used? The "I" is used to reckon with the unconscious assumptions of the audience. Their assumptions as to the

---

[97]Teles (6H).

[98]Teles (6H-7H).

[99]Cf. Diogenes 40.3 in *The Cynic Epistles*, ed. A. Malherbe, 169.

powers of the world which bring about the "I" are exposed. Thus, the selection of the "I" is an entrance into the art of self-criticism, where the audience is brought face to face with the principles and powers that constitute their world.

This understanding of the "I" should be seen in contrast to a more modern interpretation of the self as a phenomenon existing without prior relationships. Rather, this dramatic understanding of the "I" is a given, but not entirely on its own. The "I" is given in relationship to appearances or to reality. This "I" is tested through the diatribal examination as to the basic preconceptions upon which this "I" is based. This "I" is in a profound sense constituted through knowledge, built up out of the debris of opinion into the true city of the divine. The phenomenon of the "I" then was not an abstract speculation but an expression of the true existential role which a human plays in the drama of life. The "I" of Romans 7:7ff. would then not represent the solitary modern ego but a *persona dramatis* or even a *persona socialis*, becoming a spokesperson (πρόσωπον) for the contradiction and truth at the basis of human existence.

C. Romans 7:7-24: An Analysis

In returning, then, to 7:7ff., one finds that the appearance of the "I" occurs simultaneously with the recognition of the force of the Law. This takes place in the attempt to clarify the relation of the Law to sin which has already been anticipated in 5:20; 6:14, 15; 7:5-6. Now, however, this clarification becomes enacted through the drama of the "I". Indeed, διὰ νόμου reviews the ambiguous τὰ παθήματα τῶν ἁμαρτιῶν τὰ διὰ τοῦ νόμου (7:5) as well as the apocalyptic assertion διὰ νόμου ἐπίγνωσις ἁμαρτίας (3:20). Thus, the large-scale apocalyptic vision and the mythic momentum of Romans come to stand within the situation in which knowledge comes to the "I" through the Law. The knowledge which is effected is twofold: first, the original intention of the Law as God's will (οὐκ ἐπιθυμήσεις);[100] second,

---

[100]Cf. Käsemann, *Romans*, 196.

the possibility of sin within the "I" (τὴν τε γὰρ ἐπιθυμίαν οὐκ ἤδειν εἰ μὴ ὁ νόμος ἔλεγεν). This knowledge in the first aspect is already indicated in 3:21, where the intent of the Law was the promise. Yet, just as in Gal 3:21, the Law was unable to make good on that promise. Moreover, this good intent of the Law will be reiterated throughout this section (vss 12, 14, 16, 21, 22). Furthermore, it is precisely this utterance of the Law which brings the "I" to stand within the understanding of the possibility of ἐπιθυμία as encompassing the sphere of the "I". Just as sin took advantage of the introduction of the Law within Paul's mythic revision (5:20-21a), so now sin set up its base of operations διὰ τῆς ἐντολῆς in order to bring about all kinds of ἐπιθυμία ἐν ἐμοί (7:8).

Now the selection of "the last of the Ten Great Words"[101] in conjunction with the usage of the "I" is quite strategic for Paul. First of all, one should note that the issue of ἐπιθυμία in the Stoic/Cynic tradition is radically attached to the question of freedom. The mastery of ἐπιθυμία represented the feat of the truly autonomous individual. In his long treatise on freedom,[102] Epictetus demonstrates again and again that the free individual is the one who is free of hindrance, forces and desires. Freedom is not acquired by satisfying one's desire but by suppressing it.[103] The issue of living well means to come to understand that one can overcome or gain mastery of what was in one's control and to be free from anything which rendered one dependent. The task was to seek for the knowledge which enabled one to live.[104]

Philo follows this philosophical tradition in interpreting the last commandment. Indeed, he points out that the most dangerous passion is

---

[101]Philo *Spec. leg.* 4.78.

[102]Epictetus 4.1.

[103]Ibid., 4.1.175.

[104]Epictetus 4.1.64.

precisely ἐπιθυμία .[105]   He even goes so far as to say that it transcends so far the range of evil that it can be called the fountain of all evils (πηγὴ τῶν κακῶν). It is the originator of evil from which flows the calamities of the world.[106]   Desire then is the most insidious and subversive of enemies.[107]   And the reason for this is that while all of the other passions are involuntary, ἐπιθυμία originates with ourselves and is voluntary.[108]   However, this analysis of ἐπιθυμία for Philo is but the occasion for suggesting a remedy, which comes through an understanding of the Law of Moses.   Through obedience to the governance of reason (κυβερνήτη λογισμῷ), peace, order and the perfection of happy living are possible.[109]   Indeed, it seems that Philo has interpreted the Genesis story in light of this commandment.[110] Moreover, Käsemann has noted that there could well be behind this the tradition of Adam receiving the whole law with the commandment which he was given.[111]

What is significant, however, for Paul is that for vss 8ff. the positive possibility of the Law is not available for the "I".   The knowledge which is communicated is hardly liberating; rather, it exposes a cursed condition. Furthermore, this cursed situation is laid right at what Paul's intellectual contemporaries would regard as the threshold of freedom, namely, the informed "I".   The mythic history of the Law and

[105]Philo *Spec. leg.* 4.80.

[106]Ibid., 4.85.

[107]Idem, *Dec.* 142.

[108]Ibid.

[109]Idem, *Spec. leg.* 4.95.

[110]Cf. S. Lyonnet, "'Tu ne convoiteras pas' (from VII,7)," *Neotestamentica et Patristica* (Cullmann Freundesgabe; NovTSup 6; 1962) 163ff.

[111]Käsemann, *Romans*, 196.

sin is rewritten as the captive phenomenon of the "I". While the Cynic-Stoic could understand the possibility of the tyranny of false dogmata operating in the "I", such could be overthrown by true judgments.[112] In contrast with Paul, one sees only that sin has entered in a gripping fashion.[113]

Verses 8b-11 (χωρὶς γὰρ νόμου . . . δι᾽ αὐτῆς ἀπέκτεινεν) attempt to elucidate what has just preceded. However, the history of exegesis has shown that these verses are hardly pellucid. The problem, of course, rests in identifying the "I" mentioned in these verses. For whom was there the possibility of living before the Law? Adam seems a most likely possibility, since 5:12ff. seem to anticipate the fate of this section.[114] However, the most difficult issue is why Paul uses the "I" to bring out the implications of the mythic story of Adam. The concept of corporate personality, although greatly attractive, is not altogether convincing.[115] Rather, what should be considered here is the phenomenon of the "I" as the bearer and the revelation of the power of tradition. We have seen in the Excursus how the "I" for Philo can be envisioned as the embodiment of the Law.[116] Indeed, the "I" takes its stand as a true king insofar as the Law is written upon the soul.[117] We should also note that in the Cynic tradition figures of the past (e.g., Heracles, Socrates) become ways through which the Cynic fashions his own self-understanding. Tradition, in short, is tapped in order for the "I" not only to grow but even to make an authentic appearance. The

---

[112]Epictetus 4.1.86.

[113]Cf. 3:20.

[114]Cf. Käsemann, *Romans*, 197.

[115]Ibid.

[116]Excursus, pp. 64-66.

[117]Philo *Spec. leg.* 4.163-64.

topography of the "I" has a past and that is found in its valued tradition. Moreover, it is this tradition which then furnishes through its paradigms a future prospect for the "I".

Thus, we find particularly in the graphic vss 8b-10a not only a dependency upon 5:12ff. but also on the tradition that the Law has an effective presence (5:13, 20). This fateful paradox in which the "I" is caught is not merely the repetition of Adam's fate but a further disclosure of the lifeworld brought to light in 7:5. The epoch of the Letter now is conceived of as self-reckoning. The "I" does have knowledge of its fate, namely, that death and deception (vs 11) have entered its world. And, it is the Law accepted in its revelatory force by the "I" which occasions this understanding. At the same time, the Law can still be distinguished from both sin and the condition of the "I" (vss 12, 13). Paul once more through the "I" upholds the Law (3:31), while at the same time pointing out that the construction of the "I" through encounter with the Law brings about not the lifeworld of righteousness but that of death and sin (vs 13). In short, where Philo would see in the Law the possibility of empowerment of the "I" to overcome desire, the lifeworld of the "I" revealed through the Law for Paul can only entail the recognition of the distance of the "I" from the original intent of the Law. The hideous irony is that the internalization of the intent of the Law is the occasion not for accomplishment but for alienation.

Having demonstrated how the past traditions infiltrate the lifeworld of the "I", Paul now illustrates how even the future prospect of this lifeworld is fundamentally frustrated. The haunting ideal of the autonomous individual, already brought out in chap. 2, becomes verified in a perverse fashion. For, again and again, the "I" discloses through its speech its basic inability to perform what it understands as ultimately desirable. The dream underlying 2:13b, reiterated in the common assumption (οἴδαμεν) that the νόμος is spiritual, becomes a nightmare as one reads the entire fourteenth verse. Instead of the "I" as a "doer of the Law" one finds a "fleshly I", "sold under sin". Now the use of σαρκινός is a further indication that Paul is dealing with the question of the sphere or mode of existence of the "I". For Paul "flesh"

means basically that mode of existence in which the creature is fallen and
alienated from God.[118]   Πεπραμένος ὑπὸ τὴν ἁμαρτίαν ,
moreover, reinforces the condition already described in 7:8ff. Thus, in
this verse we see a fundamental cleavage between the potential of the Law
for the "I" and the reality of the "I" condition.

In the succeeding verses we find how intention, action and
awareness function within this "fleshly I". The "I" is privy to self-
knowledge, yet none of it will lead to a remedy of its condition. Rather,
the language used intensifies the dilemma. Thus, the "I" discloses that it
is not even aware of what it actually effects (κατεργάζομαι). What
it intends it fails to do, what it would avoid it does (vs 15). This
perception causes the "I" to seek the basis for this contradiction. Here the
"I" finds that even in its perverse condition the agreement with the Law is
attested (vs 16); at the same time, the "I" must admit that it is under the
control of another force, namely ἁμαρτία . Thus, in vss 16-17 Paul is
declaring that the "I" is not under its own control. Although the "I"
agrees with both Philo and the Cynic/Stoic tradition that true autonomy
comes about through a lived harmony of the individual and the divine
Law, the "I" faces up to the truth of its condition by saying that the "I"
cannot control itself. Thus, the Law as a means of self-interpretation
throws light not only on the potential for the individual but also on the
negativity within the individual, thereby concretizing vss 7 and 8 above.

From vs 18 on the "I" becomes increasingly disclosed as an
alienated observer of its own fated condition. The "I" knows (οἶδα) its
situation; it knows that "good" does not dwell in its "flesh" (vs 18a), that
a   chasm   exists   between   intention   (θέλειν)   and   act
(κατεργάζεσθαι) (vs 18b). Indeed, the reality of its performance is
that the "I" does what it intentionally opposes (vs 19). Recognizing this
situation, the "I" concludes that it is not actually the true performer of its
concrete action (vs 20). Thus, the control of sin has reached in the

---

[118]R. Bultmann, *Theology of the New Testament* (New York: Scribner's Sons,
1955) 2. 239-49.

observation of the "I" what the ancient world considered to be the core of possible human authenticity. The "I" cannot bring about the dream of the truly autonomous individual, the νόμος ἔμψυχος , the genuine performer of the culture's highest aspirations. Moreover, the irony is that this claim is made by the "I" at the point where the force of the Law is given at its deepest, that is, where the power of the Law has been internalized such that the "I" can appreciate the Law dwelling within (vs 22). Thus, vs 21 inverts the hope of Philo of seeing the Law written internally by declaring that another "Law" exists, that evil clings to the "I". Verse 23 observes (βλέπω) this tragic reality by stressing the dominance of this "other law" which is not only at war with the internalized Law of the νοῦς but even makes the "I" captive in its entire concrete existence (ἐν τοῖς μέλεσίν μου). In no way does this knowledge of the "I" situation allow for relief. Rather, from 7:7 we have had a thoroughgoing inspection of what constitutes the lifeworld of the "I" when it comes into contact with the force and power of the Law. This encounter does produce enlightenment, but of the negativity inherent in this relationship. Insofar as the "I" comes to take its stand as a bearer of the power of the Law it finds only the frustration of the promise delivered by the Law. The conclusion of 3:20 now is radically demonstrated within the very lifeworld of the "I". Furthermore, the servitude which is finally disclosed as inherent to the "I" constitution (vss 8, 11, 17, 20, 21, 23) is the enactment of what has been anticipated in 7:6. Thus, the final outcry of vs 24 dramatically sums up this fated condition.[119] The body of death

---

[119]Verse 25a actually begins the next section, as it breaks into the language of despair of vss 7-24. Verse 25b I regard, along with 8:1, to be a later gloss. While the later textual tradition does not suggest this, the theological and literary difficulties speak for it. First, 25b appears to support a theological position where the "I" is assured of being able to serve God. But that is precisely the issue refuted by the preceding text. Second, the balance as well as the summation of the sentence would indicate that what we have here is more a settled resolution of the text above. The use of ἄρα here and in 8:1 could also possibly indicate a conclusion on the part of a later writer. Also the use of the intensifier αὐτός is unnecessary in light of 7:7-24, while for a later hand it could indicate a self-assured position. 8:1 represents a conclusion actually to

refers not simply to the individual body but to the concrete sphere in which the existence of the "I" occurs.   "This" body of death is the enfleshment of the body of sin or, in other words, the   παλαιὸς ἡμῶν

ἄνθρωπος (6:6). Paul has gone quite far from the liturgical setting of these words to situate the reality of this cursed condition within the lifeworld of the "I". Perhaps even the order of the exclamation should be noted: ταλαίπωρος ἐγὼ ἄνθρωπος . While the usual translation runs "wretched man that I am," a more wooden translation might actually bring out the force of the Greek: "wretched I-man." For the key to this is that the full revelation of the "old human being" is made precisely through the disclosure of the "I".   The "I", built upon the hope of autonomy, nurtured through the knowledge of the Law, reveals its true character (πρόσωπον) as that of a slave (cf. 5:17) not of a king.

What, then, has Paul done in introducing this "I-section"? If it is more than an excursus on the Law or an apology for the Law, what is it? To answer this we must note first of all that 7:6 lays down for Paul a basic hermeneutical thesis, whereby he distinguishes responsible existence as coming about in the new epoch of the Spirit and not in that old age of the Letter. I have argued above that 7:6 sums up the preceding chapters. But I have also suggested that it provides a lead-in for what follows. I have earlier argued that the introduction of Spirit/Letter in chap. 2 had the effect of enlargening the scope to mythic proportions. In employing this antithesis, Paul is returning to the intellectual atmosphere of 2 Corinthians where the implicit cultural understanding concerning the power of tradition was found in the use of this antithesis. Now, already in chap. 2 Paul has gone to the cultural basis and hope for human performance and authenticity. And, here in 7:7ff. we have seen that through the use of the "I" Paul is examining what is the relationship of the individual to the force and power of the Law. The "I", usually seen as the focal point of liberation for the Hellenistic culture, where tradition

the entire passage. It does not touch directly the deliverance from the body of death (vs 24).   Moreover, the following verses (8:2-3) deal with present existence and not with the issue of judgment.

finds its true abode and concretization, is now disclosed in its fundamental contradiction. The hopes carried by the tradition through the Letter, the hope of illumination and genuine performance meet a grim prospect. In other words, the valued avenues of transcendence are now seen as suffocating barriers. The "I" educated by the Law, representing the highest pedagogy for humanity, reveals that the lasting effect of this education is death. We have met this conclusion before in the investigation of Galatians and 2 Corinthians. But, here under the πρόσωπον of the "I", the farthest extension of this preconception of the power of tradition for the benefit of the culture has been demonstrated.

We should also recall that while in Galatians and 2 Corinthians Paul discovered two epochs, he did not state that the epoch of the Letter has been completely eroded. On the contrary, his work is precisely to enable his readers to realize that the power of the age of death continues to linger, in an attractive, albeit illusory, fashion. Thus, in following this line of thought, we can come to a possible reason why Paul chose the "I" after 7:6. It was not to give an autobiographical report as others have seen, nor was it simply to lay bare the bankruptcy of the Jewish self-understanding (cf. 10:3) -- which it does. Rather, the reason for this was to disclose for his audience the lifeworld for which they could still maintain a possibility. The lifeworld of the "I" seen in all its cultural fascination had to be dealt with in order for the lifeworld of solidarity to appear in its fulness and clarity. The eschatological vision brought about by the Gospel (1:17) subjects all things, especially the very basic symbol of the world which is passing away, namely, the "I". In that light the "I" can manifest the forces and powers which both govern and create it. And as this investigation is set before the audience, they are given the opportunity to engage in the act of self-interpretation, of recognizing for themselves that such a mythic world is still open and operative for them. Paul thus chooses the "I" to bring his audience's world to life in order for them to see whether they want to continue to abide in this world. They are given the chance to discover on what grounds their own existence is based, not simply liturgically or ethically but at the very roots of their personal existence.

V. Romans 7:25a, 8:2-25: Language for a New World

Having argued that 7:7-24 discloses concretely the παλαιότης
γράμματος through the expression of the forces governing the
lifeworld of the "I", I now must show how the positive side of 7:6, the
καινότης πνεύματος, is brought to light in the succeeding section.
This investigation will be limited to 7:25a and 8:2-25 because, while the
topography of this new lifeworld will become readily apparent, a detailed
exegesis of the entire chapter would bring us far beyond the scope of this
investigation.[120] My focus will remain steadily upon the play of language
in this portion.   In noting the dramatic shifts which occur, one can
discover the mythic force and power of this new lifeworld. The task of
interpretation wherein Paul is heavily engaged continues with existential
and cosmic significance.   For Paul situates the task of interpreting the
lifeworld of the Spirit within the context of communal self-understanding
by linking it to the total perspective of human life and suffering. Indeed,
the quest for interpretation is so great in this section that all creation falls
under this process.   Just as in chap. 7 Paul pushed the limits of
interpretation so as to include a fundamental criticism of the "I" as the
acme of culture, so in chap. 8 Paul sees that the new lifeworld of the
Spirit enables believers to re-envision their relation to the cosmos itself.

In a most dramatic turn, the desperate cry of the "I" in 7:24
receives a response in 7:25a and 8:2.   Indeed, the eighth chapter of
Romans functions as a total response to the lifeworld presented in 7:7ff.
Where 7:7ff. has exposed the lifeworld of the Letter, so here in this
following chapter the new lifeworld of Spirit is brought forward. Thus,
the sudden exclamation of thanksgiving (7:25a) is followed by an
explanation (γάρ) which, in fact, speaks to the "I" (now in the second
person address) about the liberation from the νόμος τῆς ἁμαρτίας
καὶ τοῦ θανάτου by the νόμος τοῦ πνεύματος τῆς ζωῆς

---

[120]For those interested in a complete treatment, cf. Käsemann, *Romans*, 212ff.
And for a fuller analysis of the last portion of chap. 8 please see D. Fraikin,
"Romains 8:31-39: La Position des Eglises de la Gentilité," (Ph.D. diss.,
Harvard University, 1974).

ἐν Χριστῷ Ἰησοῦ. It is as if another voice has entered the scene established since 7:7ff. 8:2 functions as a declaration, pronouncing, in effect, that the νόμος of the Spirit has liberated the "I". The language is stylized, if not solemn, with its heaping up of phrases and explicit distinction between the νόμος of Spirit and the νόμος of sin and death. While these linguistic observations begin to suggest the emergence of a new lifeworld, the use of νόμος with πνεῦμα is rather troubling. Does it mean that the Law, upheld by Paul, is basically restored? Or, is a new law being imposed upon humanity as a whole? Is the lifeworld of the Letter reasserting itself within this new situation? Has Paul retreated from his earlier positions, which we have found in Galatians and 2 Corinthians, as well as in Romans 2? Does the νόμος τοῦ πνεύματος mean the same as νόμος τοῦ θεοῦ in 7:22, indicating that the Law is reestablished instead of ended?

A solution to this issue can be found by considering the following points. First, if νόμος τοῦ πνεύματος is equated with νόμος τοῦ θεοῦ (7:22), then 8:3a becomes quite unintelligible, if not directly contradictory. Second, if we turn to 3:27ff., where there is a dialogical setting of an imaginary interlocutor asking questions and Paul responding, we see the most curious phrases νόμος ἔργων , νόμος πίστεως (3:27). The question there is διὰ ποίου νόμου . The usage here would tend to suggest that νόμος is best understood as a principle of existence, not Torah per se.[121] The issue is on what principle does one base one's existence. Furthermore, returning to chap. 7, we can see a further illustration of the use of νόμος as indicating the principle or force under which one exists (cf. 7:23). Thus, I would suggest that νόμος τοῦ πνεύματος is analogously used and should be seen as the "governing principle" of the new lifeworld, which Paul is beginning to bring out. And the use of the verb (ἐλευθερῶ) strongly denotes that this world is radically opposed to the enslavement already detailed in 7:7ff.

---

[121]Cf. Stowers, *Paul and the Diatribe*, 248ff.

8:2, then, pronounces that the "governing force or principle" of Spirit has brought about the liberation of the "I". In that respect, we have a reiteration of 7:6, but this time with the experience of 7:7ff. brought into the picture. However, no sooner is the "I" liberated but it disappears from the conversation. For, from 8:3ff. there is definite change in perspective and person as Paul continues to speak of the lifeworld of Spirit. Does this mean the liberation of the ego is tantamount to its extinction as a significant expression of the life of the Spirit? Again we should recall that the importance of the "I" for Paul in chap. 7 was to view it as the focal point of transcendence for the Hellenistic culture, where tradition could find its true abode and concretization. As such, it was exposed for its inability to attain what it has been "educated" to do. The lifeworld in which the "I" grew and received definition was discerned as the world of sin and death. Thus, the "I" as this cultural embodiment does disappear, while, at the same time, a new relationship is given through the lifeworld of Spirit which delivers the human from the necessity of effecting its own liberation.

The issue that we face here is intimately connected with language.[122] This point can be illustrated by Gal 2:19-20. I have already remarked that Paul is trying to express the relationship to Christ through a negation of "I" in order to stress the controlling force of the Christ for his existence. Indeed, the "I" of Paul in Galatians can well be seen, from his autobiographical section, as the product of his tradition. Thus, already in Galatians we have the intimation that Paul understands "I" as more than just himself. Furthermore, the use of kerygmatic terms (Gal 2:19-20), whereby he applies them to his own fate, indicates that he has begun to reinterpret personal existence in relation to the Christ. In Romans 7:7ff. he makes full use of the understanding that the "I" is a creation of the forces of culture and sin. Thus, in noting that the "I" disappears after 8:2, we might well have an enlargement of what Paul suggests in Gal 2:19-20.

---

[122]It seems that Paul is moving from what we moderns term the "individual" to that of "person".

The principle or force for human existence has radically changed through the liberation of the Spirit. And with this liberation the language expressing the topography of human existence must necessarily change. The irruption of communal language in the text, through the decisive employment of the first and second person plural,[123] then begins to make sense if Paul is attempting to indicate that the constitution of human existence is so changed that it needs new ways of talking about how one can actually live in this new life situation.

Verses 3-4 continue the explanation begun in vs 2. The language used is once more a clue to the way in which Paul sees the new situation. Thus, vs 3a presents an anacolouthon, which is then interrupted by ὁ θεός . . . . Not only does this emphasize the unbidden action of God in sending his Son, but it dramatically points out that there is no bridge, no line of continuity from the weakened world of the Law to that of the Spirit. By comparing Gal 4:4; John 3:16ff; 1 John 4:9, we can also see that vss 3b-4 employ the language of a sending formula.[124] However, Paul has shifted the verb of sending from its traditional position as main verb to that of participle, while another verb (κατέκρινεν) receives the decided emphasis. Likewise, while the phrases ἐν ὁμοιώματι and σαρκὸς ἁμαρτίας may well stand in pre-Pauline tradition,[125] the repeated emphasis on sin[126] would appear to be a Pauline emphasis. It has already been suggested[127] that this change in emphasis throws the stress from the Incarnation to that of the crucifixion. Indeed, the closest parallels to this verse (3b) appear to be 2 Cor 5:21 and Gal 3:13-14. I have earlier suggested that Gal 3:13-14 serves to demonstrate how the

---

[123]Cf. vss 4, 9, 13, 15, 17, 22-25.

[124]Cf. Käsemann, *Romans*, 216.

[125]Cf. Phil 2:7; Rom 6:5; also 1 QS 11.9; 1 QM 4.3; 12.12.

[126] περὶ ἁμαρτίας τὴν ἁμαρτίαν ἐν τῇ σαρκί .

[127]Cf. Käsemann, *Romans*, 217.

lethal possibility of the lifeworld of the Letter has been broken in Christ. Indeed, this action allows Paul to declare that the Law was unable to give life,[128] which is the burden of the anacolouthon of 3a. Furthermore, this condemnation of sin in the flesh is done so that the δικαίωμα τοῦ νόμου might be fulfilled ἐν ἡμῖν. Not only does this hearken back to Gal 5:14, but it returns to Romans 2:26, 29, to the lifeworld possibility of keeping τὰ δικαιώματα τοῦ νόμου by the true Jew whose heart is circumcised ἐν πνεύματι. In fact, this possibility adumbrated in 2:29 is given as a present reality ἐν ἡμῖν. The fulfillment of the "demand" (δικαίωμα) of the Law, an impossibility of the lifeworld of the Law because of the σάρξ, and seen as the condition of the "I", is now declared a reality for both Paul and his audience who are included in the sphere of power (ἐν is used in a local sense) of the liberating death of Christ.

The lifeworld which comes about through the action of Christ is now described in terms of ethical action (περιπατοῦσιν . . . κατὰ πνεῦμα). Indeed, the purpose of sending the Son becomes the motivation for such praxis. The following four verses continue to demonstrate that Paul is speaking of two different lifeworlds in which human existence is concretely engaged. By introducing the notion of intelligent aim and goal in vs 5, Paul now distinguishes both worlds according to each one's future horizon as it is borne out in praxis. This future horizon is described in eschatological terms in vs 6 (θάνατος . . . ζωὴ καὶ εἰρήνη). The claim that the φρόνημα τῆς σαρκός is an enemy of God, because it does not obey the Law of God nor was it even able to, reiterates what was already shown in 7:7ff. under the aspect of the "I".

It is against this understanding of two opposing lifeworlds, where the ultimate issue of life or death is present for human action that Paul makes an interpretive application to his audience. In so doing Paul may well be referring to the community's pneumatic activity expressed by the

---

[128]Cf. Gal 3:21.

phrase πνεῦμα θεοῦ οἰκεῖ ἐν ὑμῖν and the possible prophetic utterance εἰ δέ τις πνεῦμα Χριστοῦ οὐχ ἔχει , οὗτος οὐκ ἔστιν αὐτοῦ (vs 9).[129] This present experience of Spirit is immediately related to Christ (vss 10-11) whereupon the community's future is intimately connected to the eschatological action of God in Christ. Once again Paul uses language probably taken from liturgical experience[130] as a base for envisioning the future horizon of those whose existence is the lifeworld of the Spirit.

This reflection of the future consequences found within the liturgical praxis of the community leads Paul to an exhortation of mutual encouragement (vs 12). In vs 13 one sees that this exhortation is not relegated to the present alone but is maintained within the future aspect of life/death. The following verse, which may be a prophetic utterance, interpreting those "driven"[131] by the Spirit as "sons of God" again reflects the probable experience of the community. This is, in turn, explained further by the distinction of the Spirit as one of sonship not of enslavement. Again, this interpretation is made upon the community's own ecstatic experience (vs 15), where divine sonship is discovered in the action of the Spirit upon the community (vs 16).[132] Paul, however, goes beyond Gal 4:7 in vs 17 by adding the dimension of solidarity of patience and suffering to the community's experience of their inheritance in Christ (εἴπερ συμπάσχομεν).

Thus far one can see that in 8:2ff. Paul has enunciated what is the leading or governing principle of existence which has come about through the liberating action of Christ. Indeed, one of the significant points is that Paul rigorously ties the life of πνεῦμα to the relationship in Christ. In

---

[129]Cf. 1 Cor 3:16; 12:3; 16:22; Did. 10.6.

[130] ὁ ἐγείρας Χριστὸν ἐκ νεκρῶν ; cf. 6:3ff.

[131]Cf. 1 Cor 12:2.

[132]Cf. Gal 4:6-7.

interpreting this new lifeworld of Spirit, Paul focuses upon the active
reality within the worshipping community. He extends the activity of the
Spirit beyond the experience of worship to include the entire sphere of
intelligent activity and the eschatological future of God's action in Christ.
Thus, the basis of the new self-understanding for human existence is
given definition by interpreting the present communal reality of the
worshipping community. As we have seen in Galatians and 2
Corinthians, Paul refuses to locate the ground of this new self-
understanding outside the experience of the believing community. At the
same time, he has argued, once more, that the promises of the illusory
lifeworld opposed to the Spirit are truly found in the community's own
praxis. Indeed, only there can the hopes generated for transcendence be
met and brought to fulfillment. The quest for the truly authentic
performance comes about in the lifeworld of the Spirit.

This enlarging line of interpretation continues quite markedly into
the next section (vss 18-25). The focus broadens from the present action
and limited horizon of the community to a revision of the fate of the entire
universe. Just as the present suffering with Christ will lead to future
glory, so also the παθήματα of the present time (καιρος) will bear a
different countenance in the future (vs 18). The warring of the two
lifeworlds which Paul has already brought forth under the conception of
human praxis (vss 5ff.) now is seen against an apocalyptic background.
Creation is described as awaiting eagerly the revelation of the sons of God
(vs 19). But, one should note that this is underway since the sons of God
are already brought forward in the community's activity (vs 14). The
new creation of Gal 6:15 and 2 Cor 5:17 becomes widened considerably.
The subjection of those under the cursed condition[133] is now linked to
creation itself (vs 20). And, just as ἡ γραφή subjected all under sin so
that the promise might be given to those who believe (Gal 3:22), so too
creation was subjected in the hope that it might be liberated from the
slavery of corruption into the freedom of the children of God (vs 21).

---

[133]Cf. Gal 3:22-23; also Rom 1:24.

Paul then can characterize the situation of creation in apocalyptic terms of giving birth[134] and link this universal movement to the community's present experience of waiting to reap the full benefits of their sonship (vss 22-23). In 2 Cor 4:6 we saw that for Paul a new creation, or rather, a re-creation, was underway within the experience of the Corinthian community. Now, while maintaining his eschatological reservation, Paul has brought all creation into the perspective of his radical reinterpretation. The very forces of history (vss 18,22) are reinterpreted under the light of the eschatological action where the coming glory will be revealed. Paul has gone beyond the interpretation of his day which would link the forces and powers of the cosmos to the mastering or subject "I". However, he has not given up his world's desire to see a definite connection between the human and the cosmos. He sees this connection given through the arrival of a new lifeworld of the Spirit. It is through the Spirit that both the creation and those in faith can look forward in hope (vss 20, 24-25). The apocalyptic perspective which has allowed Paul to achieve such a radical interpretation of all human history since 1:17ff. now permits a deeper penetration into the horizon of future possibility. Indeed, the creation, which has been ill used by humanity (1:20ff.) now is included in the hopeful prospect of the children of God. The καινότης

πνεύματος (7:6) carries within its horizon of hope the basis for this reinterpretation of the entire creation (πᾶσα κτίσις). The application of the solidarity of the suffering and glory with Christ is now made to creation itself. And, in so doing, Paul demonstrates that the relatedness of the community to Christ is also a hallmark of this new situation. The fellowship of suffering and promise now is writ large in the depths of creation.

Conclusion

In this chapter I have argued that Paul continues in Romans to make the act of interpretation subordinate to and instrumental of a fundamental understanding of the powers and forces of human history and culture. To

---

[134]Cf. Mark 13:5ff.

understand the strategic importance of the antithesis of Letter and Spirit in Romans 2:29, it was first necessary to investigate the apocalyptic stage of the surrounding material. From that and an extensive analysis of the diatribal argument of chap. 2, it became clear that, in summoning contemporary language, concepts and hopes, Paul endeavored to express a radically different perspective on the question of human authenticity. The antithesis of Letter and Spirit enables Paul to carry his thinking to a universal, indeed mythical, level. The issue of human authenticity thus takes place before the horizons of two antithetical lifeworlds. The longed-for dream of the autonomous self comes to reality only in the lifeworld of the Spirit.

Refining his understanding of what it means to live in this lifeworld of the Spirit, Paul reintroduces the antithesis of Letter and Spirit after an extended consideration of the forces of history as seen from the new perspective of the Christ event. The antithesis of Letter and Spirit in 7:6 then takes on the enormous proportions of two distinct epochs, which serve as possible destinies for the believing communities. In that light it was argued that 7:6 functions as a guiding hermeneutical principle for the two subsequent sections.

Now, in order to understand the particular force and meaning of 7:7-24, it was necessary to suggest that the "I" of this section functions in a fashion similar to the *persona dramatis* found in diatribal tradition. Through the use of this dramatic "I", Paul allows his audience to see for themselves the forces and pressures of the lifeworld of the Letter. Instead of presenting a vision of what was considered the pinnacle of cultural achievement, Paul discloses a process which results in self-contradiction and captivity. Only the lifeworld of the Spirit, already present in the believing community, can shatter the bonds of the Letter. Indeed, what seems to be a fleeting ideal in chap. 2 becomes a reality to be reckoned with in chap. 8, where Paul discloses the rudiments of a redefinition of human authenticity. Upon the very praxis of the life of the believing community Paul continues to reinterpret, linking its solidarity and patience with the fate of creation itself. The eschatological vision with which he begins is maintained as the lifeworld of the Spirit allows Paul to reinterpret the forces of human and cosmic existence. For Paul the act of interpretation becomes a radical participation in the new epoch of the Spirit, a fundamental response to the question of the human *incognito*.

CHAPTER FIVE

Conclusion

My investigation of Spirit and Letter in Paul began with the observation that, despite the fact that the Pauline antithesis has figured prominently in the history of interpretation, it has not been subject to an extended historical consideration. A brief synopsis of the history of interpretation illustrates an abiding historical irony in the employment of this antithesis: although the antithesis has been utilized by numerous exegetes as a fundamental principle of interpretation, the antithesis has been left usually with little or no historical foundation.

In order to avoid either a philological reduction or some theological sublimation of the meaning of this antithesis, I have attempted to let the text itself suggest interpretive leads and clues through the observation of various word-groups or verbal equivalencies and by a close analysis of the rhetorical strategies of Paul. This was done from the perspective that language is inherently historical and that the expression of language discloses to the interpreter a lifeworld of meaning which can only be understood when the interpreter enters into a questioning dialogue with the text.

From a close reading of Galatians, it becomes clear that what is at stake is nothing less than the fundamental understanding of Spirit. While Paul and his opposition base their interpretive positions upon the experience of Spirit within the communities, they part company in regard to the relationship of tradition to the experience of Spirit. In contrast to his opposition's probable vision of the continuity between Spirit and tradition, Paul views tradition in a critical light. Insofar as tradition is written, associated with works of the Law, and limited in time and space, it is an accursed power whose only promise is that of captivity. On the other hand, for those of faith, tradition is visualized as a transcending promise, reaching forward from primordial time and space to confirm the Galatians' present pneumatic experience. In Paul's eyes the historical reality of the Spirit, present within the community, opens up the meaning of tradition, rather than tradition supplying what is missing in the experience of the community. The eschatological lifeworld of Spirit allows Paul to reevaluate traditional paradigms of religious excellence as he undertakes a reinterpretation of the forces and powers which shape human existence and destiny.

Such findings prompted an extended Excursus concerning Letter, tradition and the task of interpretation. Upon the first chapter's suggestion that Paul has entered a dialogue touching upon the cultural dialectic over the experience and control of transcendence in human existence, the Excursus brought to light the variety of ways in which one would come to grips with transcendent forces and powers so as to gain some sense of identity and destiny. By plunging into the thought world of Hellenistic Judaism, we saw that a definite sense of cultural and religious continuity was achieved dramatically through a most positive understanding of Letter. Under the aspect of written Scripture, Letter functions as a storehouse of tradition for the interpreter in search of realizing the dream of freedom and autonomy. The various processes of interpretation within Hellenistic Judaism enabled the interpreter to unleash the power of the Letter for the benefit of both the individual and society. Moreover, after examining how this dialogue is actually a concentration of an even wider cultural questioning, with its constant refinement and revision of the categories of the discussion, one can better appreciate the scope and direction of Paul's response. Not only does Paul creatively address this cultural conversation, but he is, first of all, an heir to that long-standing dialectic.

The search for the unspoken issues determining the historical context of 2 Cor 3:6 entailed a close inspection of the language field, the rhetoric employed, previous and subsequent correspondence, and the probable position of the opposition. Both the opponents of Paul and the Corinthian community operate from the cultural and religious perspective that the presence of the Spirit needs objective verification and documentations. Moreover, the opponents not only assume a linkage of Spirit and Letter but, through allegorical interpretation, provide a means of tapping the spiritual power of the tradition contained in the Letter. In rejecting this viewpoint, Paul proposes that tradition does not contain or convey the Spirit. The antithesis of 2 Cor 3:6c strategically attacks the contemporary association of Letter and tradition. Moreover, this antithesis becomes a guiding principle of interpretation for vss 7-18, wherein Paul exposes the lethal lifeworld of the Letter while simultaneously demonstrating the lifegiving world of the Spirit. The dualism already apparent in Galatians reaches even greater proportions in 2 Corinthians where each of the antithetical lifeworlds stands for a powerful epoch.

Furthermore, the communal basis of interpretation, already brought out in chap. one, gains added importance. For Paul's argument stands or falls upon his contention that the Corinthians already experience the lifeworld of spirit and thus share the ground of his interpretation. While refuting the need for some sort of objective verification of Spirit, Paul casts the activity of interpretation into a universal perspective. Interpretation is not some controlled method of unveiling tradition, performed by experts and appreciated solely by initiates, but a re-creative activity of the entire community as they continue to understand the future opened up to them by the eschatological revelation in Christ.

The universal directions opened up in Galatians and 2 Corinthians continue in Romans. Having established an apocalyptic perspective, Paul historicizes, in the fashion of the sophists, Cynics and Hebrew prophets, the question of human authenticity. The introduction of Spirit and Letter in Romans 2 not only enables Paul to maintain his radical revision of contemporary assumptions concerning the constitution of the human but also suggests that the Urzeit's figure of the primordial human has come to reality in the Endzeit of the Spirit. However, it is not until 7:6ff. that the implications of the lifeworlds of Spirit and Letter are fully explored. Not only does 7:6 sharply focus the mythic revision of human history of the previous chapters, but it serves as the hermeneutical principle for understanding chaps. 7-8. By interpreting the "I" as a dramatic mode of speech within chap. 7, we can perceive how the embodiment of the highest aspirations of culture and religion is paradoxically exposed as a captive under the lifeworld of the Letter. In marked contrast, the communal language of chap. 8 signals a lifeworld where solidarity, authenticity and hope are characteristic of a radically new historical understanding. As the chapter progresses, so does Paul's interpretive scope. The cosmos itself is placed within the horizon of this new future. The lifeworld of the Spirit calls even for a reinterpretation of creation.

In tracing Paul's responses in Galatians, 2 Corinthians and Romans, we have seen how Paul uses the categories of Spirit and Letter to interpret how the human comes to terms with the forces and powers of transcendence. Moreover, it has been argued that, in dealing with each specific situation, Paul is very much in correspondence with a wider cultural debate. His responses indicate a critical awareness of the various interpretive options of his intellectual contemporaries. Paul's thought, therefore, cannot be regarded as merely an impromptu response to a specific occasion but as a creative attempt to answer questions of longstanding cultural concern. In short, an investigation of Paul's subtle use of Spirit and Letter demonstrates how much Paul is involved with the main issues of the history of religion. He thus cannot be restricted to an understanding which sees him as a charismatic but ephemeral phenomenon. Rather, subsequent research into the thought of Paul must view him within this broadened cultural perspective.

It is in this enlarged perspective that Paul's critical interpretation of tradition must be evaluated. He is indebted to the legal, philosophical and theological lines which seek to place the issue of tradition within a comprehensive perspective. Even his negative revision of tradition has its antecedents among his intellectual forebears. Thus, as he intensifies his criticism of tradition as Letter, he becomes more and more embedded in utilizing the conceptual associations of the Hellenistic world. At the same time, however, the particular development of these categories by Paul into such a dualism transcends any cultural preparation. Due to his eschatological perspective, tradition, under the aspect of Letter, not only sums up the greatest drives of his culture but illustrates its defeat. For Paul, to enter into the lifeworld of tradition is to hear the primordial call to human freedom and autonomy; it is also to be imprisoned in a world where this hope is never realized. Instead of bringing the human to transcendence, tradition confirms and objectively records the deception and determination of human existence. What Paul has treated under the notion of tradition can be seen in more modern terms under the problem of religion. Eighteen centuries before Feuerbach, Paul was suggesting that religion, insofar as it is a human attempt to control and channel transcendence, leads only to a fatal destiny for both the individual and society.

However, this negative side of Paul's thought must not allow us to forget his positive perspective. Indeed, the Letter is only seen in all its lethal power when the Spirit illuminates human destiny. It is in the act of understanding what the Spirit means for humanity that such issues come to light. In fact, for Paul it is only through the Spirit that the human is liberated to take a genuine look at those "givens" of culture or religion that predetermine the interpretive options and provide only prefabricated responses. If the interpreter is faithful to the Spirit, that is, to the reality of transcendence in one's historical experience, then the act of interpretation is essentially open-ended. The interpreter not only can hope to disclose what unspoken questions lie behind those "givens" of tradition but can recognize that the dream of human authenticity is being realized in the very activity of interpretation. Thus, Paul not only called "works", Letter, and the "I" into question but attempted to express by "hearing of faith", Spirit, and the communal language of Romans 8 the new existential reality which provoked such creative reinterpretation.

Furthermore, this hermeneutical activity is not limited to the interpretation of Scripture. Following his predecessors who saw hermeneutics as a discipline of general interpretation and understanding, Paul regards the task of interpretation to include the entire sphere of human existence. By entering the lifeworld of the Spirit, the believer is called to engage in reinterpreting even the most cosmic aspects of existence.   By the time we reach Romans 7-8 we find Paul's hermeneutical perspective encompassing a recreation of human history and society in radically existential terms.   One can say that creation was finally coming onto the scene.   Creation, for Paul, had effectively just begun.   Those he addressed were active participants in this cosmic enterprise.   Such reinterpretive exercises by Paul suggest that his thought actually prepares the way for a concept unknown to the ancients, that of creative consciousness.   Indeed, the seeds of viewing hermeneutics as a potentially revolutionary activity may have been sown by Paul's thinking.

Through close attention to how and why Paul uses language, I have attempted to pursue the interpretive activity of Paul.   In the course of this investigation I have tried to dislodge preconceptions which have long determined the common interpretation of Spirit and Letter.   The measure of success this investigation may enjoy will come about only insofar as the dialogue which has been disclosed is openly maintained and provokes further responses from history's community of interpreters.

BIBLIOGRAPHY

Attridge, H. *First Century Cynicism in the Epistles of Heraclitus*. Missoula: Scholars, 1976.

Audollent, A. *Defixionem Tabellae quotquot innoteurunt*. Paris, 1904.

Augustine. *De spiritu et littera*. Bk. 2. Chap. 37, *Retractiones*. In *Nicene and Post-Nicene Fathers*. Ed. P. Schaff; trans. P. Holmes, R. Wallis, and B. Warfield. New York: Christian Literature Society. 5: 80-114.

Barr, J. *The Semantics of Biblical Language*. Oxford: Oxford University, 1969.

Betz, H. D. *Der Apostel Paulus und die sokratische Tradition: eine exegetische Untersuchung zu einer "Apologie" 2 Korinthen 10-13*. Tübingen: Mohr, 1972.

_____. *Galatians*, Philadelphia: Fortress, 1979.

_____. "The Literary Composition and Function of Paul's Letter to the Galatians" *NTS* 21 (1975): 353-79.

_____. *Paul's Concept of Freedom in the Context of Hellenistic Discussions about the Possibilities of Human Freedom*. Berkeley: Center for Hermeneutical Studies in Hellenistic and Modern Culture, 1977.

_____. "2 Cor 6:14-7:1: An Anti-Pauline Fragment?" *JBL* 92 (1973): 88-108.

Bickerman, E. "La Chaine de la tradition Pharisienne" *RB* 59 (1952): 44-54.

Blass, F. and A. Debrunner, trans. R. Runk, ed. *A Greek Grammar of the New Testament and Other Early Christian Literature*. Chicago: University of Chicago, 1970.

Bloch, E. *Atheism in Christianity*. Trans. J. Swann. New York: Herder and Herder, 1972.

Bonner, S. *Education in Ancient Rome*. Berkeley: University of California, 1977.

Bornkamm, G. "Gesetz und Natur" In *Studien zu Antike und Christentum* 2. Munich: Kaiser, 1959.

_____. *Paul*. Trans. D. Stalker; New York: Harper & Row, 1971.

_____. "The Revelation of God's Wrath." In *Early Christian Experience*. Trans. P. Hammer. New York: Harper & Row, 1969. 47-70.

_____. "Sin, Law and Death." In *Early Christian Experience*. 87-104.

_____. *Die Vorgeschichte des sogenannten Zweiten Korintherbriefs*; Heidelberg: Winter, 1961.

Brandenburger, E. *Fleisch und Geist. Paulus und die dualistische Weisheit*. WMANT; Neukirchen-Vluyn: Neukirchener, 1968.

Bultmann, R. "Glossen im Romerbrief." In *Exegetica* Tübingen: Mohr, 1967. 278-84.

_____. " ζωοποιέω κτλ ." *TDNT* 2: 874-75.

_____. " καυχάομαι κτλ ." *TDNT* 3: 645-54.

_____. *The Old and New Man*. Trans. K. Crim. Richmond: Knox, 1967.

_____. *Der Stil der paulinischen Predigt und die kynischstoische Diatribe*. Göttingen: Vandenhoeck & Ruprecht, 1910.

_____. *Theology of the New Testament.* New York: Scribner's, 1951. 2: 239-49.

Burkert, W. "Greek Tragedy and Sacrificial Ritual." *GRBS* 7 (1966): 87-121.

_____. *Homo Necans. Interpretationem altgrieschischer Opferriten und Mythen.* RVV 32. Berlin/New York, 1972.

Calvin, J. *Commentary on the Epistles of Paul the Apostle to the Corinthians.* Trans. J. Pringle. Vol. 2. Edinburgh: Calvin Translation Society, 1849.

_____. *Institutes of the Christian Religion.* Trans. F. Battle. Vol. 2. Philadelphia: Westminster, 1960.

Cambier, J.-M. "Le Jugement de tous les hommes par Dieu seul, selon la verité, dans Rom 2:1-3:21." *ZNW* 67 (1976): 187-213.

Campenhausen, H. von. "Spirit and Authority in the Pauline Congregation." in *Ecclesiastical Authority and Spiritual Power.* Trans. J. Baker. Stanford: Stanford University, 1969. 55-75.

Church, F. F. "Rhetorical Structure and Design in Paul's Letter to Philemon." *HTR* 71 (1978): 17-33.

Cohen, B. "Letter and Spirit in Jewish and Roman Law." In *Mordocai Kaplan Jubilee Volume.* New York: Jewish Theological Seminary, 1953. 109-35.

Collange, J.-F. *Enigmes de la deuxieme Epître de Paul aux Corinthiens.* Cambridge: Cambridge University, 1972.

Conzelmann, H. *1 Corinthians.* Trans. J. Leitch. Philadelphia: Fortress, 1975.

Cumont, F. *Oriental Religions in Roman Paganism.* New York: Dover, 1956.

Dahl, N.   "The Atonement — An Adequate Reward for the Akedah? (Rom 8:32)." In *Neotestamentica et Semitica*. Eds. E. Ellis and M. Wilcox. Edinburgh: Clark, 1969. 15-29.

_____. *Studies in Paul*. Minneapolis: Augsburg, 1977.

D'Angelo, M. *Moses in the Letter to the Hebrews*. Missoula: Scholars, 1979.

Daube, D.   "Rabbinic Methods of Interpretation and Hellenistic Rhetoric." *HUCA* 22 (1949): 239-64.

Davies, W. D. *Paul and Rabbinic Judaism*. (London: SPCK, 1965.

_____. *Torah in the Messianic Age and/or the Age to Come*. Philadelphia: SBL, 1952.

Deissmann, A. *Bible Studies*. trans. A. Grieve. Edinburgh: Clark, 1931.

_____. *Light from the Ancient East*. Trans. L. Strachan. Grand Rapids: Baker, 1978.

_____. *Neue Bibelstudien*. Marburg: Elwert, 1897. 76-79.

Delling, G. " τελέω κτλ ." *TDNT* 8: 61-87.

Dillon, J. *The Middle Platonists*. Ithaca: Cornell, 1977.

Donfried, K. ed. *The Romans Debate*. Minneapolis: Augsburg, 1977.

Dudley, D. R. *A History of Cynicism*. London: Methuen, 1937.

Dunn, J.   "2 Corinthians 3:17 — 'The Lord is the Spirit.'" *JTS* 21 (1970): 309-20.

Ebeling, G. "Geist und Buchstabe." *RGG*^{3} 2: 1290-96.

Edelstein, L. and I. Kidd. *Posidonius*. Vol. 1. Cambridge: Cambridge University, 1972.

Fiorenza, E. Schussler, ed. *Aspects of Religious Propaganda in Judaism and Early Christianity*. Notre Dame: Notre Dame University, 1976.

Fraikin, D. "Romains 8:31-39: La Position des Eglises de la Gentilité." Ph.D. diss., Harvard University, 1974.

Fridrichsen, A. "Quatre conjectures sur le texte du Nouveau Testament." *RHPR* 3 (1923): 439-42.

Gadamer, H.-G. *Dialogue and Dialectic*. Trans. P. Smith. New Haven: Yale University, 1980.

_____. *Philosophical Hermeneutics*. Trans. and ed. D. Linge. Berkeley: University of California, 1977.

_____. *Truth and Method*. Trans. and ed. G. Barden and J. Cumming. New York: Seabury, 1975.

Gaiser, K. *Protreptik und Paränese bei Platon*. Stuttgart: Kohlhammer, 1959.

Georgi, D. "Folly." *IDBSup*: 340-41.

_____. *Die Gegner des Paulus im 2. Korintherbrief*. WMANT; Neukirchen: Neukirchener, 1964.

_____. *Weisheit Salomos, Jüdische Schriften aus hellenistischrömischer Zeit* 3. Gütersloh: Gütersloher Verlagshaus Gerd Mohn, 1980.

Goodenough, E. R. *By Light, Light*. New Haven: Yale University, 1935.

_____. "The Political Philosophy of Hellenistic Kingship." *Yale Classical Studies* 1 (1928): 55-102.

Golden, J. "The Magic of Magic and Superstition." In *Aspects of Religious Propaganda in Judaism and Early Christianity*. Ed. E. Schussler-Fiorenza. Notre Dame: Notre Dame University, 1976. 115-48.

Grant, R. M. *The Letter and the Spirit*. London: SPCK, 1957.

Guthrie, W. K. C. *A History of Greek Philosophy*. 2 vols. Cambridge: Cambridge University, 1965-77.

_____. *The Sophists*. Cambridge: Cambridge University, 1971.

Hadas, M. *Hellenistic Culture*. New York: Norton, 1959.

Hahn, F. "Das Gesetzeverständnis in Römer - und Galaterbrief." *ZNTW* 67 (1976): 29-63.

Havelock, E. *The Liberal Temper in Greek Politics*. New Haven: Yale University, 1964.

Heinemann, F. *Nomos und Physis*. Basel: Reinhart, 1945.

Heinemann, I. "Die Lehre vom ungeschriebenen Gesetz im jüdischen Schriftum." *HUCA* 4 (1927): 149-71.

Hengel, M. *The Atonement*. Trans. J. Bowden: Philadelphia: Fortress, 1981.

_____. *Judaism and Hellenism*. Trans. J. Bowden. Philadelphia: Fortress, 1974. Vols. 1-2.

Hickling, C. "The Sequence of Thought in 2 Corinthians, Chapter 3." *NTS* 21 (1974/75): 380-95.

Hirzel, R. *Agraphos Nomos 20, der Abhandlungen der philologisch-historischen Classe der königl. sächischen Gesellschaft der Wissenschaften* 1. Leipzig: Teubner, 1900.

Holstad, R. "Cynic Hero and Cynic King". Thesis, University of Uppsala, 1948.

Holladay, C. *Theios Aner in Hellenistic Judaism*. Missoula: Scholars, 1977.

Holmberg, B. *Paul and Power*. Philadelphia: Fortress, 1980.

Hooker, M. "Beyond the Things that are Written? St. Paul's Use of Scripture." *NTS* 27 (1980/81): 295-309.

Hubner, H. "Gal 3:10 und die Herkunft des Paulus." *Kerygma und Dogma.* 19 (1973): 215-31.

Joachim of Fiore. *Concordia.* Facsimile ed., 1519. Frankfurt am Main: Minerva, 1964.

Käsemann, E. *Commentary on Romans.* Trans. G. Bromily. Grand Rapids: Eerdmans, 1980.

_____. "The Spirit and the Letter." In *Perspective on Paul.* Philadelphia: Fortress, 1969. 138-66.

Kennedy, G. *The Art of Persuasion in Greece.* Princeton: Princeton University, 1963.

_____. *The Art of Rhetoric in the Roman World.* Princeton: Princeton University, 1972.

Kim, C.-H. *The Familiar Letter of Recommendation.* Missoula: Scholars, 1972).

Klassen, W. "Anabaptist Hermeneutics: The Letter and the Spirit." *MQR* 40 (1966): 83-96.

Koester, H. "NOMOS PHUSEOS, The Concept of Natural Law in Greek Thought." In *Festschrift for E. R. Goodenough* (1968): 521-41.

_____. " φύσις κτλ ." *TDNT* 9: 251-77.

Krämer, H. J. *Arete bei Platon und Aristoteles.* Amsterdam: Schippers, 1967.

Kuhn, K. G. *Konkordanz zu den Qumrantexten.* Göttingen: Vandenhoeck & Ruprecht, 1960.

Kümmel, W. *Romer 7 und die Bekehrung des Paulus.* Leipzig: Hinrichs, 1929.

Kustas, G. *Diatribe in Ancient Rhetorical Theory.* Berkeley: Center for Hermeneutical Studies in Hellenistic and Modern Culture, 1976.

Lausberg, H. *Handbuch des literarischen Rhetorik.* Munich: Heuber, 1973. Vols. 1-2.

Lesky, A. *A History of Greek Literature.* Trans. J. Willis and C. de Heer. New York: Crowell, 1966.

Lieberman, S. *Hellenism in Jewish Palestine.* New York: Jewish Theological Seminary, 1962.

Lietzmann, H. *Handbuch zum Neuen Testament 9, An die Korinther 1-2.* Tübingen: Mohr [Siebeck], 1949.

Lochler, W. "Himmelsbrief." *RGG*^{2} 2 (1928): 1902.

Lohse, E. Trans. and ed. *Die Texte aus Qumran.* Munich: Kosel, 1971.

Loisy, A. *L'Epître aux Galates.* Paris: Nourry, 1916.

Long, A. *Hellenistic Philosophy.* London: Duckworth, 1974.

Lührmann, D. *Das Offenbarungsverständnis bei Paulus und in paulinischen Gemeinden.* Neukirche-Vluyn: Neukirchener, 1965.

_____. *Der Brief an die Galater.* Zurich: Theologischer, 1980.

Lull, D. *The Spirit in Galatia.* Chico, CA: Scholars, 1980.

Luther, M. *Lectures on the Psalms.* In *Luther's Works.* Ed. H. Oswald. Trans. H. Bouman. Vols. 10-11. St. Louis: Concordia, 1974-76.

_____. *Lectures on Romans.* In *Luther's Works.* Ed. H. Oswald. Trans. W. Tillmann and J. Preus. Vol. 25. St. Louis: Concordia, 1972.

Luz, U. *Das Geschichtsverständnis des Paulus*. Munich: Kaiser, 1968.

Lyonnet, S. "'Tu ne convoiteras pas' (Rom 7:7)." *Neotestamentica et Patristica*. Cullmann Freundesgabe; NovTSup 6. 1962: 163ff.

MacDonald, D. "There is no Male and Female: Galatians 3:26-28 and Gnostic Baptismal Tradition." Ph.D. diss., Harvard University, 1978.

Malherbe, A. ed. *The Cynic Epistles*. Missoula: Scholars, 1977.

Neusner, J. *Early Rabbinic Judaism*. Leiden: Brill, 1975.

_____. *Method and Meaning in Ancient Judaism*. Missoula: Scholars, 1979.

Nilsson, M. *Greek Folk Religion*. Philadelphia: University of Pennsylvania, 1978. 102-20.

Norden, E. *Agnostos Theos, Untersuchungen zur Formengeschichte religioser Rede*. Stuttgart: Teubner, 1956.

O'Neil, E. trans. *Teles*. Missoula: Scholars, 1977.

Pagels, E. *The Gnostic Paul*. Philadelphia: Fortress, 1975.

Patte, D. *Early Jewish Hermeneutic in Palestine*. Missoula: Scholars, 1975.

Pearson, B. *The Pneumatikos-Spermatikos Terminology in 1 Corinthians*. Missoula: Scholars, 1973.

Pereira, F. "The Galatian Controversy in the Light of the Targums." *Indian Journal of Theology* 19-20 (1970/71): 13-29.

Plummer, A. *A Critical and Exegetical Commentary on the Second Epistle of St. Paul to the Corinthians*. Edinburgh: Clark, 1966.

Poettcker, H. "Meno Simon's Encounter with the Bible." *MQR* 40 (1966): 112-26.

Preisendanz, K.   "Fluchtafel (Defixion)."   *Reallexikon für Antike und Christentum* 8 (1972): 1-29.

Quell, G., and S. Schulz " σπέρμα κτλ ."   *TDNT* 7: 536-47.

Räisänen, H.   "Des 'Gesetz des Glaubens' (Röm 3:27) und das 'Gesetz des Geistes' (Röm 8:2)" *NTS* 26 (1979: 101-17.

Reese, J. M.   *Hellenistic Influence on the Book of Wisdom and Its Consequences.* Rome: Biblical Institute, 1970.

Reitzenstein, R.   *Hellenistic Mystery Religions.*   Trans. J. Steely Pittsburgh: Pickwick, 1978.

Richardson, P.   "Spirit and Letter: A Foundation of Hermeneutics." *EvangQuart* 45 (1973): 208-18.

Robinson, J.   "Die Hodajot-Formel in Gebet und Hymnus des Frühchristentums." In *Apophoreta, Festschrift für E. Haenchen zu seinem 70 Geburtstag.* Berlin: Topelmann, 1964; 194-235.

Röhrich, L. "Himmelsbrief." *RGG³* (1949): 338-39.

Romilly, J. de. *Magic and Rhetoric in Ancient Greece.* Cambridge, MA: Harvard University, 1964.

Royce, J. *The Problem of Christianity.* Chicago: University of Chicago, 1968.

Schmithals, W. *Gnosticism in Corinth.* Trans. J. Steely. Nashville: Abingdon, 1971.

Schneider, B. "The Meaning of St. Paul's Antithesis `The Letter and the Spirit.'" *CBQ* 15 (1953): 163-207.

Schneider, N. *Die rhetorische Eigenwart der paulinischen Antithese.* Tübingen: Mohr, 1970.

Schoeps, H. *Paul.* Trans. H. Knight. Philadelphia: Westminster, 1961.

Schrenk, G. " γράμμα κτλ ." *TDNT* 1: 742-73.

Schulz, S. "Die Decke des Moses." *ZNW* 49 (1948): 1-30.

Schütz, J. H. *Paul and the Anatomy of Apostolic Authority*. Cambridge: Cambridge Unversity, 1975.

Schweizer, E. " πνεῦμα κτλ ." *TDNT* 6: 389-455.

Smith, J. Z. "Wisdom and Apocalyptic." In *Religious Syncretism in Antiquity*. Ed. B. Pearson. Missoula: Scholars, 1975. 131-56.

Speyer, W. "Fluch." *Reallexikon für Antike und Christentum* 7 (1969): 1160-1288.

Stendahl, K. "The Apostle Paul and the Introspective Conscience of the West." In *Paul among the Jews and Gentiles*. Philadelphia: Fortress, 1976; 78-96.

Stowers, S. "A Critical Reassessment of Paul and the Diatribe: The Dialogical Element in Paul's Letter to the Romans." Ph.D. diss., Yale University, 1979.

Strugnell, J. "A Plea for Conjectural Emendation in the New Testament." *CBJ* 36 (1974): 543-58.

Thesliff, H. *An Introduction to the Pythagorean Writings of the Hellenistic Period*. Abo: Acta Academica Aboensis, 1965.

Thyen, H. *Der Stil der jüdisch-hellenistischen Homilie*. Göttingen: Vandenhoeck & Ruprecht, 1955.

Vermes, G., trans. *The Essene Writings from Qumran*. Gloucester: Smith, 1973.

Vogel, C. de. *Pythagoras and Early Pythagoreanism*. Assen: Van Gorcum, 1966.

Watson, N. "The Interpretation of Romans 7." *AusBibRev* 21 (1973): 27-39.

Weiss, J. *Die Aufgaben des neutestamentlichen Wissenschaft in der Gegenwart.* Göttingen: Vandenhoeck & Ruprecht, 1911.

White, J. *The Body of the Greek Letter.* Missoula: Scholars, 1972.

Wilken, R., ed. *Aspects of Wisdom in Judaism and Early Christianity.* Notre Dame: Notre Dame University, 1975.

Willcox, M. "'Upon the Tree' — Deut 21:22-23 in the New Testament." *JBL* 96 (1977): 85-99.

Wuellner, W. "Paul's Rhetoric of Argumentation in Romans." *CBQ* 38 (1976): 330--51.

INDEX

A

Abraham, 15-16, 22, 23, 28-31, 56-60, 155

Adam, 166-167, 180

APOCRYPHA:

  Baruch

    3:14, 72n.111

    3:29-37, 72n.110

  2 Esdras

    7:46, 47n.118

  1 Macc

    2:51-52; 2:52, 15-16 nn.37-38

  2 Macc

    7:24, 9n.22

  Sirach

    Prol 1-4, 71n.98

    Prol 14, 71n.100

    Prol 29ff., 71n.102

    Prol 31, 71n.99

    Prol 36, 71n.100

    6:37, 71n.101

    24:23, 72

    32:35, 153n.32

    39:1-3, 71n.103

    39:6, 72n.104

    39:8, 72 nn.105-106

    39:9, 72n.106

    41:8-10, 72n.106

    44:19-21, 15-16 nn.37-38

    44:1-51:29, 72n.107

    51:23ff., 72n.108

  Wisdom of Solomon

    2-5, 73n.113

    3:1-6, 73n.113

    3:7-9, 73n.113

    4:10-15, 73n.113

    6, 73n.113

    6.21-25, 78n.134

    7, 56n.6, 73n.113

    11:23, 151n.27

    13:1-15:17, 147n.14

    14:8-31, 147n.11

    15:1-2, 150n.22

    15:1-3, 151n.27

    15:3, 74n.113

    17:1, 74n.113

    17:20, 74n.113

    18:4, 159n.64

Arnim, H. von, 100 nn.243-244, 101n.247

Attridge, H., 94n.209, 203

Audollent, A., 34n.77, 203

autonomous self, xix, 64-66, 91, 103, 148, 178, 181-184, 194

B

Barr, J., xv n.16, 203

Betz, H., xiv, xiv n.14, xvi, xvi nn.18,21, 2n.3, 3n.4b, 7n.14, 8n.17, 10n.25, 11 nn.30-31, 14n.34, 15n.35, 15n.36, 18n.39, 23n.48, 24n.51, 27, 27n.57, 36n.84, 45n.108, 46, 46n.117, 48 nn.121-122, 49 nn.124-126, 51 nn.131-132, 52, 52 nn.133-134, 117n.22, 122n.37, 123n.40, 203

Bornkamm, G., xviii n.26, 109n.6, 146, 146nn.5-7,8, 147nn.10, 12, 15, 148nn.16-17, 155, 155n.42, 156n.50, 165n.74, 204

Brandeburger, E., xiv, xiv n.13, xv n.16, 204

Bultmann, R., xvii, xvii n.24, 3, 3n.4a, 130n.69, 150n.21, 159n.62, 182n.118, 204

Burkert, W., 42n.97, 205

C

Calvin, J., xiii, xiii n.8, 205

Church, F., xvi, xvi n.19, xvii, 205
Cohen, B., xvi, xvi n.22, 91n.200,
    142, 205
competency, 114, 118, 119
communal interpretation, xx, 5,
    25-26, 30, 37, 124, 138, 140, 142,
    190-192, 198, 199, 201-202
Conzelmann, H., 117nn.22-3, 205
cosmos (universal
    interpretation), 1, 49, 100-103,
    142, 186, 193, 199

D
Dahl, 33n.75, 206
Deismann, A., 32n.73, 36n.84, 206
Delling, G., 5n.9, 206
diatribal elements, 3-5, 12n.34,
    150-152, 157-164, 173-174,
Dillon, J., 101n.248, 206

E
EARLY CHRISTIAN LITERATURE
    1 Clement - 50.1-5, 42n.98
    Didache - 10:6, 191n.129
    Eusebius, Prep. Evan.
        8.10.2, 68n.83
        8.10.4, 68n.82
Ebeling, G., xii n.3, 206
Edelstein, L., 101n.249, 102n.252,
    206

F
Fraikin, D., 186n.120, 207
freedom, 51, 95, 134, 137-138, 139,
    178
future, xxi, 141-142, 192

G
Gadamer, H., xv n.16, 207
Gaiser, K., 88n.185, 207
Georgi, D., xiv, xiv n.12, xx,
    58n.18, 61nn.39-40, 62, 62nn.44,

46, 63n.54, 67, 67 nn.76-77, 68
    nn.79-81, 69 nn.88, 90, 74n.113,
    109, 124, 124 nn.44-45, 125, 125
    nn.46-52, 126 nn.53-75, 127nn.58-
    60, 62, 128, 129, 130, 130n.70,
    132n.74, 133, 133nn.80-81,
    135n.87, 136, 136nn.90-91, 139,
    207
Goodenough, E., 66n.72, 207,
    97n.220, 207
Grant, R., xii, xii nn.5-6, 100n.242,
    108n.3, 208
GREEK AND LATIN AUTHORS
    Andocides - De Myst. 85, 85
    Antig. - Car. 129, 19n.40
    Antiphon - On Truth,
        OP 1364,
            frag 1 84n.164
            frag 2 84n.165
    Aristophanes - Clouds
        11.1075ff., 84n.162
    Aristotle - Meta.
        987B11, 97n.223
        987B28, 97n.224
        1090A20, 97n.224
        Rhet
            1368B.1-13, 91n.201
            1373B.1, 92n.202
            1373B.10ff,. 92n.203
            1375A.ff., 92n.204
            1376B.21, 9n.23
    Arrian - Frag. 11 (174), 175n.94
    Cicero
        De div.
            1.24.50-51, 42n.98, 43n.103
            1.125, 102n.252
        De deorum nat., 49n.127
        De fato - 39-44, 100n.245
        De leg. - 1.33, 96n.220
        De off. - 1.56, 96n.220
        Resp. - 1.10.16, 96n.220
        Tim. - 1.1, 96n.220

Tusc. dis.
  1.17.39, 96n.220
  1.48.116-17, 42n.98,
    44n.107
Critias
  Sisyphus frag 25, 82n.160
Democritus
  frag. 47, 174;181; 245;
    248, 83n.160
Demosthenes
  Ag. Lept. 107, 33n.74
  In Arist.,
    no. 25,15-20, 83n.160
Dio Cassius
  Hist. 44.51.2, 33n.74
Dio Chrysostum
  1.27, 168n.77
  31.70, 33n.74
  80, 33n.74
Diodorus Siculus. - *Hist.*
  1.1-5, 102n.253
  1.1.3, 102n.254
  1.1.4-5, 102n.255
  1.2.1-2, 102n.256
  1.2.2, 103n.260
  1.2.3, 103n.257
  1.2.5, 103n.258
  1.2.6, 103n.259
  13.26.3, 83n.160
  13.69.2-3, 33n.74
Diogenes Laertius
  6.11, 85n.169
  7.37.166, 9n.22
  7.88, 99, 99n.236
  7.119, 100n.239
  7.121, 100n.240
  7.122, 100n.240
  7.128, 100n.241
  7.135, 100n.246
  7.136, 98n.232
  7.148-49, 98n.233
  7.156, 98n.234
  8.15,17, 98n.229

8.25-35, 96n.220
8.33, 98n.228
9.55, 82n.158
Epictetus - *Diss.*
  1.1.14-17, 150n.21
  1.6.20, 99n.238
  1.20.7, 158n.56
  2.1.28, 159n.60
  2.6.16, 150n.21
  2.8.11-14, 152n.28
  2.9.19-22, 156n.49
  2.9.19, 159n.61
  2.12.3, 158n.54
  2.12.20, 158n.56
  2.16.11-28, 150n.21
  2.19.24-28, 156n.48, 158n.61
  3.22.2-3, 168n.79
  3.22.17, 158n.55
  3.22.80, 150n.21
  4.1 178, 178n.102
  4.1.64, 178n.104
  4.1.86, 180n.112
  4.1.175, 178n.103
  4.7.12ff., 175, 175n.95
  4.8.10ff., 157n.51
  4.8.17, 153n.32, 163n.71
  4.8.18, 169n.81
  Ench. - 17, 175n.93
Euripides
  Bacchae
    11, 112n.12
  Suppl.
    429ff., 85
Gorgias
  Helen,
    6 (DK 2.290), 84n.162
Herodotus,
  Hist. 1.82, 33n.74
Heraclitus
  frag. 114, 85n.167
Hesiod
  Erga 276, 85n.167
Isocrates

Panegyricus **28ff.**, 83n.160
Josephus
  Ant.
    1.17, 63n.53
    1.21ff., 56n.5
    1.154-55, 15n.37
    1.154, 56n.2
    1.155-156, 56n.3
    1.155, 56n.4
    1.183, 15n.37
    3.75, 63n.49
    3.77, 63n.49
    3.88, 63n.49
    3.89-90, 61n.35
    3.90, 62 nn.41-42
    3.99ff., 127n.61, 131,
      131n.72
    3.101, 62 nn.45, 47
    3.138, 63n.50
    3.317, 67n.77
    3.322, 67n.77
    8.171, 172, 19n.40
    13.290, 297, 10n.27
    20:38, 9n.22
  C.Ap.
    2.14, 19n.40
    2.151-163, 65n.69
    2.178, 61n.36
    2.279, 67n.74
    2.293, 159n.64
Libanius
  Declamatio **42.24,** 42n.101
Lucan
  Pharsalia **2.304-9,** 43n.103
Lysias
  Second Oration **18-19,** 83n.160
Nicomachus of Gerasa
  Arith., Intro. **1.3.3-6,** 96n.220
Ovid
  Metamorphosis
    4.1.389ff., 42n.99
    11.810-15, 105n.265

    15.153ff., 96n.220
    15.745ff., 105n.265
Philo
  De Abr.
    3, 58n.22
    4, 58n.21
    5-6, 17n.38
    5, 58n.23, 59n.24
    6, 59n.25
    11, 59n.26
    23, 59n.27
    25, 64n.58
    61ff., 59n.28
    68-88, 57n.11
    68, 59n.29
    82, 59n.29
    89, 64n.58
    261, 58n.16, 64n.59
    262-74, 15n.37
    262-70, 17n.38
    271-72, 59n.30
    275-76, 17n.38, 46n.112
    275, 59n.31
    276, 60n.32
  De agr. **27, 157,** 68n.84
  De conf. ling. **196-98,** 65n.66
  De Dec.
    1, 61n.33, 62n.43
    15, 61 nn.34-35
    19, 61n.35
    32, 61n.35
    39, 61n.35
    41, 61n.35
    45-49, 61n.35
    142, 179 nn.107-108
  De fug.
    166-69, 70n.95
  De gig
    23ff., 70n.94
    55, 70n.97
    61, 64n.58
    64, 65n.67

62-64, 70n.92
De opif.
   3, 61n.38, 64n.58, 67n.78
   100, 98n.231
De plant.
   36, 68 nn.84-85
De post. Caini
   51, 68n.84
De praem., 31n.69
   27. 15n.37
   79ff. 155n.39
   152 57n.7
De sacr. Abelis et Caini
   7, 76-79 70n.96
De somn.
   2.175, 34n.79, 64n.61
De spec. leg.
   1.314-23, 120n.30
   4.78, 178n.101
   4.80, 179n.105
   4.85, 179n.106
   4.95, 179n.109
   4.160-69, 65
   4.163-64, 180n.117
   4.163, 65n.70
   4.164, 66n.71
De Virt.
   194, 58n.20
   198, 64n.58
   213, 17n.38
   214, 57nn.12-13
   216-219, 15n.37
   216, 57 nn.14-15, 58n.16, 64n.59
   217, 58 nn.17-18
   218, 58n.19
   219, 17n.38, 57 nn.8-9, 64n.58
Hypoth.
   6.6.9, 67n.74
Leg. all
   3.118, 30n.67
   3.4,236, 68n.84

Mig. Abr.
   85, 62n.47
   93, 67n.77
   127-130, 16n.38
   129-131, 15n.37
Quis heres
   90-95, 15n.37
   96-99, 57n.11
   167, 62n.47
   265, 58n.18
   266, 58n.18
Quod Deus
   50, 64n.62
   159-61, 65n.67
Quod prob.
   62ff., 65n.63
   68, 65n.64
   71, 65n.65
Vit. cont.
   28, 69n.87
   64, 69n.86, 70n.91
   78, 30n.67, 69n.89
Vit. Mos.
   1.4, 61n.37
   1.158-59, 64n.60
   1.162, 64n.60
   2.14, 67n.75
   2.4, 65n.69
   2.40, 70, 70n.93
   2.43, 67n.77
   2.48, 61n.38
   2.69-70, 61n.37
   2.70ff., 127n.61, 131n.71,
   2.97, 63n.50
Philostratus,
  Vita Apol.
   8.7.2, 32n.72
Plato
  Critias
   119C-120D, 33n.74
  Ep.2
   312D, 87n.182
   314A-C, 88n.183

Ep.7
  341Bff., 87, 87n.180
  344D, 87n.181
Laws
  644D, 90n.198
  659D, 90n.194
  680A, 88n.186
  713C-E, 88n.187
  793B-C, 89n.188
  822E-823A, 90n.195
  865A, 90n.197
  874E-875A, 89n.190
  875D, 89n.193
  957C-E, 91n.199
  957D, 66n.72
Phaedrus
  243,247, 120n.30
  249, 120n.30
  274B, 86n.171
  274E, 86n.172
  275D, 87n.173
  276A, 87, 87 nn.174-175
  276C, 87n.176
  277A, 87n.177
  278C, 87n.178
Prot.
  313Dff., 111n.10
  320ff., 82n.158
  326D, 82n.159
  337C, 85n.168
Rep
  367A, 9n.23
  1.336Bff., 83n.161
  492Aff,. 84n.163
Thaet
  142D, 19n.40
Tim
  20E-25D, 19n.40
Pliny
  Nat. hist.
    34.36, 96n.220
Plutarch

CQ
  8.7.727, 96n.220
Pseudo-Heraclitus
  9th Letter
    1.2, 153n.32
    1.17, 94n.212
    11.4-5, 94n.210, 95n.216
    11.4-7, 95n.216
    11.8-19, 95n.216
    11.9-10, 94n.211
    11.21-22, 95n.213
    11.22-23, 95n.214
Quintillian
  Inst. Orat.
    4.1.5ff., 111n.11
    7.6.4-8, 93n.206
Seneca
  Ep. 77.17, 159n.60
  Ep. 90, 101
  90.3, 8, 10, 18-19,
    24, 27, 29, 31, 101n.250
  90.5, 6, 102n.251
  Ep. 108.34, 96n.220
  Nat. quaest. **7.32.2,** 96n.220
Sextus Empiricus
  Math. **9.127,** 97n.227
Sophocles
  Antigone, 76 85
Teles
  Peri autarkeias
    5H, 175, 175n.96
    6H, 8H, 20n.43
    6H, 176, 176n.97
    6H-7H, 176, 176n.98
Thucydides
  Hist.
    1:20, 19n.40
    1.76.2, 83n.162
    2.63.2, 83n.162
    3.40.4, 83n.162
    4.60.1, 83n.162
    5.85-111, 83n.162

5.104, 83n.162

Virgil
  Aeneid
    6.755ff., 104n.264
  Fourth Eclogue
    4ff., 104n.262
    46ff., 104n.263

Xenophon
  Anab.
    3.3.9-15, 110n.7
  Cyropaedia
    7.5.70-74, 110n.7
  Mem
    4.4.12ff., 83n.160

Guthrie, W., 81n.152, 82 nn.155-8, 85n.166, 86n.170, , 96n.217, 97 nn.222, 225-226, 208

H
heavenly letter, 62, 74-77
HEBREW SCRIPTURE
Daniel
  8:19, 146n.7
Deuteronomy
  17:18-20, 65n.68
  21:23, 34, 39, 41, 42, 43
  27:26, 33, 34, 35, 36
  28:58, 34n.78, 35, 35n.80
  28:61, 34n.78
  29:20, 34n.78
  29:26, 34n.78
  30, 64
  30:14, 21, 65n.64
  30:15, 19, 64n.62
Exodus
  28:30, 30n.67
  31:18, xiii n.7
  32:4,6, 135n.89
  33-34, 127
  34, 116, 127, 131, 134-135, 137, 140
  34:29ff., 131
  34:30, 133n.83

34:33,35, 134, 135n.87
34:34, 136
Ezekiel
  11:19(LXX), 115
  36:26(LXX), 115
Genesis
  1:26, 138n.97
  15:6, 17n.38, 28, 29, 30n.68
  26:5, 17n.38
Habakuk
  2:4, 28, 37, 37n.88, 78n.132
Isaiah
  3:13-15, 151n.25
  53:1, 20, 20n.42
  54:1, 51
  66:18ff, 153n.31
Jeremiah
  4:4, 163n.73
  38:33(LXX), 115, 156
Joel
  2:11, 111n.9, 114, 114n.15
Leviticus
  18:5, 37, 37n.89
Numbers
  21:18, 79n.140
Proverbs
  24:12, 152n.29
Psalms
  62:13, 152n.29
  142(3):2(LXX), 12n.32
2 Samuel
  12:7, 151n.25
Zephaniah
  1:18, 146n.7
Hegel, G., xiii,n.10, 72n.109
Heinemann, F., 81 nn.152-153, 208
Hengel, M., 42n.100, 43n.102, 43n.104, 43n.106, 72n.109, 208
human drive for transcendence, xix, xxii, 105, 162-163

I
"I", 24, 24 nn.48, 51, 173, 174-185,

186-190, 194
identity, 23, 25, 30, 60

K

Kasemann, E., xi, xi nn.1-21,
   79n.111, xiii n.10, xxii, 145n.3,
   156n.43, 158 nn.58-59, 159n.63,
   160n.65, 163, 163n.72, 165, 165
   nn.75-76, 169n.83, 177n.100, 179,
   179n.111, 180n.114, 186n.120, 189
   nn.124, 127, 209
Klassen, W., xiii n.9, 209
Koester, H., 81n.153, 209
Kramer, H., 88n.184, 209
Kummel, W., 172, 172n.89, 174,
   210

L

Lausberg, H., 111n.11, 134n.85,
   210
Lesky, A., 81n.153, 82n.154,
   82n.158, 87n.179, 210
letter,
   and imperial destiny, 104-105
   and power of interpretation, 66-
   70
letters of recommendation, 111,
   113, 114, 118-121, 122, 126
Loisy, A., 28n.58, 210
Long, A., 99, 99 nn.235-237, 210
Luhrmann, D., 2, 2n.2, 15n.36, 210
Lull, D., 18n.39, 210
Luther, M., xiii, xiii n.8, 210
Lyonnet, S., 179n.110, 211

M

MacDonald, D., 48n.120, 211
Malherbe, A., 120n.30, 176n.99,
   211
Meyer, M., 24n.48
Moses, 70, 116, 127, 131-132, 133,

135, 136

N

Neusner, J., 10n.27, 211
NEW TESTAMENT
 1 Corinthians
   1:4, 110n.7
   1:7-8, 117
   1:8, 117
   2:4b, 117
   2:10, 117
   2:12ff., 123
   2:12, 117
   2:15-16, 117
   3:13, 117
   3:16, 191n.129
   4:5, 117, 150n.21
   4:6, 123n.39
   5:9, 117n.22
   7:29, 117
   7:31, 117
   8:1, 123n.39
   9:14, 123n.42
   10:6ff., 117
   10:7-11, 135n.89
   10:11, 117
   10:23, 123n.39
   12:2, 191n.131
   12:3, 191n.129
   12:8ff., 117
   13:12-13, 117
   14:5, 123n.39
   14:23-25, 117
   15:20ff,. 117
   15:57, 110n.7
   16:22, 191n.129
 2 Corinthians
   1:1ff., 110n.6
   1:1-2:13, 109n.6
   1:3, 110n.7
   2:13, 109n.6
   2:14ff., 118, 131, 133, 136, 137

2:14-7:4, 109n.6
2:14-6:13, 109n.6
2:14-3:6, 113, 116
2:14-16, 110, 110n.7, 111n.9,
 118, 120n.29, 140
2:14-16b, 112
2:14-15, 114, 138n.95
2:14, 114, 120n.30
2:15-16, 114
2:15, 114
2:16, 114
2:16c, 111, 113
2:17ff., 134
2:17, 111, 113, 114, 118,
 118n.24, 120n.30, 134
3, 125, 144, 157, 162, 165
3:1ff., 122
3:1-6, 124
3:1-3, 114
3:1, 111, 113, 118
3:2-3, 111, 140
3:2, 118, 120n.30
3:3, 113, 118, 119n.27, 131,
 138n.95
3:3c, 115
3:4, 112, 119, 119n.26, 134
3:5-6a, 119
3:5, 112-114, 118
3:6ff., 148
3:6, xix-xx, 2, 107-110, 116,
 118, 119, 131n.73, 134, 141,
 144, 145, 163, 198
3:6b, 129
3:6c, xx, 112, 129, 130, 131,
 139, 140, 199
3:7ff., 119, 127, 144
3:7-18, xx, 109, 116, 119, 130,
 131, 199
3:7-11, 149n.20
3:7-9, 132
3:7-8, 131
3:7, 131, 132, 134, 136
3:8, 120, 132, 133

3:9, 120, 131, 132, 133
3:10, 132n.76, 133
3:11, 120, 131, 133, 134, 136
3:12, 120, 134, 134n.86, 135
3:13, 134, 135, 136, 137
3:14, 135n.87, 148
3:14a, 135, 136, 138
3:14b, 135, 136, 137
3:14c, 136
3:15, 136
3:16, 137
3:16-17, 135n.87
3:17a, 137, 137n.92
3:17b, 137, 137n.93
3:18, 134, 138, 138n.96, 140,
 141
4:1, 120, 134
4:2, 120, 120n.29
4:3-6, 138n.95
4:3, 120, 135, 150n.21
4:4, 138n.96
4:5-6, 138n.97, 142
4:5, 119n.25
4:6, 193
4:7-12, 120
4:7, 134
4:16, 120, 134
5:6, 134
5:11, 134
5:12, 119n.25, 121
5:17, 192
5:21, 42, 189
6:14-7:1, 109n.6, 117n.22
7:2-4, 109n.6
7:5-16, 109n.6
7:5, 109n.6
8, 109n.6
8:16, 110n.7
9, 109n.6
9:15, 110n.7
10-13, 109n.6, 116, 122,
 122n.35
10:1, 122n.36

10:2, 122
10:3-6, 123
10:8, 122
10:10a, 122
10:10b, 122
10:11, 122n.36
10:12, 122, 123
10:12b, 123
10:13, 123
10:15, 123n.38
10:15b, 123n.39
10:18a, 123
11:4, 6n.11
11:7-11, 123n.42
11:23ff., 123n.41
12:1-9, 123n.43
12:16, 123n.42
12:19b, 123, 123n.39
Galatians
1:1, 9n.19, 23
1:2, 5n.8
1:4, 41n.95
1:6ff., 5
1:6-9, 5n.8, 6n.11
1:6-7, 9n.22, 13
1:6, 9n.22, 12, 25n.52, 110n.7
1:7, 9n.23
1:8-9, 32
1:8, 13
1:10-2:21, 5n.8
1:10-2:14, 22
1:10, 13
1:11-12, 23
1:11, 5n.8
1:12-2:14, 8n.17, 9
1:12, 9n.20, 9n.21, 10, 12
1:13-2:21, 34
1:13-14, 13, 23, 23n.46
1:13, 5n.8, 10n.26
1:14, 10n.24
1:15-16, 9n.21, 23n.46
1:16, 23

1:18-24, 10
1:20, 5n.8, 32
2:1-10, 10
2:3ff., 13
2:4, 10n.29,
2:10-21, 10
2:11-14, 10, 13
2:14, 10n.28, 10n.29
2:14b, 12
2:15-21, 11n.31
2:15-16, 11-15, 18, 22
2:15-16d, 14, 17
2:16, 8, 11n.31, 19, 20, 22
2:17-21, 13, 13n.34,
2:17, 11n.31
2:17a, 13, 13n.34
2:17b, 13n.34
2:17c, 13n.34
2:18, 13n.34
2:18a, 13
2:18b, 13
2:19-20, 11n.31, 23-25, 170n.86, 188
2:19, 13n.34, 24n.50
2:19a, 24
2:20, 24, 41n.95
2:20a, 13n.34
2:20b, 14n.34
2:20d, 24n.50
2:21, 11n.31, 14n.34
2:21a, 13, 14n.34
2:21b, 13, 14n.34, 44
3, 144
3:1ff., 36
3:1-14, xviii, 1, 2, 44, 45, 52
3:1-5, 3-6, 7, 8, 14n.34, 22, 24-26, 30, 50
3:1, 5n.10, 7, 7n.14, 8, 21, 25, 31, 39, 40
3:1a, 3
3:1b, 3, 5
3:1c, 3

3:2-5, 2n.1, 8
3:2, 2, 5n.10, 6, 8, 13, 18, 20,
   21, 22n.45, 31n.70, 36, 37,
   42n.101, 52
3:2a, 4
3:2b, 4
3:3, 5, 5n.9, 5n.10, 7, 18
3:3a, 4
3:3b, 4
3:4, 5n.10
3:4a, 4
3:4b, 4, 7n.15
3:5, 2, 5, 5n.9, 6, 13, 18, 20,
   22n.45, 31n.70, 36, 42n.101,
   53
3:5a, 4
3:5b, 4
3:6ff., 15, 17, 26, 27, 50
3:6-14, 8, 23n.47, 27, 45, 47
3:6-12, 27
3:6-9, 26n.55, 27n.56, 29, 31,
   31n.70, 36, 41
3:6-7, 29, 29n.66
3:6, 7n.14, 15
3:7-9, 28
3:7-8, 37n.87
3:7, 29n.62, 29n.63, 38n.90
3:8, 2, 7n.14, 26, 29n.62, 35,
   38, 38n.90
3:8-9, 29
3:9, 29, 29n.62
3:10ff., 40, 149n.20
3:10-13, 26n.55
3:10-12, 27n.56, 31, 39, 40, 43
3:10, 8, 31-36, 34n.76, 37n.89,
   38n.90, 39
3:10b, 40
3:11-12, 37
3:11, 38, 38n.90
3:11a, 37n.86
3:11b, 28
3:12, 38n.90
3:13-14, 38, 189

3:13, 7n.14, 33n.75, 34, 38n.91,
   42-44, 148
3:13a, 39, 40
3:13b, 39, 40, 41
3:14, 2n.2, 27, 39, 41
3:15-18, 45
3:16ff., 148
3:17ff., 34, 167
3:17-21, 13
3:19, 135n.88
3:21b-22, 46
3:21, 148, 178, 190n.128
3:21b, 13
3:22-23, 192n.133
3:22, 23n.47, 47, 135n.88,
   138n.94, 149n.20, 192
3:23-24, 47, 49
3:23, 47
3:24, 47
3:25, 47
3:26-28, 48n.120
3:29, 48
4:1ff., 47
4:1-3, 49
4:3, 47n.119, 48
4:4-5, 38n.91, 49
4:4, 49, 189
4:5, 38n.91
4:6-7, 49, 191n.132
4:7, 191
4:8-10, 47n.119
4:9-10, 13, 18, 48
4:9, 49, 97n.221
4:21ff., 26
4:21-31, 1, 13, 50
4:21, 13, 18, 31n.70, 34n.79,
   42n.101, 50
4:22ff., 30
4:23, 50
4:24ff., 35
4:24b-26, 51
4:26, 51
4:28, 51

4:30, 51
5:2, 13
5:3, 18
5:4, 13
5:14, 190
6:12-13, 13
6:12, 13
6:15, 53n.135, 192
6:16, 53n.135
James
    2:20-26, 15n.37
John
    3:16ff., 189
1 John
    4:9, 189
Mark
    13:5ff., 193n.134
Philemon
    4, 110n.7
Philippians
    1:3, 110n.7
    2:7, 189n.125
Romans
    1, 151
    1:8, 110n.7
    1:16, 149, 152
    1:17ff., 193
    1:17, 28n.60, 149, 185
    1:18, 146, 146n.7, 147, 148n.19
    1:18ff., 146, 147, 150, 151, 157
    1:18-3:20, xxi, 144, 146, 149, 150n.21, 151
    1:18-2:29, 165
    1:19, 147n.9, 150
    1:20ff, 193
    1:20, 146n.5, 147n.9
    1:21, 147, 147n.9, 150
    1:23, 147
    1:24, 147, 192n.133
    1:25, 147
    1:26, 147
    1:28, 146n.5, 147, 147n.9, 150

1:29ff, 146n.5
1:32, 147n.9, 149n.21, 150
1:32a, 150
2, 143, 144, 145, 174, 184, 187, 194, 199
2:1-5, 150n.21
2:1, 149n.21, 154n.36
2:2, 149, 150, 153, 160, 161
2:3, 145n.2, 149n.21, 150, 151, 153
2:4-5, 153
2:4, 151
2:5, 152, 163
2:6, 152, 153, 155
2:7-11, 152, 154
2:7-8, 152
2:9-10, 152
2:9, 152, 155
2:10, 152
2:11ff., 157
2:11, 152, 154
2:12ff., 154
2:12-15, 154, 156
2:12-13, 157
2:12, 154
2:12b, 155
2:13, 145n.2, 155, 160, 161
2:13b, 181
2:14-15, 145n.2, 150n.21, 154, 154n.37, 155, 157, 161, 161n.67
2:14, 145n.2, 155, 156
2:15, 150n.21, 156, 163
2:16, 150n.21
2:17ff., 158
2:17-24, 145n.2, 154, 154n.37, 157, 161n.68
2:17-20, 157, 158, 161
2:17, 154, 157, 159
2:18c, 159
2:19ff., 159
2:19a, 159

2:20, 157
2:20c, 159
2:21-22, 158
2:22b, 158
2:23ff., 159
2:23, 159
2:24, 158, 160
2:25-29, 154
2:25, 154n.37, 161n.68
2:25a, 161, 161n.66
2:26-27, 145n.2, 163
2:26, 161, 190
2:27, 154n.37, 161, 162, 164
2:28-29, 145n.2, 154n.37, 164
2:28, 163n.70, 163, 164
2:28b, 163
2:29, xxi, 144, 145, 150n.21, 163, 171, 190, 194
3:1-20, 148
3:3-4, 148n.19
3:3, 148n.19
3:9, 146, 173n.92
3:10ff., 146
3:10-18, 148
3:19-20, 148
3:19, 148
3:20, 12n.32, 177, 180n.113, 183
3:21-26, 149
3:21, 178
3:27ff., 187
3:27, 22n.45, 187
3:31, 181
4:1ff., 28n.60
4:1, 173n.92
5-6, 165, 170, 171
5, 174
5:1-11, 166
5:12ff., 180
5:12, 166
5:13, 167, 181
5:14, 166
5:15, 166, 167

5:16, 166, 167
5:17, 166, 167, 184
5:18, 167
5:19, 166, 167
5:20-21a, 178
5:20, 167, 170n.87, 177, 181
5:21, 167
6, 174
6:1, 167
6:2, 167
6:3ff., 171, 191n.130
6:3, 167
6:4, 167, 171
6:5, 168n.77, 189n.125
6:6, 168, 170, 184
6:7, 168
6:9, 168
6:10, 170n.86
6:12ff., 169
6:12-23, 168
6:14, 166, 168, 177
6:15ff., 171
6:15, 168, 169
6:16ff., 170
6:16, 168
6:17, 110n.7
6:19, 168
6:20, 168
6:22, 168
7-8, xxi, 143, 165, 200, 202
7, xxi, 186, 187, 188, 200
7:1ff., 165, 169
7:1-6, 174
7:1-5, 165
7:2-3, 169, 170
7:2c, 170n.88
7:3d, 170n.88
7:4, 169, 170
7:4d-6, 173
7:4e, 171
7:5, 170, 177
7:5-6, 169, 170, 177
7:5, 166, 181

7:6ff., 199
7:6, xxi, 143, 144, 165, 166,
    170, 171, 172, 184, 185,
    186, 188, 194, 200
7:6a, 166
7:6b, 166, 170
7:6c, 166
7:6d, 166
7:7ff., 143, 144n.1, 165n.76,
    172, 177, 184, 186, 188, 190
7:7-25, xxi
7:7-25a, 172, 173
7:7-24, 172, 177, 183n.119,
    186, 194
7:7, 173, 183
7:7b, 173
7:8ff., 179, 182
7:8b-11, 180
7:8b-10a, 181
7:8, 173, 178, 182, 183
7:9-10, 173
7:9, 173
7:10, 173
7:11, 173, 181, 183
7:12, 178, 181
7:13, 173, 181
7:14, 173, 178
7:14a, 173
7:15, 173, 182
7:16-17, 182
7:16, 178, 182
7:17, 173, 183
7:18, 182
7:18a, 182
7:18b, 182
7:19, 173, 182
7:20, 173, 182, 183
7:20a, 173
7:21, 178, 183
7:22-23, 173
7:22, 173, 178, 183, 187
7:23, 170n.87, 173, 183, 187

7:24, 173, 183, 183n.119, 186
7:25a, 173, 183n.119, 186, 187
7:25b, 183n.119
8, 186, 194, 200
8:1, 183n.119
8:2ff., xxii, 144n.1, 191
8:2-25, xxi, 172, 186
8:2-3, 183n.119
8:2, 186, 187, 188
8:3ff., 188
8:3-4, 189
8:3b-4, 189
8:3a, 187, 189, 190
8:3b, 189
8:4, 189n.123
8:5ff., 192
8:5, 190
8:6, 190
8:9, 189n.123, 191
8:10-11, 191
8:12, 191
8:13, 189n.123, 191
8:14, 192
8:15, 189n.123, 191
8:16, 191
8:17, 189n.123, 191
8:18-25, 192
8:18, 192
8:19, 192
8:20, 192, 193
8:21, 192
8:22-25, 189n.123
8:22-23, 193
8:22, 193
8:24-25, 193
8:31-39, 186n.120
10, 25n.53
10:3, 20, 185
10:5, 20
10:6-7, 20
10:6, 30n.67
10:8, 21

10:9-10, 21
10:14, 20
10:16-17, 19, 20
10:17, 20
10:18, 20
15:4, 7n.14
16:25, 150n.21
1 Thess
  1:2, 110n.7
  1:3, 19-21
  1:5, 150n.21
  1:7, 19
  1:8, 20
  2:13-16, 20n.41
2 Timothy
  2:8, 150n.21
nomos (Law), 18, 20, 22, 33, 34-36, 37, 39, 40, 45-46, , 48, 50, 70, 80, 81-86, 148, 156, 165, 167, 169-170, 172, 177-185
Norden, E., 159n.63, 211

O
objective verifiability, xx, 122, 139
orality (oral power),
  oral message, 40-41, 44, 47

P
Pagels, E., xii, xii n.4, 211
Pearson, B., 20n.41, 211
personification, 26, 29, 35, 47, 54, 174-177
Poettcker, H., xiii n.9, 211
PSEUDEPIGRAPHA
  2 Baruch
    4:1-6, 51n.130
    48:38,40, 156n.46
    48:47, 154n.38, 156n.46
    57, 16n.38
    57:2, 15n.37, 156n.46
    54:17ff., 148n.18
    78:1, 76n.125
    81:4, 76n.126

82:1, 76n.127
83:7-8, 76n.128
84:7, 76n.129
84:7ff, 150n.22
84:9, 76n.130
85:1-3, 76n.131
87:1, 76n.125
1 Enoch
  33:3-4, 75n.120
  47:3, 75n.121
  52:7, 151n.24
  81:2, 75n.122
  82:2-3, 75n.119
  91:7, 146n.7
  103:2ff., 75n.123
  104:12ff., 75n.119
4 Ezra
  7:34ff., 150n.22
  7:72, 156n.46
Jubilees
  1:29, 74n.114
  4:5, 74n.115
  4:17-20, 74n.116
  5:13ff., 75n.118
  6:17, 74n.115
  6:22, 74n.115
  10:17, 75n.117
  14:6,20; 23:10; 24:11, 15-16nn.37-38
  15:9ff., 16n.38
  19:9, 75n.117
  21:10, 46n.113
  30:20, 75n.117
  30:22, 75n.118
  50:13, 74n.115
Letter of Aristeias
  142, 19n.40
  170-71, 36n.83
  178, 310-11, 36n.83
  312-16, 36n.83
  313, 322, 36n.83
  311, 63n.52
  313ff., 63n.52

Psalms of Solomon
   12:6, 45n.110
Sibylline Oracles
   3.195, 159n.64
Testament of Joseph
   20, 45n.110

Q
QUMRAN
   CD   1.1-2.1, 78n.133
      2.2, 78, 78n.135
      2.14, 78n.136
      2.17-4.12, 78n.138
      6.2-7, 79n.140
   1Q
      pHab 2.1ff,. 78n.132
      pHab 6:12-7.5, 77
      pHap 7.17-8.3, 37n.88,
         78n.132
   1QH
      1.15-20, 79n.143
      1.19, 80n.144
      1.21, 79n.143
      1.24, 80n.145
      2.13, 80n.146
      2.17-18, 80n.143
      3.9, 80n.149
      3.19, 80n.149
      3.22, 80n.147
      3.25-29, 80n.149
      4.27, 80n.143
      4.5, 79n.143
      5.11, 80n.143
      5.15, 80n.143
      5.25, 80n.143
      7.10, 80n.143
      7.14, 80n.143
      10.7, 79n.143
      11.9, 10, 80n.143
      11.11, 80n.143
      11.12, 80n.143
      11.13, 80n.143

      11.19, 79n.143
      12.13, 79n.143
      12.34, 79n.143
      14.8, 79n.143
      14.25, 80n.143
      16.10, 80n.143
      18.6, 80n.143
      18.11, 79n.143, 80n.148
      18.14, 80n.143
      18.24, 79n.143
      18.27, 80n.143
   1QM
      4:3; 12:12, 189n.125
   1QS
      3.18-4.26, 78n.139
      5.5, 163
      5.8-9, 78n.139
      5.9, 79n.141
      6.7, 80n.150
      8.15, 80n.151
      11.9, 189n.125

R
RABBINIC LITERATURE
   M. Abot
      1.1, 90n.196
   Mek Exod
      20:18, 46n.114
Reese, J., 73n.112, 212
Reitzenstein, R., xv, xv n.17, 212
Richardson, P., 108n.3, 212
Robinson, J., 111n.8, 212
Rohrich, L., 62n.46, 114n.17, 212
Romilly, J. de, 32n.71, 212

S
Schneider, N., xvii, xvii n.25, 212
Schoeps, H., 37n.85, 212
Schrenk, G., xiii n.11, 7n.14, 7n.14,
   63n.55, 213
Schussler-Fiorenza, E., xiv n.15,
   207

Schutz, J., 9n.18, 9n.18, 213
Schweizer, E., xiii n.11, 213
scripture and magic curse, xviii,
    30, 44, 52,
solidarity, xxii, 30,
Stendahl, K., 172n.90, 213
Stowers, S., xvi, xvi n.20, xvii, 3,
    3n.5, 4, 4 nn.6-7, 21n.44, 46
    nn.115-116, 50n.128, 149n.21, 151
    nn.23, 26, 152n.30, 153n.33, 158,
    158 nn.52-53, 57, 169n.82,
    173n.91, 187n.121, 213

T
Thesliff, H., 96n.218, 213
tradition,
  and magic, 28, 47
V
Vogel, C. de, 96n.218, 213

W
Weiss, J., xvii, xvii n.23, 214
Wilcox, M., 33n.75, 214
written/unwritten dialectic, 84-91

STUDIES IN THE BIBLE AND EARLY CHRISTIANITY

1. Hugh M. Humphrey, **A Bibliography for the Gospel of Mark, 1954-1980**

2. Rolland Wolfe, **The Twelve Religions of the Bible**

3. Jean LaPorte, *Eucharistia* **in Philo**

4. Peter Gorday, **Principles of Patristic Exegesis: Romans 9-11 in Origen, John Chrysostom, and Augustine**

5. Marcus J. Borg, **Conflict, Holiness and Politics in the Teachings of Jesus**

6. Watson E. Mills, **Glossolalia: A Bibliography**

7. Matthew Baasten, **Pride According to Gregory the Great: A Study of the Moralia**

8. Douglas E. Oakman, **Jesus and The Economic Questions of His Day**

9. John Anthony McGuckin, **The Transfiguration of Christ in Scripture and Tradition**

10. Raymond A. Martin, **Syntax Criticism of the Synoptic Gospels**

11. Thomas A. Robinson, **The Bauer Thesis Examined: The Geography of Heresy in the Early Christian Church**

12. John Chrysostom, **Commentary on Isaiah 1-8**, Duane A. Garrett (trans.)

13. John Chrysostom, *A Comparison Between A King and A Monk/Against the Opponents of the Monastic Life*: **Two Treatises by John Chrysostom**, David G. Hunter (trans.)

14. Amy-Jill Levine, **The Social and Ethnic Dimensions of Matthean Salvation History: "Go nowhere among the Gentiles..." (Matt. 10:5b)**

15. Allan Fitzgerald, **Conversion Through Penance in the Italian Church of the Fourth and Fifth Centuries: New Approaches to the Experience of Conversion from Sin**

16. William Lane Craig, **Assessing the New Testament Evidence for the Historicity of the Resurrection of Jesus**

17. Jack Lewis (ed.), **Interpreting 2 Corinthians 5:14-21: An Exercise in Hermeneutics**

18. Raymond A. Martin, **Syntax Criticism of Johannine Literature, The Catholic Epistles, and The Gospel Passion Accounts**

19. Peter W. Macky, **The Centrality of Metaphors to Biblical Thought: A Method for Interpreting the Bible**

20. David A. Fiensy, **The Social History Of Palestine In The Herodian Period: The Land Is Mine**

21. Dale Miller and Patricia Miller, **The Gospel of Mark as Midrash on Earlier Jewish and New Testament Literature**

22. Terrance Callan, **Psychological Perspectives On the Life of Paul: An Application of the Methodology of Gerd Theissen**

23. Carolinne White, **The Correspondence (394-419)Between Jerome and Augustine of Hippo**

24. J. Arthur Baird, **A Comparative Analysis of the Gospel Genre: The Synoptic Mode and Its Uniqueness**

25. Isabel Ann Massey, **Interpreting The Sermon On The Mount in the Light of Jewish Tradition As Evidenced in the Palestinian Targums of the Pentateuch**

26. Tom Robinson and David J. Hawkin, **Self-Definition and Self-Discovery In Early Christianity**

27. James D. Price, **The Syntax Of Masoretic Accents In The Hebrew Bible**

28. Dan Cohn-Sherbok, **Rabbinic Perspectives On The New Testament**

29. Christine Trevett, **A Study of Ignatius of Antioch in Syria and Asia**

30. Verna E. F. Harrison, **Grace and Human Freedom According to St. Gregory of Nyssa**

31. Pearse Cusack, **An Interpretation of the Second Dialogue of Gregory the Great: Hagiography and St. Benedict**

32. Ernst R. Wendland, **Comparative Discourse Analysis and the Translation of Psalm 22 in Chichewa, a Bantu Language of South-Central Africa**

33. Arthur A. Dewey, **Spirit and Leter in Paul**

34. To be announced.

35. Julia M. O'Brien and Fred L. Horton, Jr. (eds.), **The Yahweh/Baal Confrontation and other Studies in Biblical Literature and Archaeology: Essays in honour of Emmett Willard Hamrick**